Family Dispute Resolution from a Cultural Perspective

Family Dispute Resolution from a Cultural Perspective:

South Sudanese Australian Legal Consciousness

By

Buol Garang Anyieth Juuk

Cambridge Scholars
Publishing

Family Dispute Resolution from a Cultural Perspective:
South Sudanese Australian Legal Consciousness

By Buol Garang Anyieth Juuk

This book first published 2023

Cambridge Scholars Publishing

Lady Stephenson Library, Newcastle upon Tyne, NE6 2PA, UK

British Library Cataloguing in Publication Data
A catalogue record for this book is available from the British Library

ISBN (10): 1-5275-2872-3
ISBN (13): 978-1-5275-2872-7

TABLE OF CONTENTS

PREFACE

This book was inspired and informed by my work experience for over seventeen years in the community sector as a senior Family Dispute Resolution Practitioner FDRP (Family Mediator) and Support Service Coordinator, focusing on the Culturally and Linguistically Diverse communities (CALD) as well as the wider Australian community. My work experience and involvement in supporting these cultural groups aroused my interest to study and understand more about how family law disputes are resolved or not resolved by these communities, as well as their experiences and concerns as they traversed the challenges of navigating a formal family law system different to their informal customary law.

Through these experiences and my increasing interest in the areas of family law over the last seventeen years, I became alert to the increasing concerns of the South Sudanese community, families, and community leaders who stated that the challenges they faced in resolving family disputes were not being addressed. In addition, many families did not want to see their members departing from their traditional ways of resolving family disputes and taking newfound freedoms which might lead to separation or divorce. However, at the same time, they were not certain how to resolve those disputes without tampering with the legal system in case one of the parties resorted to involving the authorities such as the police or a family court.

Being from the same community, and of a refugee background myself, I had some understanding of the experiences of South Sudanese former refugees. My experience of forced migration began when I left home at the age of fifteen and went to live in the Pinyudo refugee camp in Ethiopia. I later became one of over twenty-six thousand unaccompanied minors known as the lost boys of the Sudan, many of whom found their way to the United States (US) and Australia.[1] I walked thousands of miles to Ethiopia in late 1987 and remained there until 1991. Due to the internal war in Ethiopia, we were left with no other option but to return to Southern Sudan. In late 1993,

---

[1] Buol Garang Anyieth Juuk, *From Tyranny to Triumph : Once a Sudanese Refugee, Now a Proud Citizen of Australia and South Sudan / Buol Garang Anyieth Juuk ; Edited by Don Sinnott*, ed. D. H. Sinnott (West Lakes, S.Aust: Seaview Press, 2011).

I crossed the border to Uganda and stayed there until 1995. Due to the Lord Resistance Army (LRA) activities in northern Uganda which created insecurity for refugees in the camps, I decided to move to northern Kenya where the largest population of South Sudanese refugees were residing. In 2004, I finally resettled in Australia. These journeys were full of challenges but were later marked by gaining good employment, raising a happy family, and academic success. They were both personal and a testament to how a refugee's life can be very tough and inspiring. I have witnessed and experienced most of that which my participants have experienced, particularly during the flight into forced migration.

My position as a South Sudanese refugee has influenced my choice of research methods. The South Sudanese community is sensitive to discussing issues related to families and the community with outsiders as, in most cases, they believe the information collected may be used against them at any stage by government agencies or other communities.

The only way they can participate with full confidence is when the information is delivered through community and church leaders. With this in mind, this research has adapted a community driven approach, which involves giving the Jieng community the opportunity to become informed and to understand the benefits of the research. This was realised by approaching and meeting with and briefing community leaders, church leaders, key people such as elders and professionals. As part of the requirement by the Ethics and Behavioural Committee to provide letters of permission from the church and community leaders agreeing to promote the research project on behalf of the researcher, the church representative in Australia wrote a letter of permission as did a representative of the African Communities Council of South Australia. This was significant and likely played a role in the large turnout during the focus groups.

South Sudanese communities do not have a homogenous family and customary law practice; therefore, this study specifically examines the experiences of South Sudanese "Jieng" (known to many as Dinka) families. Many people in Australia and around the world are familiar with the word *Dinka*, however, the term was invented by outsiders, and no one knows the precise origin of the word. The people now known as the "Dinka" call themselves "Muonyjang" or "Jieng", their actual name is Jieng; therefore, I will use Jieng instead of Dinka throughout the book. Given the nature and complexities of South Sudanese experiences, this book takes an interdisciplinary approach that integrates perspectives from law, the social-legal area, and the fields of refugee and migration studies.

CHAPTER ONE

INTRODUCTION

1.1. Introduction

Australia is a multicultural society comprising a rich diversity of cultures, languages, religions and ethnicities with one in four persons born overseas.[1] Although many immigrants come from countries and continents with similar laws to Australia, this may not be the case for those former refugees who emigrated from African communities, in particular South Sudan, where customary laws are followed. South Sudan is the newest country on Earth, gaining independence on 9 July 2011, through a referendum held on 9 January 2011 in the Republic of Sudan.[2] The referendum was agreed upon as a result of the Comprehensive Peace Agreement (CPA) signed in 2005 between the Sudan People Liberation Movement (SPLM) representing the region of Southern Sudan, and the National Congress Party (NCP) which represented the government of Sudan. After independence, South Sudan adopted a decentral system of government with ten states. There are sixty-four ethnic groups in South Sudan, each of which has an individual and distinct body of functioning customary law.[3]

Australia has over approximately thirty thousand[4] former refugees from South Sudan, and this number continues to grow. Family law disputes in South Sudan are traditionally resolved within families or the community

---

[1] Australia Bureau of Statistics (ABS), "Culturally Diversity in Australia," 2011 Census (2011).

[2] Christopher Zambakari, "In Search of Durable Peace: The Comprehensive Peace Agreement and Power Sharing in Sudan," *The Journal of North African Studies* (2012).

[3] Akechak Jok, R Leitch, and Carrie Vandewint, "A Study of Customary Law in Contemporary Southern Sudan," *Juba: World Vision International and the South Sudan Secretariat of Legal and Constitutional Affairs* (2004).

[4] Julie Robinson, "Sudanese Heritage and Living in Australia: Implications of Demography for Individual and Community Resilience," *Australasian Review of African Studies, The* 32, no. 2 (2011).

and have relied on customary legal practices, rather than government statutory authorities.[5] Despite previous research on South Sudanese settlement challenges in Australia, little is known about the experiences and challenges South Sudanese families encounter in a legal environment that is significantly different from that of their home country. Thus, this book intends to fill this gap in the literature in two ways: by analysing the experiences of South Sudanese Jieng families in relation to marriage, divorce, and the care arrangements for children in South Sudan and Australia from their own perspective; and by exploring ways of making family dispute resolution among the Jieng families living in Australia more appropriate and relevant to Jieng cultures. Jieng (Dinka) people constitute the largest ethnic group in South Sudan, numbering over three million in a country of around twelve million people;[6] it is estimated in Australia that forty-three per cent of the South Sudanese population are of Jieng background.[7]

Family dispute resolution is the central theme of this book and the reason for which the empirical data was collected. This book is significant because it will contribute to the growing body of research on non-Australian perspectives of South Sudanese settlement in Australia. While other researchers have highlighted several of the settlement problems faced by South Sudanese former refugees, none has focused on the important issue of how family law problems are resolved. This book will also make a vital contribution to our understanding of how the Australian legal system works (or does not work) within the context of legal pluralism. While formally, Australia has the one legal system based on statutory law, in practice it appears that different communities within Australia resolve legal issues using their own sense of legal norms and values. On the one hand, it may be the case that family law issues are being adequately resolved within South Sudanese Australian communities; however, on the other hand, it may be that gendered violence and child welfare issues are not being addressed. Therefore, this book will contribute to our understanding of social integration and family well-being of South Sudanese families and other groups in Australia.

---

[5] John Wuol Makec, *The Customary Law of the Dinka (Jieng): A Comparative Analysis of an African Legal System* (Khartoum: J. W. Makec, 1986).
[6] Sudan Government, "5th Sudan Population and Housing Census 2008," (Khartoum Sudan: Central Bureau of Statistics, 2009).
[7] (ABS), "Culturally Diversity in Australia."; ibid.

The book identifies strategies that may assist in prevention and early intervention in Jieng families and other cultural groups before statutory Australian family law becomes necessary. Further, the book may also shed light on approaches to mediating conflicts between customary laws and Australian laws in other cultural groups, including the Australian Indigenous peoples. Thus, the book will provide knowledge to service providers, practitioners, and communities concerning how to best support South Sudanese families and other groups with similar practices in Australia. In this way, it will have direct relevance for family law practitioners across Australia, as well as mediators, the judiciary, and other court personnel who work with family law litigants from a range of cultural backgrounds. Finally, the general perspective suggested that a community-based dispute resolutions model may be a solution for the South Sudanese and other similar groups in Australia, which would empower Jieng communities to resolve disputes through culturally appropriate means such as the restorative family dispute resolution model (RFDR).

This book comprises eight chapters including the conclusion and explores South Sudanese Jieng families' experiences of how disputes related to marriage, divorce, and living arrangements for children after separation are resolved. Through engaging interactions with South Sudanese Jieng participants (focus groups and individuals), this book is intended to provide a wider understanding of the South Sudanese experience of dispute resolution in Australia. The study creates opportunities for Jieng families to share their experiences of solving family law disputes in Australia within a legal system that is very different to South Sudanese customary law. The voices of South Sudanese refugees are often overlooked, which may be due to their refugee status, and also reflects language and cultural barriers. Their narratives will document how South Sudanese and immigrant families experience family law issues, and why many South Sudanese families are reluctant to use the formal legal system. Understanding these barriers and the South Sudanese experience in accessing the formal family law system is important for policy makers. This book has also identified ways in which family law issues can be mediated that take into consideration South Sudanese culture. This understanding is significant for service providers who are working with or supporting South Sudanese families. Finally, this book has significance for South Sudanese refugee families, since they will have the opportunity to understand each other's experiences of going to family dispute challenges in Australia.

Chapter Two presents a brief history of South Sudan, including the unrest since 1955, and the South Sudanese people's experiences of war and forced migration. It also discusses the movement of refugees and migrants from South Sudan to Australia. It is important to examine this historical context in order to fully understand how South Sudanese people experience family dispute resolution in Australia. This chapter further explores the legal system of South Sudan. It firstly demonstrates that the legal system has been unstable, during times of war, or indeed non-existent. As a result of the long-standing internal wars and military regimes, the rule of law in Sudan collapsed. Since Sudan's independence, there has been a complete absence of rule of law, including the separation of powers and the protection of human rights. Consequently, the people of Sudan have been living in a somewhat lawless society led by soldiers and rebel groups, where they had no access to human rights, legal protection, or justice.

Chapter Three provides an overview of the customary law in South Sudan, in particular, investigating how Jieng communities resolve family customary law disputes. South Sudan has a plural legal system which incorporates both statutory and customary law, and which is very different to that of Australia. It is necessary to understand how family law disputes would normally be resolved within Jieng communities in South Sudan in order to understand the legal consciousness of Jieng former refugees once they arrive in Australia. Most family disputes in South Sudan would be resolved through customary law. Therefore, the first task of this chapter is to discuss what exactly customary law is and how it differs from statutory law, focusing specifically on the resolution of marriage, divorce, and child custody disputes in Jieng communities. There has been previous work on Jieng customary law,[8] but none has focused on the resolution of disputes related to marriage, divorce, and child custody. There has also been a strong critique about the negative impact of customary law, especially on women and children, and customary law has also been seen to clash with international human rights instruments. This chapter examines these critiques and explores the role of international human rights instruments under customary law in South Sudan.

Chapter Four provides a brief account of Australian family law and its progression from its English heritage to its application in contemporary multicultural Australia. The chapter gives a historical narrative of the major changes to family law in Australia and offers a brief overview of the progress toward the rights of the child and recognition of non-traditional families. In particular, it focuses on the ways in which family disputes are

---

[8] Makec, *The Customary Law of the Dinka (Jieng): A Comparative Analysis of an African Legal System.*

resolved. It then examines the published research on the experiences, challenges, and opportunities encountered by South Sudanese former refugees in relation to the resolution of family disputes within the family law system in Australia. In order to do this, this chapter examines how Australian law operates, or does not operate, within the context of legal pluralism.

While this chapter provides the essential background for the following chapters which present an original empirical analysis of the experiences of Jieng former refugees living in Australia, it also makes a significant contribution in its own right. There have been many amendments to the *Family Law Act 1975*, including recent changes which recognised same sex marriage. However, little attention has been paid to the existence of legal pluralism within Australia, including the way in which refugee, migrant, and Indigenous social groups need to interact with both formal and customary legal systems.

Chapter Five presents the findings of the empirical data and analysis. The chapter discusses and analyses how family disputes are currently resolved or not resolved here in Australia through formal family law systems such as courts and family dispute resolution (Family Mediation). The study found that the most common type of problems experienced were disputes over the care of children, in particular regarding who is traditionally—or according to the *Family Law Act 1975*—supposed to take care of the children after separation. Other common issues included intervention orders and police involvement in family matters which were described by participants as a hindrance to the participation of family members and elders in the dispute resolution process. Male participants further stated they were concerned about the misuse of freedom by women and a lack of understanding of the law and its consequences. Furthermore, participants revealed that they did not trust government agencies to resolve their family matters, and the majority believed that the Department of Child Protection and domestic violence services were created to separate families and remove children to create employment for job-seekers in the sector. Most participants stated they had attempted several times to have their disputes resolved by elders, close relatives, and their community, but they had been unsuccessful.

Chapter Six presents participants' efforts to reach resolution using traditional dispute resolution processes through families and communities. Efforts at resolution were largely contrary to the methods expected within the formal Australian legal system. In order to examine how Jieng communities resolved disputes outside of the formal legal system, this chapter investigates, in turn, each type of family dispute that arose from the interviews such as bride wealth and co-parenting issues. Finally, the chapter critically assesses the use of traditional methods of resolution by highlighting their problems. Participants were asked about the status of their family and marriage life before they came to Australia and what they believed had changed since. During the interviews and focus group meetings, participants discussed specific issues related to separation, divorce, and disputes over the care of children. Participants were asked additional questions, including what actions were taken to resolve those problems and their satisfaction with the outcome. These issues were then discussed in-depth, exploring the reasons behind their decisions and whether any services were helpful or not throughout the process.

The chapter analyses several of the disputes encountered by families in trying to achieve resolutions. It also questioned whether legal pluralism or restorative (community-based) dispute resolution, normally led by elders, may be an appropriate solution in resolving family disputes among South Sudanese families and other non-European groups, particularly Indigenous Australians.

Chapter Seven offers a solution to the resolution of family dispute problems under Australian family law faced by South Sudanese Jieng families and other similar groups in Australia. It provides a possible policy solution that may be used by the family law sector and service providers across the community. It offers several strategies concerning important perspectives on engaging South Sudanese Jieng communities and other similar groups through the restorative family dispute resolution approach (Community-Based Mediation). This chapter also examines all alternative formal family dispute resolution systems and legal pluralism, which studies revealed were options previously suggested but not acted upon.

Jieng participants, most of whom were community leaders, stressed that family cohesion was their main priority, and that the involvement of external services was seen as likely to lead to divorce rather than reconciliation. Venturing outside of the community to engage family law services was regarded as a "last resort." Therefore, the general perspective suggested that a community-based dispute resolution model may be a solution for South Sudanese communities and other non-European groups, particularly Indigenous Australians. The chapter further provides a brief background of restorative dispute resolution (Community-Based Mediation) and family dispute resolution in Australia and several challenges with CALD families in utilising the services as briefly discussed in Chapter Four.

The concluding chapter, Chapter Eight, brings together the whole book by exploring how disputes related to marriage, divorce, and co-parenting are resolved or not resolved among the South Sudanese Jieng communities in Australia. It offers concluding remarks and strategies on the significant perspectives in engaging the South Sudanese Jieng communities and other similar groups through the restorative dispute resolution approach.

CHAPTER TWO

SOUTH SUDANESE SETTLEMENT IN AUSTRALIA: HISTORICAL BACKGROUND

The Sudan has been at war with itself for over five decades. The civil war erupted in the 1950s during which time Sudan was still under Anglo-Egyptian and British colonial rule. This initial period of conflict was resolved in 1972.[1] Eleven years later, a second protracted war started and ended in 2005.[2] The Comprehensive Peace Agreement (CPA) signed in 2005 eventually led to the independence of South Sudan in July 2011.[3] Again, peace did not last long. South Sudan experienced only a short period of relative stability before further civil unrest erupted in December 2013.[4] This latest internal war was due to political differences within the ruling party, the Sudan People's Liberation Movement (SPLM). This protracted period of civil war displaced and dispersed the South Sudanese across the borders of what was then Sudan into neighbouring countries and as far as Australia, the USA, and to some parts of Europe. This chapter presents an overview of the contemporary history of South Sudan. It examines the South Sudanese people's experiences of wars and forced migration since 1955 and provides contextual information to understand the circumstances that led to the resettlement of many South Sudanese refugees in Australia.

The chapter also provides the historical circumstances of the challenges encountered by early refugees and migrants before their arrival in Australia. The chapter further explores the legal system of South Sudan. It firstly

---

[1] Robert O Collins, *A History of Modern Sudan* (Cambridge University Press, 2008).

[2] Hilde F Johnson, *South Sudan: The Untold Story from Independence to the Civil War* (IB Tauris, 2016).

[3] Sayyid Muhammad Abu Rannat, "The Relationship between Islamic and Customary Law in the Sudan 1," *Journal of African Law* 4, no. 1 (1960).

[4] Jan Arno Hessbruegge, "Customary Law and Authority in a State under Construction: The Case of South Sudan," *African Journal of Legal Studies* 5, no. 3 (2012).

shows that the legal system has been either unstable during times of war or non-existent since due to long-standing civil war and military regimes, the rule of law in Sudan collapsed. Since Sudan's independence, there has been a complete absence of rule of law, including the separation of powers and the protection of human rights. Consequently, the people of Sudan have been living in a somewhat lawless society led by soldiers and rebel groups, where they have no access to human rights, legal protection, or justice.[5] Consequently, the people of South Sudan have no understanding of, or no faith in, the legal system, nor are they likely to access it to resolve their family problems.

Prior to the independence of South Sudan on 9 July 2011, Sudan was geographically the largest country in Africa, containing over 40 million people.[6] Its population is also highly diverse. Sudan consisted of more than 500 ethnic groups, speaking approximately 145 different languages and dialects.[7] This diversity reflects the division of the country into North and South Sudan. Present day South Sudan is inhabited by diverse ethnic groups who identify as ethnic-Africans. In North Sudan, most people identify as Arabs, although many are of African descent. The South Sudanese speak many languages; those most commonly spoken are the *lingua franca*, the "Juba Arabic," ethnic languages or dialects, and English. The main religion in the South is Christianity. The main language in North Sudan is Sudanese Arabic, which is a type of Arabic, and the main religion is Islam. [8] There are also other languages, dialects, religious beliefs, and traditions practiced throughout both North and South Sudan.[9]

[5] Johnson, *South Sudan: The Untold Story from Independence to the Civil War*.

[6] Peter Malcolm Holt and Martin W Daly, *A History of the Sudan: From the Coming of Islam to the Present Day* (Routledge, 2014); ibid.; ibid.

[7] England : Ashgate Aldershot, *The Multi-Cultural Family*, ed. Ann Laquer Estin (Aldershot, England: Aldershot, England : Ashgate, 2008).

[8] Holt and Daly, *A History of the Sudan: From the Coming of Islam to the Present Day*.19

[9] Francis Deng, *Customary Law in the Modern World: The Crossfire of Sudan's War of Identities* (Routledge, 2009).

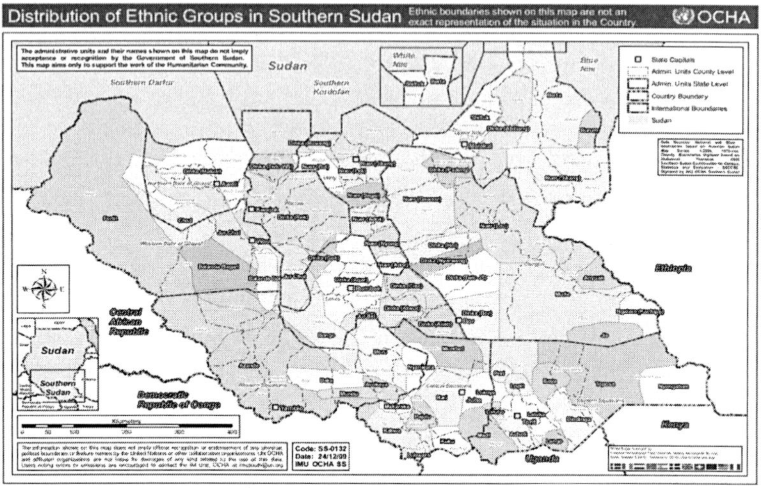

Figure 2.1: Demographic Map of South Sudan

Figure 2.1 shows the distribution of ethnic groups across South Sudan. In South Sudan, there are sixty-four ethnic groups, mostly consisting of Indigenous peoples broadly categorised into the *Nilotic, Nilo-Hamitic, and Sudanic* groups.[10] The Nilotic people are the largest ethnic group in South Sudan, and their original home can be traced to the Nile Valley from where they disperse across South Sudan and neighbouring regions.[11] They mostly speak the Nilotic language which is part of a large ethnic sub-group of the Nilo-Saharan language. It is mainly spoken in Eastern African countries including South Sudan, Kenya, Northern Tanzania, Uganda, and South-Western Ethiopia.[12] The major Nilotic groups in Australia is the Jieng

10 Santino Atem Deng, "Fitting the Jigsaw: South Sudanese Family Dynamics and Parenting Practices in Australia" (Victoria University, 2016).

11 Francis M Deng, "Customary Law in the Cross-Fire of Sudan's War of Identities," *Washington DC: Institute of Peace* (2006).

12 James Wani-Kana Lino Lejukole, "" We Will Do It Our Own Ways": A Perspective of Southern Sudanese Refugees Resettlement Experiences in Australian Society" (2009).

(known to many as Dinka).[13] The next largest is the Nuer (Naath), followed by the Shullok (Collo), Acholi, and many other small ethnic groups.[14]

The second group in South Sudan consists of the Nilo-Hamites, who are mainly located the central and eastern parts of the Equatorial and Upper Nile regions of South Sudan. This group speak Bari, Otuho (Lotuko), and several other dialects. Whereas the Nilotic people rear farm animals, the Nilo-Hamites depend mostly on subsistence farming.[15] The third group of people in South Sudan are the Sudanic. This group lives mainly in the East-Western Equatorial and Western Bahr El Ghazal regions and comprised of Azande, Balanda, Madi, Muru, and a few others.[16] Similar to Nilo-Hamites, the Sudanic group are also subsistence farmers.

While these are the three main ethnic groups within South Sudan, there are also many others. Table 2.1 lists all the sixty-four ethnic groups, and each has its own distinctive customary law system. The Nilotic, Nilo-Hamites and Sudanic peoples are known as the Indigenous peoples of South Sudan. Many other groups also immigrated to South Sudan before and after its independence in 2011. This diversity means that South Sudan is still strongly divided. There have been barriers in identifying all of the ethnic and cultural groups in South Sudan, as well as problems incorporating all groups within a unified nation.[17] The first national census was scheduled for 2015 but was cancelled due to ongoing civil unrest.[18]

In South Sudan, many of the ethnic groups live in semi-independent homesteads that are clustered into villages. The homesteads are inhabited by immediate and extended family members. The way in which groups are structured and regulated varies according to ethnic identity. Some groups (the Shilluk, Azande, and Anyuak) have been traditionally administered by a King, whereas others are overseen by Chiefs. Most groups followed traditional beliefs before the arrival of Christianity, especially within groups located in rural areas, and many have continued with their traditional

---

[13] Ibid.

[14] Mohamed Fadlalla, "Customary Laws in Southern Sudan: Customary Law of Dinka and Nuer," *New York: iUniverse* (2009).

[15] Jok Madut Jok, *Diversity, Unity, and Nation Building in South Sudan* (US Institute of Peace, 2011).

[16] Jay Marlowe, *Belonging and Transnational Refugee Settlement: Unsettling the Everyday and the Extraordinary* (Routledge, 2017).

[17] Kok, op.cit. 29

[18] Douglas Hamilton Johnson, *The Root Causes of Sudan's Civil Wars: Peace or Truce* (Boydell & Brewer Ltd, 2011).

practices.[19] Some communities continue to believe in the power of spirits; for instance, the Jieng believe in a supreme God (Nhialic) in the sky, and fortune-tellers, diviners, rainmakers, and spear-masters are highly regarded members of the community.[20]

Within South Sudanese culture, the division of labour has been traditionally structured around gender, age, and individual status within the family, clan, and the larger community.[21] Traditionally, men have largely been the head of the family, protectors of their own families as well as of the clan and wider community, while women are homemakers and carers for the general well-being of the family. This family structure, however, has changed in response to the civil wars, as with the deaths of so many male heads of families, women have had to step into the vacuum.[22] Every ethnic group in South Sudan has its own way of introducing young men and women to adulthood,[23] for instance, the Jieng and Nuer communities use marking an individual's someone's forehead and the wearing of special beads to denote being initiated into adulthood and being able to marry and have a family.[24] For most people in South Sudan, marriage is seen as an important milestone which involves not just a couple but also the entire immediate and extended family members on both the paternal and maternal side of the family,[25] and as will be examined in the following Chapter, traditional norms around marriage also extends to the practice of early and forced marriage, polygyny and levirate marriage.[26]

---

19 Tracy E. Higgins, *Future of African Customary Law*, ed. Paolo Galizzi and Jeanmarie Fenrich (Cambridge University Press, 2011).

20 Deng, *Customary Law in the Modern World: The Crossfire of Sudan's War of Identities*.24

21 Francis Mading Deng, *The Dinka of the Sudan* (New York: New York, Holt, Rinehart and Winston, 1972).

22 Julia A Duany and Wal Duany, "War and Women in the Sudan: Role Change and Adjustment to New Responsibilities," *Northeast African Studies* 8, no. 2 (2001).

23 Deng, *The Dinka of the Sudan*.

24 Ibid.

25 Ibid.

26 Stephanie Beswick, "" We Are Bought Like Clothes": The War over Polygyny and Levirate Marriage in South Sudan," *Northeast African Studies* 8, no. 2 (2001).

Table 2.1: List of 64 Ethnic Groups with Distinctive Customary Law in South Sudan

1. *Acholi*	2. *Adio (Makaraka*	3. *Aja*
4. *Anyuak (Anyuaa*	5. *Atuot (Reel)*	6. *Atuot (Reel)*
7. *Azande*	8. *Bai*	9. *Baka*
10. *Balanda-Boor*	11. *Balanda-Bviri*	12. *Banda*
13. *Bari*	14. *Binga*	15. *Bongo*
16. *Didinga*	17. *Dinka (Jieng)*	18. *Dongotona*
19. *Feroghe*	20. *Gollo*	21. *Ifoto*
22. *Imatong*	23. *Indri*	24. *Jiye*
25. *Jur (Beli & Modo)*	26. *Jurchol (Luo)*	27. *Kakwa*
28. *Kara*	29. *Keliku*	30. *Kuku*
31. *Lango*	32. *Larim (Boya)*	33. *Logir*
34. *Lokoya*	35. *Lopit*	36. *Lotuka (Otuho)*
37. *Lugbwara*	38. *Lulubo*	39. *Maban*
40. *Madi*	41. *Mananger*	42. *Mangayat*
43. *Moro*	44. *Moro Kodo*	45. *Mundari*
46. *Mundu*	47. *Murle*	48. *Ndogo*
49. *Ngulngule*	50. *Nuer (Naath)*	51. *Nyangatom*
52. *Nyangwara*	53. *Pari*	54. *Pojullo*
55. *Sere*	56. *Shatt*	57. *Shilluk (Chollo)*
58. *Suri (Kachipo)*	59. *Tenet*	60. *Tid*
61. *Toposa*	62. *Uduk*	63. *Woro*
64. *Yulu*		

2.1. Socio-Political History

Before its partition, Sudan was geographically located in the northern part of the African continent. It shares borders with Egypt and Libya to the north; Uganda and Kenya to the south; Ethiopia and Eritrea to the east; and the Democratic Republic of the Congo, Chad, and the Central African Republic to the west; and Egypt to the north.[27] For almost 200 years, South Sudan has been subjected to exploitation by its northern neighbours. Arab Muslim raids into South Sudan looking for slaves as well as gold, ivory and timber laid the foundation for future cultural, racial and economic conflict.[28]

These tensions were exacerbated by European invaders seeking trade for commodities and new markets.[29] In 1820, the Ottoman-led Egyptian army invaded Sudan, and the country became an occupied territory of Egypt for the next sixty-five years. After the Ottoman Empire's death, the Egyptians were unable to provide a cohesive regime in Sudan whose people, always on the lookout for a possible revolt, overthrew Egyptian rule in 1885 under the leadership of Mahdi.[30]

This respite from foreign intrusion was short-lived as Egypt, led by British colonial forces, again conquered Sudan in 1889. Sudan was then subjected to the combined rule of the Anglo-Egyptian forces for the next sixty-six years, between 1889 and 1955. During this time, the country was also known as Anglo-Egyptian Sudan.[31]

Colonial rule recognised the division between the predominantly Islamic north and the Christian/Ethnic African south, and the country was largely governed as two distinct states.[32] Following British withdrawal in 1956 and Sudan's independence, a supposed system of power-sharing was implemented.[33] However, this arrangement continued the focus of government and military

[27] Peter Malcolm Holt, *A Modern History of the Sudan: From the Funj Sultanate to the Present Day* (London: Weidenfeld & Nicolson [1961], 1961).
[28] Jane Kani Edward, "Sudanese Women Refugees: Transformations and Future Imaginings," (2007).
[29] Holt and Daly, *A History of the Sudan: From the Coming of Islam to the Present Day*.
[30] Abu Rannat, "The Relationship between Islamic and Customary Law in the Sudan 1."
[31] Gabriel R Warburg, "Historical Discord in the Nile Valley," (1992).
[32] Richard Gray, "A History of the Southern Sudan, 1839-1889," (1961).
[33] Douglas H. Johnson, *The Root Causes of Sudan's Civil Wars*, ed. Institute International African (Bloomington: Bloomington : Indiana University Press, 2003).

power in the north.[34] South Sudan has a long history of oppression which is the outcome of colonisation, the lack of political representation, and the concentration of power within the north. The basis of this oppression did not substantially change with independence of Sudan.[35]

In 1953, Egypt and Britain forged an agreement that promised Sudan's independence within the following three years, and Sudan achieved independence on 1 January 1956.[36] During the process toward independence, the South Sudanese were given assurance by the then power brokers in North Sudan that they would be given a federal system of the government in the south after independence.[37] Despite all these promises, the newly appointed leadership upheld religious and Arabic ideology and ignored cultural differences that existed amongst the people of Sudan.[38]

As a consequence of the new government's breach of their promises, the people in South Sudan rebelled against the government. This conflict later evolved into a civil war that would last over a decade.[39] General Ibrahim Abboud seized took power in a military coup in November 1958, notifying Sudanese citizens over the radio of his ascent to power.[40] The new regime continued the war in the south, and expelled hundreds of missionaries from Sudan.[41] Consequently, the leadership of Abboud, *"opted for intensified Arabization and Islamization of non-Muslims"*,[42] which further escalated the conflict between the North and the South. However, the Anglo-Egyptian colonial powers used legal pluralism to govern the country. Thus, what

---

[34] William Twining, "Human Rights: Southern Voices Francis Deng, Abdullahi an-Na'im, Yash Ghai and Upendra Baxi," *Law, Social Justice and Global Development Journal*.
[35] Gray, "A History of the Southern Sudan, 1839-1889."
[36] K Michael Barbour, "The Sudan since Independence," *The Journal of Modern African Studies* 18, no. 1 (1980).
[37] Ibid.
[38] Deng, *Customary Law in the Modern World: The Crossfire of Sudan's War of Identities*.
[39] Douglas H. Johnson, "Judicial Regulation and Administrative Control: Customary Law and the Nuer, 1898–1954," *J. Afr. Hist.* 27, no. 1 (2003).
[40] Alison J. Ayers, "Sudan's Uncivil War: The Global–Historical Constitution of Political Violence," *Review of African Political Economy* 37, no. 124 (2010).
[41] Scopas S Poggo, "General Ibrahim Abboud's Military Administration in the Sudan, 1958-1964: Implementation of the Programs of Islamization and Arabization in the Southern Sudan," *Northeast African Studies* 9, no. 1 (2002).
[42] Ibid.

follows is the overview of Sudan's legal history from colonial rule to the present day.[43]

2.2. Legal History

The legal history of Sudan and South Sudan reflect the divisions and conflicts that have long afflicted these regions. In 1821, the Ottoman Empire invaded Sudan and established foreign rule known as the Turco-Egyptian administration.[44] This administration ruled the country until 1885, when it was deposed by a fundamentalist Islamic movement under the leadership of Mohammed Ahmed. Ahmed became the Mahdi, meaning the Islamic Messiah.[45] Although Sharia Law was imposed by Mahdi, much of the rural north was administered by customary laws that claimed to reflect Islamic principles but were mostly Indigenous.[46] Southern Sudan continued to follow customary practices which had their basis within traditional religious beliefs.[47] After joint British-Egyptian forces overthrew the Mahdist state in 1898, the British-dominated Anglo-Egyptian administration ruled the country until independence on 1 January 1956.[48]

The British established a formal legal system based on English common law, which was modified to an extent to reflect the local conditions of the Sudan.[49] The British tried to respect the Islamic beliefs that dominated in the north and recognised the application of Sharia Law in personal matters. They also recognised that most of the north observed customary practices that differed from orthodox Sharia. In response, they established a system

---

[43] Raphael Koba Badal, "Religion and Conflict in the Sudan: A Perspective," *Bulletin of Peace Proposals* 21, no. 3 (1990).
[44] Richard Leslie Hill, "On the Frontiers of Islam: Two Manuscripts Concerning the Sudan under Turco-Egyptian Rule 1822-1845," (1970).
[45] Alice Moore-Harell, "The Turco-Egyptian Army in Sudan on the Eve of the Mahdiyya, 1877-80," *International Journal of Middle East Studies* 31, no. 1 (1999).
[46] Ibid.
[47] MW Daly, "'Summing Up'islam and Politics in Sudan Islam, Secularism and Politics in Sudan since the Mahdiyya. By Gabriel Warburg. London: Hurst, 2003. Pp. Xvii+ 252.£ 45 (Isbn 1-85065-588-X);£ 19.95, Paperback (Isbn 1-85065-590-1)," *The Journal of African History* 45, no. 02 (2004).
[48] Aharon Layish and Gabriel R Warburg, *The Reinstatement of Islamic Law in Sudan under Numayrī: An Evaluation of a Legal Experiment in the Light of Its Historical Context, Methodology, and Repercussions* (Brill, 2002).
[49] Mark Fathi Massoud, *Law's Fragile State: Colonial, Authoritarian, and Humanitarian Legacies in Sudan* (Cambridge University Press, 2013).

of informal justice which allowed for the administration of customary law.[50] In the south, where communities were largely unaffected by Islam, the British allowed for the continuation of customary laws.[51]

The British attempted to extend English common law through the adoption of a penal code and code of criminal procedure which was applied by the statutory courts.[52] At the level of the local courts, customary law was still applied, but it was also guided by statutory law in criminal matters. A code of civil justice allowed the statutory courts to apply customary law as deemed appropriate. Thus, while customary law continued to be recognised, it was incorporated into a formal legal system.

While the customs and traditions of the southern Sudanese ethnic groups were the primary source of law,[53] the colonial rulers took some steps to improve the operations of customary law alongside their laws in the Sudan. First, customary laws operating in Sudan were formally recognised by colonial powers. Customary laws were also addressed with the passage of the *Civil Justice Ordinance 1929* and the Chief's *Courts Ordinance 1931.*[54]

The second set of laws was a novel development which formally recognised chiefs' legal authority to exercise customary jurisdiction in their traditional tribal areas.[55] Section (6) of the *Civil Justice Ordinance* 1929 provided that, "*the Chiefs Court shall administer the Native Law and custom prevailing in the area over which the Court exercises its jurisdiction provided that such Native Law and Custom is not contrary to justice, morality or order.*"[56] Thus, the continuation of customary laws in the colonial era of the Sudan was affirmed.

Many years of British colonial rule left Sudan with a legal system derived from different sources. In the predominantly Islamic north, personal law pertaining to marriage, divorce, inheritance, adoption, and family disputes

---

[50] Mohammed Ibrahim Khalil, "Sudan Legal System and Problem of Law Reform" (paper presented at the Sudan Law Reform, Odmurman, 2008).
[51] Ibid
[52] Mohammed Ibrahim Khalil, "Sudan Legal System and Problem of Law Reform," *Law Reform in Sudan*, no. OMDURMAN. Ahfad University for Women (2008).
[53] Natale Olwak Akolawin, "Personal Law in the Sudan—Trends and Developments," *Journal of African Law* 17, no. 2.
[54] Khalil, "Sudan Legal System and Problem of Law Reform."
[55] Mohamed Hassan Fadlalla, *Short History of Sudan* (Iuniverse, 2004).
[56] Akolawin, "Personal Law in the Sudan—Trends and Developments."66

were adjudicated in Sharia Courts.[57] In contrast, customary law was practiced in the southern region of Sudan and among other non-Muslim populations, as discussed above. The main legal influence of the British consists of precedents of common law which are used in some cases.[58] Most lawyers and judges were also British trained. Soon after Sudan gained independence in 1956, a discussion was initiated by the new government for a need to reform or remove the legal system imposed by British colonisation. As a result, a commission was formed to review the legal system and to recommend the appropriate legal framework to be used in Sudan.[59] The commission was in the process of preparing a revision of the legal system when it was disrupted by further political conflict. Due to the influence from neighbouring Egypt and the fear of continuation of the British laws, a group of military officers led by Jaafar Nimeiri and the Free Officers' Movement, carried out the 1969 Military coup against the elected civilian government. The regime, which viewed Gamal Abdul Nasser's government in Egypt as a model, dissolved the existing legal review commission and formed a new one dominated by twelve Egyptian jurists.[60]

Subsequently, following the unsuccessful 1971 coup attempt against the Nimeiri government and increasing political disillusionment with Egypt, the Minister for Justice formed a new committee of Sudanese lawyers tasked with examination of the Egyptian-based codes. As a result of this review, the government repealed these codes in 1973, returning Sudan's legal system to its pre-1970 common law basis.[61] Furthermore, the Sources of Judicial Decisions Bill called for a section within the civil procedure code, which allowed judges to apply the concept of "*equality and good conscience*" in the absence of a provision of law, to be repealed. This was permitted provided that it be replaced by the Quran or standards of conduct based on the words and practice of the prophet Muhammad.[62] In September 1983, President Nimeiri issued several decrees, known as the September laws, which imposed Sharia Law. The legislation to facilitate the

[57] Ilias Bantekas and Hassan Abu-Sabeib, "Reconciliation of Islamic Law with Constitutionalism: The Protection of Human Rights in Sudan's New Constitution," *Afr. J. Int'l & Comp. L.* 12 (2000).
[58] Egon Guttmann, "The Reception of the Common Law in the Sudan," *International & Comparative Law Quarterly* 6, no. 03 (1957).
[59]Abdullahi A. An-na' Im and Francis M. Deng, "Self-Determination and Unity: The Case of Sudan," *Law & Policy* 18 (1996).
[60] Ibid
[61] Ibid
[62] Guttmann, "The Reception of the Common Law in the Sudan."

implementation of Sharia Law was approved by the People's Assembly in November 1983 without debate.[63] The imposition of Islamic law was bitterly resented by secularised Muslims and the predominantly non-Muslim population of the south.[64]

The abolition of the 1983 September laws was the primary goal of the Sudan People Liberation Movement (SPLM), which refused end hostilities in the south until its demand were met.[65] The Sudan People's Liberation Army (SPLA) and its political wing, the Sudan People's Liberation Movement (SPLM), launched a revolution struggle against the Khartoum government on 16 May 1983 with the goal of creating a new secular Sudan where religion was separated from state. John Garang, the leader of SPLA/M, was an important factor in the peace settlement between the north and south.[66] Garang argued that the conflict between the two was "*more about cultural, economic, and political marginalization of the peripheries than race and religion.*"[67] Garang sought a unified Sudan that was no longer controlled by the concentration of power in the north.[68]

In 1989, Sadiq al Mahdi reluctantly indicated his willingness to consider repealing the September decrees. He announced that on 1 July 1989, the cabinet would consider draft legislation repealing the September laws and would meet with SPLM leaders to resolve the ongoing civil war peacefully. However, another military coup occurred within twenty-four hours before the Sadiq al Mahdi government was due to vote on the abrogation of the September laws. A new military regime led by General Omar Hassan Hamid al Bashir initially indicated they would retain the freeze of the implementation of the September laws, but Bashir changed his mind. Bashir enlisted al Turabi, the leader of the National Islamic front (NIF) after Nimeiri's overthrow, to prepare new laws based on the Islamic principles.

---

[63] Ibid.
[64] Ibid.
[65] M. Weller et al., *Settling Self-Determination Disputes: Complex Power-Sharing in Theory and Practice* (Martinus Nijhoff Publishers, 2008).
[66] Jok, Leitch, and Vandewint, "A Study of Customary Law in Contemporary Southern Sudan."
[67] Ibid.
[68] LB Lokosang, *South Sudan: The Case for Independence and Learning from Mistakes* (London: Xlibris Corporation, 2010).

In January 1991, Bashir issued a decree that Islam law would be applied in the court throughout the north but not in southern Sudan.[69]

During Nimeriri's administration, the judiciary system had been divided into two sections: a section led by the Chief Justice, and the Sharia segment led by the Chief Qadi.[70] Both criminal and civil cases were adjudicated by the civil courts. All matters of personal status, such as inheritance, marriage, divorce, and family relations were adjudicated by the sharia courts, comprising religious judges trained in Islamic law.[71] The consolidation of the Civil and Sharia courts were made through executive order which created a single High Court of Appeal to replace both the former Supreme Court and the Office of Chief Qadi.[72] Judges were required to apply civil and sharia law as if they were a single code of law.[73] In addition, the High Court of Appeal, as well as all lower courts, was required to apply Islamic law exclusively.[74]

As a result, the judicial system of Sudan was independent in theory. However, since 1958, due to the country's continuous military government, there has been no stability in the legal system as each regime that came to power imposed its own changes and removed the policies of predecessors.[75] For instance, in July 1989, a decree which gave the president powers to appoint and dismiss all judges, was issued.[76] This example illustrates the

---

[69] G Norman Anderson, *Sudan in Crisis: The Failure of Democracy* (University Press of Florida, 1999).
[70] Liv Tønnessen and Liv Tønnessen, "Gendered Citizenship in Sudan: Competing Debates on Family Laws among Northern and Southern Elites in Khartoum," *The Journal of North African Studies* 13, no. 4.
[71] Layish and Warburg, *The Reinstatement of Islamic Law in Sudan under Numayrī: An Evaluation of a Legal Experiment in the Light of Its Historical Context, Methodology, and Repercussions*.47
[72] Abdelsalam Hassan, "History of Law Reform in Sudan," *REDRESS*, no. Khartoum. Sudan (2008).
[73] Ibid.
[74] Jure Vidmar, "South Sudan and the International Legal Framework Governing the Emergence and Delimitation of New States," *Tex. Int'l LJ* 47 (2011).
[75] Bantekas and Abu-Sabeib, "Reconciliation of Islamic Law with Constitutionalism: The Protection of Human Rights in Sudan's New Constitution."
[76] Ibid

collapse of the legal system in Sudan as a whole and, in particular, how the war affected South Sudan at that time.[77]

Consequently, in 2005, an agreement was achieved between the Sudan ruling party, the National Congress Party (NCP), and the Sudan People Liberation Movement/Army (SPLM/A) representing Southern Sudan and other marginalised areas known within the Comprehensive Peace Agreement (CPA).[78] SPLA had fought for independence from the oppressive regime of Omar al Bashir. Under Bashir, Sharia Law, the Arabic language and Arabic culture was imposed on the south. The imposition of the Islamic regime on communities within southern Sudan was the primary source of conflict with the north.[79] The CPA exempted South Sudan from Sharia's Law. Debate flared concerning the status of Sharia Law in the national capital, Khartoum. Many argued that the exemption from Sharia Law should also be extended to Khartoum. However, the NCP, the ruling party in the north, insisted that Sharia Law be applied in Khartoum, and this provision was eventually agreed upon.[80]

2.2.1. First Civil War 1955 - 1972

The first civil war erupted in 1955 and ended in 1972. The consequent peace agreement provided South Sudan with regional autonomy and recognised the dominant Christian belief systems alongside traditional beliefs.[81] However, the peace was short-lived, and war resumed following Nimeiri's imposition of Islamic law and the breach of the peace agreement by dividing the South into three regions.[82] The political leaders of the north claimed a predominantly Arab-Islamic identity, which led to conflict with the native African and partly Christian South. The conflict was led by the Sudan People's Liberation Army and the Sudan People's Liberation Movement (SPLA/M), which now sought liberation of the entire country rather than

---

[77] Danijela Milos, "South Sudanese Communities and Australian Family Law: A Clash of Systems," *Australasian Review of African Studies, The* 32, no. 2 (2011).
[78] Ibid
[79] Amir H Idris, *Sudan's Civil War: Slavery, Race, and Formational Identities* (Lewiston: Edwin Mellen Press, 2001).
[80] Zambakari, "In Search of Durable Peace: The Comprehensive Peace Agreement and Power Sharing in Sudan."
[81] Abel Alier, *Southern Sudan: Too Many Agreements Dishonoured*, vol. 13 (Ithaca Press, 1992).
[82] Ibid.

mere secession of the south.[83] SPLA/M called for a "New Sudan," which would not be divided by race, ethnicity, culture, religion or gender. Encouraged by this vision, marginalised groups in the north, including the Nuba of Southern Kordofan and the Ingessana, or Funj, of the Southern Blue Nile, which had retained an African cultural identity alongside an Africanised version of Islam, also joined the conflict in support of the South.[84]

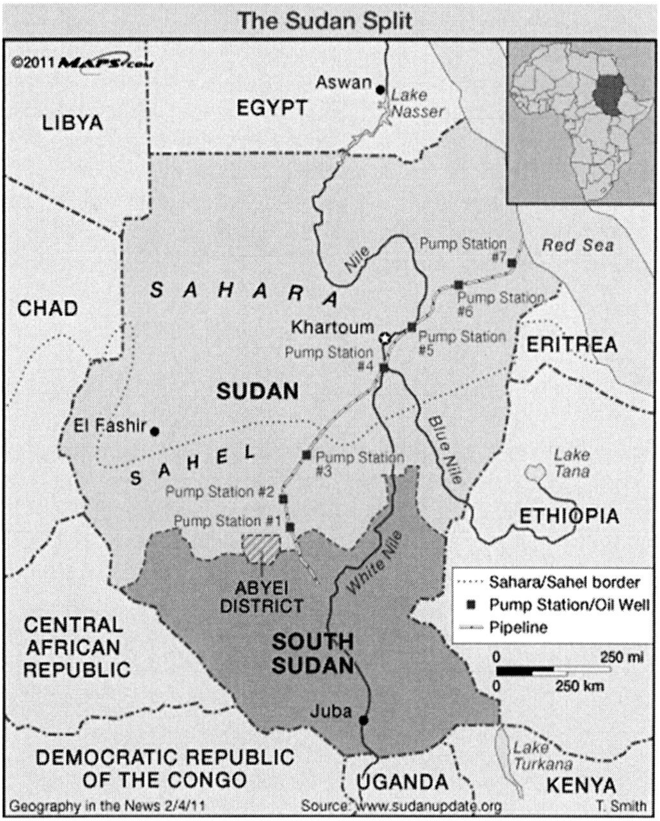

Figure 2:2. Map of the Split Sudan

[83] Jok Madut Jok and Sharon Elaine Hutchinson, "Sudan's Prolonged Second Civil War and the Militarization of Nuer and Dinka Ethnic Identities," *African Studies Review* 42, no. 02 (1999).
[84] Ibid.

Nevertheless, the conflict resumed in 1983 upon the introduction of Sharia across the Sudan. The imposition of the Islamic law over the ethnic African and Christian majority in the southern region of the Sudan resulted in the rebellion which become known as Sudan's second civil war.[85]

2.2.2. The Second Civil War 1983 - 2005

A struggle for South Sudan's independence commenced in 1955 until 1972.[86] The war concluded in 1972, with a peace accord which allowed the south a regional autonomous government. This government recognised the freedom of belief and religion since the majority of people in Sudan's southern region believed in Christianity and traditional African religions.[87] This peace and tranquillity lasted for only eleven years until another war reignited in 1983. This war was in reaction to president Nimeiri's imposition of Islamic law, in addition to the partition of Southern Sudan into three regions, which constituted a unilateral abrogation of the peace agreement.[88]

The partition of the south and the imposition of Islamic law triggered a return to armed struggle under the Sudan People's Liberation Army and the Sudan People's Liberation Movement (SPLA/M).[89] As a result of this conflict, the dominant Arab-Islamic leadership imposed its Islamic culture upon the largely Indigenous and Christian south.[90] The SPLM/A's declared objective, unlike in the first war, was not the secession of the south from the north, but the liberation of the whole country from Arab-Islamic domination. The SPLM/A called for the creation of a "New Sudan," in which there would be no discrimination according to race, ethnicity, culture, religion, or gender.[91] This vision of equality appealed to the marginalised

---

[85] Mawut Achiecque Mach Guarak, *Integration and Fragmentation of the Sudan: An African Renaissance* (AuthorHouse, 2011).

[86] Jaclyn Christine Garcia, "The Future of South Sudanese Women: Restructuring Customary Law in South Sudan" (Brandeis University, 2011).

[87] Øystein H Rolandsen and Martin W Daly, *A History of South Sudan: From Slavery to Independence* (Cambridge University Press, 2016).

[88] Jay Marlowe, "South Sudanese Diaspora in Australasia," *Australasian Review of African Studies, The* 32, no. 2 (2011).

[89] Alex De Waal, "When Kleptocracy Becomes Insolvent: Brute Causes of the Civil War in South Sudan," *African Affairs* 113, no. 452 (2014).

[90] Ibid.

[91] Catherine Vanner, Spogmai Akseer, and Thursica Kovinthan, "Learning Peace (and Conflict): The Role of Primary Learning Materials in Peacebuilding in Post-War Afghanistan, South Sudan and Sri Lanka," *Journal of Peace Education* 14, no. 1 (2017).

regions of the north, which remained African in race, ethnicity, and culture, but maintained an Africanised version of Islam. In the mid-1980s, the Nuba of Southern Kordofan and the Ingessana, or Funj, of the Southern Blue Nile joined the south in the struggle.[92]

The Sudan People's Liberation Army (SPLA), and its people political wing the Sudan People's Liberation Movement (SPLM), were formed under the leadership of John Garang de Mabior. The SPLA/SPLM began to resist the policies of the northern and Islamic based government in Khartoum.[93] Garang was a former senior military officer within Sudan's army, and formed this rebel group in response to the government's policies and action in the south.[94] This new rebel movement was a significant catalyst for the second civil war in 1983, which resulted in the displacement of millions of South Sudanese people to neighbouring countries.[95]

Under Garang, the SPLA and SPLM fought the northern government forces.[96] Conflict occurred largely in the south, with devastating consequences. Government militia burnt entire villages to the ground, and murdered thousands of people living in villages in the south; millions were forced to flee.[97] Many hundreds of women and girls were raped, kidnapped, or taken as slaves to the north.[98]

The second civil war officially ended with a peace agreement signed in 2005. However, the devastation that occurred still resonates. In January 2011, South Sudanese nationals, including thousands who had resettled in other countries, voted on whether to become independent from the north. This reignited debate over control of oil and set off further violence in southern regions.[99] The two major civil wars between the north and South Sudan account for more than forty years of protracted conflict since the

---

[92] Idris, *Sudan's Civil War: Slavery, Race, and Formational Identities*.92
[93] A Boswell, "Sudan: Will the North Survive If the South Secedes," *Retrieved January* 24 (2011).
[94] Amel Aldehaib, *Sudan's Comprehensive Peace Agreement Viewed through the Eyes of the Women of South Sudan* (Institute for Justice and Reconciliation, 2010).
[95] Zambakari, "In Search of Durable Peace: The Comprehensive Peace Agreement and Power Sharing in Sudan."
[96] S. F. Beswick, "Islam and the Dinka of the Southern Sudan from the Pre-Colonial Period to Independence (1956)," *Journal of Asian and African Studies* 35, no. 4.
[97] Clemence Pinaud, "South Sudan: Civil War, Predation and the Making of a Military Aristocracy," *African Affairs* 113, no. 451 (2014).
[98] Ibid
[99] Boswell, "Sudan: Will the North Survive If the South Secedes."

country gained independence in 1956.[100] On one level, the warfare can be understood as a conflict between the Islamic Arabs of the north and southern ethnic African Christians. However, this conceptualisation is rather simple. The history of civil wars goes further than conflict between ethnic or religious identities, as there have been contentious debates about access to natural resources—most notably oil.[101]

The war intensified noticeably after Omar Bashir's coup d'état.[102] By 2001, an estimated two million people had been killed by war-related violence and famine, and a further million people were displaced. Bashir was indicted in 2009 by the International Criminal Court for crimes against humanity and war crimes and, in 2010, on charges of genocide. However, it was only in 2019 that Sudan's ruling military council agreed to transfer Bashir to Hague for trial.[103]

The plight of South Sudanese people gained international exposure in the late 1990s and early 2000s. This was largely due to the experiences of the "Lost Boys," a few thousand of whom were resettled in the US in early 2000s.[104] It is worthwhile noting that the author of this book is one of these Lost Boys referenced in many books, including his own.[105] The Lost Boys made their way by foot to refugee camps in Ethiopia and Kenya where they spent years enduring adverse conditions that meant scarce resources, limited security, and few opportunities for education.[106] Others found places of asylum in Egypt, Syria, and other neighbouring African countries. It was from these places that tens of thousands of forcibly displaced South Sudanese people were offered opportunities for resettlement in countries

---

[100] Hessbruegge, "Customary Law and Authority in a State under Construction: The Case of South Sudan."

[101] Tiernan Mennen, "Legal Pluralism in Southern Sudan: Can the Rest of Africa Show the Way?," *Africa Policy Journal* 3, no. 1 (2007).

[102] Julie Flint and Alex De Waal, *Darfur: A New History of a Long War* (Zed Books, 2008).

[103] Allard Duurma and Tanya R Muller, 'The Icc Indictment Against Al-Bashir And Its Repercussions For Peacekeeping And Humanitarian Operations In Darfur' (2019) 40(5) *The World Quarterly* 890.

[104] Melinda B Robins, "'Lost Boys' and the Promised Land Us Newspaper Coverage of Sudanese Refugees," *Journalism* 4, no. 1 (2003).

[105] Juuk, *From Tyranny to Triumph : Once a Sudanese Refugee, Now a Proud Citizen of Australia and South Sudan / Buol Garang Anyieth Juuk ; Edited by Don Sinnott.*

[106] Ibid.

signatory to the *United Nations 1951 Refugee Convention,* including Australia.

2.3. South Sudan Independence

South Sudan attained independence from the Republic of Sudan on 9 July 2011, after almost fifty years of continuous civil war.[107] Independence came pursuant to the Comprehensive Peace Agreement (CPA), signed six years earlier. The CPA comprised of six protocols agreed to between 2002 and 2004 and provided the basis for governance during the Interim Period (9 July 2005 – 9 July 2011).[108]

The Republic of South Sudan has a pluralist legal regime that reflects the country's turbulent history. The transitional constitution recognises five sources of law: the transitional constitution itself; written law; customs and traditions of the people; the will of the people; and "any other relevant source."[109] Prior to independence, Sudanese law was in force on the territory of what is now the Republic of South Sudan. Religious laws govern personal matters while civil matters are formally governed by statute although, in practice, resort is often made to unwritten rules and traditional community justice systems to resolve disputes. The *1998 Constitution of Sudan* designated sharia as the primary source of Sudanese law, leading judges to infuse their rulings with Islamic principles in order to interpret and apply religiously neutral laws in accordance with sharia principles.

Since independence, the parliament of South Sudan has faced the enormous task of amending, adapting, and updating existing laws and enacting new ones. This is to create a legal system that embraces the cultural identities of the new country, while providing the stability necessary to reduce ethnic tension and foster investment.[110] The difficulty of setting an agenda and pursuing a clear legislative strategy presents an additional obstacle.

The current framework within which the justice system is to operate in South Sudan differs from that previously applicable in three major ways.

---

[107] Cherry Leonardi et al., *Local Justice in Southern Sudan* (United States Institute of Peace, 2010).

[108] (ABS), "Culturally Diversity in Australia."

[109] Ibid.

[110] Alexander P. Danne, "Customary and Indigenous Law in Transitional Post-Conflict States: A South Sudanese Case Study," *Monash University Law Review* 30, no. 2.

Firstly, sharia is no longer a source of law. Secondly, during the Interim Period, English and Arabic were the official working languages; however, since independence the official working language has been English only. Thirdly, the justice system departs from inquisitorial procedures in favour of the new statutory court system which includes more adversarial features. However, the changed framework has yet to be adopted throughout the system and implementation of these changes has not been unproblematic. In particular, as of December 2013, the reform towards the adversarial model has not yet been integrated into the daily functioning of the courts, and it appears that many trials continue to be conducted according to inquisitorial procedures.[111] Further, Arabic has continued to be used in court; the switch to English has only posed significant practical problems, since many judges, prosecutors, and legal practitioners were trained in Khartoum and are not yet familiar with English legal terminology.[112]

2.4. Resettlement of Refugees and Other Migrants in Australia

This section provides a brief historical perspective of immigration and resettlement of refugees and migrants in Australia. This is important to enhance our understanding of the arrival of other refugees and the problems they encounter in trying to integrate into Australian society. Since 1945, when Australia's first immigration department was established, approximately seven million permanent migrants have settled in Australia.[113] The literature indicates that until recently, and due to the White Australia Policy, most immigrants came from Great Britain and Ireland.[114] The privileging of British immigration has resulted in mainstream culture reflecting Anglo-Celtic language, cultural norms, values and attitudes. Australian political and legal systems also have their roots in Great Britain.

---

[111] Christopher Zambakari, "South Sudan and the Nation-Building Project: Lessons and Challenges," *International Journal of African Renaissance Studies-Multi-, Inter-and Transdisciplinarity* 8, no. 1 (2013).

[112] Ibid.

[113] Keith Jacobs, *Experience and Representation: Contemporary Perspectives on Migration in Australia* (Routledge, 2016).

[114] Roger White and Bedassa Tadesse, "Immigration Policy, Cultural Pluralism and Trade: Evidence from the White Australia Policy," *Pacific Economic Review* 12, no. 4 (2007).

Arguably, this history has also shaped the perceptions and attitudes of Australians towards other groups of migrants and refugees in Australia.[115]

The White Australia Policy was dismantled in the late 1960s and early 1970s. This has resulted in a move away from the belief that immigrants should share cultural similarities and shared values with mainstream Australian cultural in order to ensure easy integration into Australian society. In 1973, the *Racial Discrimination Act* made the selection of immigrants based on race illegal.[116]

2.4.1. Early and Present Immigration to Australia

Aboriginal people inhabited and flourished in Australia for over 60,000 years, before the arrival of the first fleet of Europeans on Australian shores.[117] Their societies were very diverse, with about 600 language groups spread across the continent. The arrival of Europeans resulted in devastating consequences, commencing in 1788.[118] British colonial law did not recognise the Aboriginal people as possessing sovereignty over Australia, nor did it recognise Aboriginal customary law.[119]

Australia's cultural transformation began with immigration from Great Britain.[120]

This was then followed by immigrants from other parts of Europe, as well as other regions including China, the Pacific Islands, Lebanon, Afghanistan and India.[121] The numbers of British migrants, however, continued to lead

[115] Ibid.
[116] Caroline B Brettell and James F Hollifield, *Migration Theory: Talking across Disciplines* (Routledge, 2014).
[117] Julie Matthews, "Schooling and Settlement: Refugee Education in Australia," *International studies in sociology of education* 18, no. 1 (2008).
[118] Campbell McLachlan, "The Recognition of Aboriginal Customary Law: Pluralism Beyond the Colonial Paradigm: A Review Article," *International and Comparative Law Quarterly* (1988).
[119] Ibid.
[120] White and Tadesse, "Immigration Policy, Cultural Pluralism and Trade: Evidence from the White Australia Policy."
[121] Stephen Constantine, "British Emigration to the Empire-Commonwealth since 1880: From Overseas Settlement to Diaspora?," *The Journal of Imperial and Commonwealth History* 31, no. 2 (2003).

until 1973 when the White Australian Policy of 1901 was abolished.[122] This policy allowed only White European settlers, but was supplemented by the post-World War II migration from the other parts of Europe, Middle East, Asia and South America and most recently, by arrivals from Africa, including from South Sudan.[123]

The arrival of refugees from Central and Eastern Europe who were fleeing various communist and authoritarian regimes occurred between the period 1920-1940 and 1947-1953.[124] From the mid-1950s, immigrants started to arrive from Hungary and Czechoslovakia after their respective political and failed uprisings. In the 1970s, waves of refugees arrived from South and East Asia resulting from the wars in that region.[125] In the 1980s, many refugees fleeing from political turmoil, civil and military upheavals, were resettled from South America, and, in the 1990s, from El Salvador and Yugoslavia,[126] followed by refugees from Africa and the Middle East in the late 1990s.[127] Most of these forced migrations resulted from armed conflicts, human rights abuses, and natural and other man-made disasters such as famine, all of which forced people out of their home countries.[128] Globally, there are about sixty-eight million internally Displaced Persons (IDPs), while twenty-five million people are officially recorded as refugees and three million are asylum seekers.[129] According to the United Nations High Commissioner for Refugees (UNHCR) 1951 Convention:

> a “refugee” is a person who is owing to a well-founded fear of being persecuted for reasons of race, religion, nationality, membership of a particular social group, or political opinion, is outside the country of his

[122] Robert Schweitzer et al., "Trauma, Post-Migration Living Difficulties, and Social Support as Predictors of Psychological Adjustment in Resettled Sudanese Refugees," *Australian and New Zealand Journal of Psychiatry* 40, no. 2 (2006).
[123] Jay M Marlowe, "Beyond the Discourse of Trauma: Shifting the Focus on Sudanese Refugees," *Journal of refugee studies* 23, no. 2 (2010).
[124] Nigar G. Khawaja and Karla Milner, "Acculturation Stress in South Sudanese Refugees: Impact on Marital Relationships," *International Journal of Intercultural Relations* 36, no. 5 (2012).
[125] Farida Fozdar and Lisa Hartley, "Refugee Resettlement in Australia: What We Know and Need to Know," *Refugee Survey Quarterly* 32, no. 3 (2013).
[126] Ibid.
[127] Ibid.
[128] Khawaja and Milner, "Acculturation Stress in South Sudanese Refugees: Impact on Marital Relationships."
[129] Tamirace Fakhoury, "Multi-Level Governance and Migration Politics in the Arab World: The Case of Syria’s Displacement," *Journal of Ethnic and Migration Studies* 45, no. 8 (2019).

> nationality, and unable to or owing to such fear, is unwilling to avail himself of the protection of that country.[130]

As signatory to the Geneva Convention 1951 on the protection and the status of refugees, and as a member of international community and the United Nations (UN),[131] Australia has a collective obligation and responsibility not only to protect refugees but also to find a solution to these humanitarian needs.[132] Australia has two core resettlement categories: skilled migration and family migrants; and a humanitarian program for refugees and others in refugee related situations.[133] The majority of Sudanese and South Sudanese, in particular, have arrived in Australia under the humanitarian program.[134] Australian resettles refugees via two programs. First, the Onshore Protection / Asylum program is intended to protect refugees already in Australia, especially those who are found to be refugees according to the UNHCR convention.[135] The second program is the Offshore Resettlement Program, which allows for the off-shore processing of refugees, who are then able to resettle in Australia on protection and humanitarian visas. The majority of South Sudanese who have resettled in Australia have arrived under this second program.

This program is further divided into two categories: refugees, and Special Humanitarian Program (SHP).[136] Someone is considered a refugee within the first category if they may be subjected to persecution in their home country, and they are now outside their homeland. Refugees also need to be

---

[130] James C Hathaway, *The Rights of Refugees under International Law* (Cambridge University Press, 2005).

[131] Andreas Zimmermann, Jonas Dörschner, and Felix Machts, *The 1951 Convention Relating to the Status of Refugees and Its 1967 Protocol: A Commentary* (Oxford University Press, 2011).

[132] Edward Newman and Joanne Van Selm, "Refugees and Forced Displacement," *International Security, Human Vulnerability, and the State, UNU Press, Tokyo Japan* (2003).

[133] Fozdar and Hartley, "Refugee Resettlement in Australia: What We Know and Need to Know."138

[134] Gail Mason and Mariastella Pulvirenti, "Former Refugees and Community Resilience 'Papering Over'domestic Violence," *British Journal of Criminology* 53, no. 3 (2013).

[135] Ibid

[136] Claire Murphy, "Asylum Seeker Policy in Australia: Sending Refugees Back to Persecution" (Murdoch University, 2014).

recommended by the UNHCR as needing resettlement.[137] The Special Humanitarian Programs (SHP) covers people who are not identified as refugees as such, but are nevertheless outside their home country, are subject to great discrimination amounting to serious human rights violations, and have immediate family members in Australia who have already been granted protection visas.[138] The SHP requires the refugee to be supported by a sponsor who must be an Australian citizen / permanent resident or an eligible New Zealand citizen, or through sponsorship by an Australian-based organisation.[139] Decisions concerning who can be resettled upon the SHP are normally based on UNHCR recommendations concerning resettlement needs, and on the capacity of the sponsor to assist in resettlement. The government also consults with humanitarian organisations and immigration and border protection authorities in Australia.[140]

Currently, Australia is resettling non-European refugees and migrants, including the thousands of South Sudanese refugees on humanitarian visas through the UNHCR and its overseas missions in Africa.[141] According to Robinson, there were over thirty thousand people of Sudanese heritage living in Australia by June 2010.[142] However, it should be noted that the Australian Bureau of Statistics (ABS) indicates that there were only 26,199 South Sudanese/Sudanese-born in Australia during the 2011 census.[143] The difference in numbers is likely because the ABS figures considered only those who were born in South Sudan and Sudan before arriving in Australia, while Robinson's research included those of Sudanese heritage who were born in countries of refuge in Africa, as well as those who were born in Australia to South Sudanese and Sudanese parents. It should be noted, however, that before South Sudan became independent, the majority of South Sudanese identified themselves as Sudanese, hence, it is arguable that

137 Klaus Neumann et al., "Refugee Settlement in Australia: Policy, Scholarship and the Production of Knowledge, 1952– 2013," *Journal of Intercultural Studies* 35, no. 1 (2014).

138 Murphy, "Asylum Seeker Policy in Australia: Sending Refugees Back to Persecution."

139 Ibid.

140 Ibid.

141 Kate E Murray, "Sudanese Perspectives on Resettlement in Australia," *Journal of Pacific Rim Psychology* 4, no. 01 (2010).

142 Robinson, "Sudanese Heritage and Living in Australia: Implications of Demography for Individual and Community Resilience."

143 Ibid

the population of Sudanese from the north is very small in the stated above figure.

As a result, the ethnic dynamic of Australian society has dramatically and irrevocably changed since the 1940s. According to the last Census, one in four Australians were born overseas.[144] This means that Australia is a multicultural country which has a rich diversity of cultures, ethnic identities, religions, and languages. Although many immigrants come from countries and continents with similar laws to Australia, especially Europe, this may not be the case for those who were resettled from Africa,[145] in particular, from South Sudan where customary laws are followed.

Before exploring the arrival of Sudanese refugees and other African groups, it is necessary to define and differentiate between migrants and refugees. This definition is important, as the experiences of migrants and refugees may differ significantly, and this study deals primarily with the specific experiences of South Sudanese refugees who have resettled in Australia over the last twenty years. A refugee, according to the UN Refugee Convention of 1951,[146] is defined as "a person who: owing to well-founded fear of being persecuted for reasons of race, religion, nationality, membership of a particular social group or political opinion, and is outside the country of his/her nationality and is unable, or owing to such fear, is unwilling to avail himself of the protection of that country".[147] Conversely, migrants make a conscious choice to leave their country of origin and can return there without a problem.[148] If life in their chosen destination does not work out as they had hoped, or if they become homesick, it is safe for them to return home.

---

[144] Anthony Moran, "Post-Multicultural Australia? Cosmopolitanism Critique and the Future of Australian Multiculturalism," in *The Public Life of Australian Multiculturalism* (Springer, 2017).
[145] Elizabeth Wendy Harte, "Settlement Geography of African Refugee Communities in Southeast Queensland: An Analysis of Residential Distribution and Secondary Migration," (2010).
[146] Ivor C Jackson, "The 1951 Convention Relating to the Status of Refugees: A Universal Basis for Protection," *Int'l J. Refugee l.* 3 (1991).
[147] Louise Wilhelmine Holborn, Philip Chartrand, and Rita Chartrand, *Refugees, a Problem of Our Time: The Work of the United Nations High Commissioner for Refugees, 1951-1972*, vol. 2 (Scarecrow Press, 1975).
[148] John W Berry et al., "Comparative Studies of Acculturative Stress," *International migration review* (1987).

However, the question arises: are the South Sudanese who resettled in Australia, many of whom are now Australian citizens, still considered as refugees? According to UN Convention on Refugees, resettlement is the term used to describe "the transfer of refugees from the country in which they have sought refuge to another State that has agreed to admit them."[149] Resettlement is intended to protect refugees whose life, liberty, safety, health, or other human rights are at risk in the country where they sought refuge. For this reason, when refugees are permanently resettled, they are no longer stateless and have all their rights protected by the third country like Australia. For the purpose of this book, I will adopt the term "former refugees."

2.4.2. South Sudanese in Refugee Camps

As stated early in this chapter, Sudan's first civil war began shortly after independence from joint British-Egyptian colonial rule in 1956 and continued until 1972 with a peace accord reached by two warring parties known as the Addis Ababa agreement.[150] A second civil war broke out in 1983 and continued until 2005 when a similar agreement was reached in the Kenyan town of Naivasha, referred to as the Comprehensive Peace Agreement (CPA).[151] The toll from both wars is estimated to have reached two million deaths and four million people have been either internally displaced or forced to flee to neighbouring countries.[152]

During the second civil war that erupted in 1983, thousands of South Sudanese were forced to leave their hometowns and villages.[153] Many families became separated as individuals ran into the bush in different directions with no time to check the whereabouts of their family members. Thousands trekked in groups to neighbouring countries including Ethiopia,

---

[149] UN General Assembly, "Convention Relating to the Status of Refugees, 28 July 1951, United Nations, Treaty Series, Vol. 189," *Retrieved April* 20 (2015).
[150] Jane Shakespeare-Finch and Kylie Wickham, "Adaptation of Sudanese Refugees in an Australian Context: Investigating Helps and Hindrances," *International migration* 48, no. 1 (2010).
[151] An-na' Im and Deng, "Self-Determination and Unity: The Case of Sudan."
[152] Ibid
[153] Monash Legal Service Inc Springvale, "Comparative Analysis of South Sudanese Customary Law and Victorian Law," (Melbourne Australia: Springvale Monash Legal Service Inc., 2008).

Kenya, and Uganda, where makeshift shanty towns became permanent refugee camps for many years, and indeed still exist.[154]

At the refugee camps, there was a lack of communication infrastructure which hindered efforts to locate relatives and clansmen, and many spent years not knowing whether family members or relatives had survived. The majority of the South Sudanese who are now in Australia previously lived in the Kakuma and Dadaab refugee camps in Kenya, the Gambella in western Ethiopia,[155] while others lived in various refugee camps in Northern Uganda. The greater part of those spent many years in these camps without adequate food, water, clothing, sanitation, and with limited education and employment opportunities.[156]

A great number of South Sudanese who were living in Northern Sudan sought refuge in Egypt, but unlike the other three countries mentioned before, there were no refugee camps there. Instead, they were allowed to live in the wider community, but under poor living conditions. Sudanese nationals were granted the right to live and work freely in Egypt by the 1978 Treaty of Wadi El Ni.[157] Consequently, living conditions were very harsh and those who could find work were sometimes subjected to demanding work conditions and long hours with little pay.[158]

While in Egypt, Sudanese-born refugees were allowed to register with the United Nations High Commissioner for Refugees (UNHCR) to request permanent resettlement in the USA, Canada, Australia, and a few other countries in the West. In the mid-1990s, the UNHCR began resettling the

---

[154] Jane Kani Edward, "South Sudanese Refugee Women: Questioning the Past, Imagining the Future," in *Women's Rights and Human Rights* (Springer, 2001).

[155] Australia Government, "Sudanese Community Profile," (Canberra: Department of Immigration and Citizenship, 2007).

[156] *Migration and Refugee Law : Principles and Practice in Australia*, ed. John Vrachnas (Port Melbourne, Vic.: Port Melbourne, Vic. : Cambridge University Press, 2008).

[157] H Furnes et al., "Pan-African Magmatism in the Wadi El-Imra District, Central Eastern Desert, Egypt: Geochemistry and Tectonic Environment," *Journal of the Geological Society* 153, no. 5 (1996).

[158] Edward, "Sudanese Women Refugees: Transformations and Future Imaginings."

first Sudanese refugees from Kakuma and Dadaab refugee camps to the USA, Canada, Europe and Australia.[159]

2.4.3. South Sudanese Arrival in Australia

While Australia is meant to be a multicultural country, some South Sudanese people still experience challenges in integrating into Australian society according to Australian Bureau of Statistics 2011 (ABS).[160] Australia's African community is small. It has a population of about 337,791, which is 1.6 percent of the total national population.[161] This chapter concentrates on the recent refugees from South Sudan, most of whom are humanitarian entrants.

Although Australia is a multicultural society which encourages ethnic diversity with integrated cultures, the mainstream culture is generally individualistic, i.e., where an individual is considered as autonomous and independent of others. There is formal gender equality and no one is above the law.[162] Consequently, mainstream Australian culture is contrary to South Sudanese Jieng culture which is collectivistic in nature, holds that individuals are interdependent with strong links, and respect for the family and community members at large is important. These differences may cause a culture clash as the Jieng community is hierarchical, authoritarian, and patriarchal with specific gender roles.[163]

Between 1997 and 2010, Australia resettled over approximately thirty thousand Sudanese-born people who arrived through the offshore humanitarian program.[164] Through this program, individuals register as refugees with the UNHCR and, if they meet the resettlement criteria, they are granted a visa to permanently settle in Australia and can apply for

---

[159] Bram J Jansen, "Between Vulnerability and Assertiveness: Negotiating Resettlement in Kakuma Refugee Camp, Kenya," *African Affairs* 107, no. 429 (2008).

[160] Ibolya Losoncz, "Blocked Opportunity and Threatened Identity: Understanding Experiences of Disrespect in South Sudanese Australians," *Australasian Review of African Studies, The* 32, no. 2 (2011).

[161] Ibid

[162] Khawaja and Milner, "Acculturation Stress in South Sudanese Refugees: Impact on Marital Relationships."

[163] Aparna Hebbani, Levi Obijiofor, and Helen Bristed, "Intercultural Communication Challenges Confronting Female Sudanese Former Refugees in Australia," (2010).

[164] Government, "Sudanese Community Profile."

citizenship after four years.[165] However, between 2001 and 2007, Sudanese born people comprised forty to seventy percent of Australia's offshore humanitarian program.[166] Among these, seventy-four percent arrived under the Special Humanitarian Program (SHP). As previously mentioned in this chapter, there is a subcategory for people living outside their country of origin who are considered to have suffered substantial discrimination amounting to a gross violation of human rights in their home country, and who had relatives or family members living in Australia.[167] Consequently, the numbers dropped in 2009/2010 when the Department for Immigration and Citizenship (DIAC) re-assessed priorities and committed to an increased refugee intake from other countries. The small number of visas currently allocated to South Sudanese-born persons has meant for longer waiting times for those in Africa to join their relatives and friends in Australia.[168]

The 2011 census revealed that the state of Victoria hosted the largest number of Sudanese-born Australians (totalling thirty-six percent).[169] The majority of Sudan's refugees in Australia are Christian (eighty-three percent), with smaller populations identifying as Muslim (twelve percent) and other (five percent). Most people from Sudanese backgrounds (fifty percent) arrived as part of a family group of three or more people, whilst twenty percent arrived as a family of six or more.[170] A further thirty-seven percent arrived alone, reflecting the scattering of family members due to war.

2.5. Conclusion

This chapter has provided a detailed account of the people of South Sudan and highlighted that there are sixty-four ethnic groups in the nation with different sets of customary laws. The chapter has briefly provided Sudan's

---

[165] Farida Fozdar and Brian Spittles, "The Australian Citizenship Test: Process and Rhetoric," *Australian Journal of Politics & History* 55, no. 4 (2009).

[166] Shakespeare-Finch and Wickham, "Adaptation of Sudanese Refugees in an Australian Context: Investigating Helps and Hindrances."

[167] Carol Pavlish and Anita Ho, "Human Rights Barriers for Displaced Persons in Southern Sudan.(World Health)," *Journal of Nursing Scholarship* 41, no. 3 (2009).

[168] Jessica Rebecca Bishop, *To Be a Family: Changes Experienced within South Sudanese Families in Australia* (University of Melbourne, Department of Social Work, 2011).

[169] Ibid.

[170] Ibid.

political history and legal system commencing with the colonial period, independent Sudan, and South Sudan. It has explained the motivation for Sudanese refugees to flee their homes and find refuge in countries such as Australia. It has also provided an account of their experiences before fleeing the country, including the constant fighting between the government and rebels, and the many military coups and changes in government and laws which demonstrated that Sudanese citizens were being persecuted and forced out of their homes. These experiences of persecution stay with refugees after resettlement and are likely to translate into a distrust of governments, legal systems, and government officials, which may eventually progress to difficulties with settling into a new country. The chapter concluded that the journey of the South Sudanese to a number of neighbouring countries as refugees, and their subsequent settlements to Australia and other Western countries can come with challenges such as cultural and legal problems.

CHAPTER THREE

CUSTOMARY LAW (FAMILY LAW) IN SOUTH SUDAN

3.1. Introduction

This chapter provides an overview of customary law in South Sudan, and analyses how Jieng communities resolve family customary law disputes. South Sudan has a pluralistic legal system which incorporates both statutory and customary law, and is very different from Australia's. It is necessary to understand how family law disputes would normally be resolved within Jieng communities in South Sudan in order to understand the legal consciousness of Jieng former refugees once they arrive in Australia.

Most family disputes in South Sudan would be resolved through customary law.[1] Therefore, the first task of this chapter is to discuss what exactly customary law is and how it differs from statutory law, while focusing on the resolution of marriage, divorce, and child custody disputes in Jieng communities. There has been previous work on Jieng customary law,[2] but none have focused on the resolution of disputes related to marriage, divorce and child custody. The available literature is predominantly from an anthropological perspective[3] rather than from a family customary law context. An exception is that of Fadlalla, who examined the work of Makec,[4] the author of *The Customary Law of the Jieng (Dinka): A Comparative Analysis of an African Legal System.*[5] Fadlalla published a comparative analysis of Nuer and Dinka customary law based on the restatement of customary Dinka (Jieng) law of the Bhar el ghazal region Act 1984.

[1] Santino Atem Deng, "South Sudanese Youth Acculturation and Intergenerational Challenges" (paper presented at the Annual Conference, 2016).
[2] "Fitting the Jigsaw: South Sudanese Family Dynamics and Parenting Practices in Australia."
[3] Ibid
[4] John Wuol Makec, *The Customary Law of the Dinka People of Sudan: In Comparison with Aspects of Western and Islamic Laws* (Afroworld Pub. Co., 1988).
[5] Ibid.

However, the author fell short on the diversification of Jieng customary law in the other region of the Upper Nile where another large Jieng population reside. These studies provide detailed ethnographic descriptions of the Jieng people. Hence, this chapter provides a significant contribution to our understanding of customary law and how its approach differs from statutory law in dispute resolutions among all Jieng communities in South Sudan.

The chapter provides a brief discussion on the evolution of Jieng customs and culture. This discussion is important to examine the changes and modifications that Jieng customs and culture have undergone in South Sudan and Sudan respectively. This is relevant to examine the possible legal clash between the observance of Jieng customary law and Australian family law which will be discussed in detail in a later chapter. Further, the chapter analyses the Jieng conceptualisation of the family and how this influences dispute resolution processes among Jieng communities.

Finally, there is sometimes a tendency by socio-legal scholars to over-romanticise customary law, or to treat it as a concept which is static and unchanging.[6] However, there has also been a strong critique about the negative impact of customary law, especially on women and children, and it has also been seen to clash with international human rights instruments. Accordingly, this chapter examines these critiques and explores the role of international human rights instruments under customary law in South Sudan.

3.2. Customary Law in South Sudan

South Sudan has a pluralistic legal system which incorporates both statutory and customary law. This division is also referred to as formal and informal legal systems.[7] Customary law is recognised in the constitution of South Sudan, and it is an equivalent of family law in other countries like Australia. In South Sudan, there are sixty-four ethnic groups, each of which has an individual and distinct body of functioning customary law. As a result, this chapter will focus mainly on Jieng (Dinka) customary law and will adopt

---

6 Heike Krieger, "A Conflict of Norms: The Relationship between Humanitarian Law and Human Rights Law in the Icrc Customary Law Study," *Journal of Conflict and Security Law* 11, no. 2 (2006).

7 Hessbruegge, "Customary Law and Authority in a State under Construction: The Case of South Sudan."113

the use of "Jieng Customary Law" (JCL) instead of South Sudanese customary law.

Customary law is defined as a common rule that reflects shared social norms and values that have become recognised within a legal system based upon a common understanding of rights and obligations.[8] It generally exists in an informal, unwritten form that is passed down orally from generation to generation.[9] Customary law is adhered to among South Sudanese because each individual recognises the benefits of behaving in accordance with other individual's expectations. Thus, it is argued that sources of recognition of customary law are reciprocity, loss of reputation, and status.[10] In contrast, formal legal systems are based on written legal protocols, rather than social conventions. Adherence to formal legal rules is reinforced by the power of elite individuals or institutions. Recognition of customary law and participation in its enforcement by members of an ethnic or cultural group arises when the substantial benefits from doing so can be internalised by each individual; that is, incentives must be mostly positive for customary law to prevail.[11] Following from the above definition, it is clear that customary law is different to statutory law in South Sudan and it is important to explore those differences before embarking on a general analysis of customary law.

3.2.1. Differences between Customary Law and Statutory Law

Customary law differs from statutory law in South Sudan in several ways. Firstly, it is the law that is perceived as subordinate to statutory law in the hierarchy; that is, it is basic law that is applied in a functioning society.[12] There are a number of issues that customary law covers which include family matters such as: bride wealth payments and ceremonies; adultery and penalties involved; divorce and relevant payments; and child custody.[13]

---

[8] Fadlalla, "Customary Laws in Southern Sudan: Customary Law of Dinka and Nuer."

[9] Ibid

[10] Ibid

[11] Mohamed Hassan Fadlalla, *Customary Laws in Southern Sudan: Customary Laws of Dinka and Nuer* (iUniverse, 2009).

[12] Jok, Leitch, and Vandewint, "A Study of Customary Law in Contemporary Southern Sudan."

[13] Paul Philip Howell, *A Manual of Nuer Law: Being an Account of Customary Law, Its Evolution and Development in the Courts Established by the Sudan Government* (Routledge, 2018).

Property disputes are also covered under customary law and include inheritance and land disputes, as well as procedural laws and laws of obligation such as contracts and liability.[14] The application of customary law also depends on the type of matter at hand. Customary laws that relate to personal issues, such as Jieng divorce laws, are only applied to the individuals involved. For personal issues, individuals may use their own personal customary laws rather than rely on local laws. For matters that have a territorial basis, such as incurring marriage liability, the law that is applied is that which relates to any individual within the jurisdiction of the relevant customary laws.[15]

Secondly, South Sudanese customary law is inquisitorial. Chiefs are community leaders who are widely known and respected and, in some instances, chosen by the people.[16] Therefore, the expectation is that a known leader will personally investigate the case and take into account public opinion and culture. Chiefs will often listen to debates and views within their communities, and decisions reflect wider social, economic, and political positions.[17] They can also actively engage in the investigation of the case rather than simply hearing the facts and applying the law.[18] Chiefs may refer to written laws, especially when assigning a penalty, but the law is treated as something that is flexible and contextual rather than being fixed and universal.[19] This is contrary to a statutory legal system, where the judge is not necessarily known to the parties and will not investigate the case, but will hear the facts and arguments and apply a decision based on legal rules.[20]

---

[14]Ibid.

[15] Adeogun Tolulope Jolaade and Isola Abidemi Abiola, "Patriarchy and Customary Law as Major Cogs in the Wheel of Women's Peace Building in South Sudan," *Journal of Gender, Information and Development in Africa (JGIDA)* 5, no. 1 (2016)..

[16] Buol Juuk, "South Sudanese Dinka Customary Law in Comparison with Australian Family Law: Legal Implications for Dinka Families," *Australasian Review of African Studies, The* 34, no. 2 (2013).

[17] Leonardi, Cherry et al, 'The politics of customary law as ascertainment in South Sudan' (2011) 63 *Journal of Legal Pluralism* 111, 123.

[18] Manfred Hinz, "The Ascertainment of Customary Law: What Is Ascertainment of Customary Law and What Is It For? The Experience of the Customary Law Ascertainment Project in Namibia," *The Experience of the Customary Law Ascertainment Project in Namibia (July 19, 2012). Oñati Socio-Legal Series* 2, no. 7 (2012).

[19] Leonardi et al, op.cit.

[20] Fadlalla, "Customary Laws in Southern Sudan: Customary Law of Dinka and Nuer."

Thirdly, whereas statutory law is adversarial, South Sudanese customary law system often adopts a conciliatory approach to dispute resolution.[21] The objectives of South Sudanese customary law are not retributive but restitutive and can be summarised as "the maintenance of peace or equilibrium and the restoration of the status through the payment of damages."[22] In contrast, Western statutory legal systems attempt to ascertain the truth, even though the truth may not bring satisfaction or resolution for the parties. Danne explains that, "African dispute resolution has been described as placing a premium on improving relations on the basis of equity, good conscience and fair play, rather than the strict legality often associated with Western justice."[23] Therefore, in South Sudan, in criminal matters, the court may order the offender to pay compensation to the victim's family to restore equilibrium. This is considered to be more effective than applying penal sanctions, as it seen to enhance social cohesion, maintain a sense of obedience to social norms, and reinforce shared values.[24]

Fourthly, customary law does not clearly divide criminal law from civil law.[25] Criminal and civil cases are both dealt with in the same way using customary law. The rationale for this approach is the desire to restore social equilibrium through the payment of damages.[26] What this means is that in criminal law cases as well as civil, payments of fines are used as punishments, where the wrongdoer can repay the victim by financial means. These payments may include "many cows, or money" depending on the customs and values of the community, while statute law focuses on the punishment of the wrongdoer.[27] This is a significant difference in the process and the conceptualisation of the law and family disputes. What this implied is that, since the majority of disputes in South Sudan are resolved through customary law and courts, most Jieng families and other South

---

[21] Danne, "Customary and Indigenous Law in Transitional Post-Conflict States: A South Sudanese Case Study."
[22] Milos, "South Sudanese Communities and Australian Family Law: A Clash of Systems."
[23] Danne, "Customary and Indigenous Law in Transitional Post-Conflict States: A South Sudanese Case Study."
[24] Makec, *The Customary Law of the Dinka People of Sudan: In Comparison with Aspects of Western and Islamic Laws*.
[25] Fadlalla, "Customary Laws in Southern Sudan: Customary Law of Dinka and Nuer."
[26] Peter Nyot Kok, "The Customary Law of the Dinka People of Sudan: In Comparison with Aspects of Western and Islamic Laws," (1990).
[27] Ibid.

Sudanese only understand the law to work in the same way as it does in their home country of South Sudan.[28] Furthermore, prison sentences are not the preferred option among South Sudanese cultures and the legal system, especially in the case of customary law, as it is seen to exacerbate a breach in social relations.[29] In cases where prison sentences are considered, compensation is usually directly commensurable, often resulting in the prisons containing poor individuals who cannot pay their fines.[30] The other difference is that, customary law is not written or documented, and this reflects the values and customs of a community that is constantly evolving, which means courts cases are not recorded and decision and precedents are not noted, instead its becomes oral traditions.[31]

3.2.2. Family Dispute Resolution using Restorative Approach.

In South Sudan and other African states, traditional customary practices have regulated dispute resolution since immemorial and in certain cases these practices have been significant and are currently presented as form of restorative justice.[32] Griffiths and Corrado argued that "Aboriginal peoples and communities have served as the catalysts for the development of a wide range of innovative, community-based restorative justice practices."[33] On the other hand, Daly claims there has been an orientalist of appropriation of indigenous justice practices, widely in the service of enhancing advocates' positions. For the states with indigenous dispute resolution process, designing laws that give legal effect to the best interest of children and alternative instruments has involved policy choices regarding whether to incorporate these indigenous modes into new laws. In South Sudan however, family dynamics are predominately traditional, values and beliefs,

---

[28] David Pimentel, "Rule of Law Reform without Cultural Imperialism? Reinforcing Customary Justice through Collateral Review in Southern Sudan," *Hague Journal on the Rule of Law* 2, no. 01 (2010).

[29] Jeffery L. Deal, "Torture by "Cieng": Ethical Theory Meets Social Practice among the Dinka Agaar of South Sudan," *American Anthropologist* 112, no. 4.

[30] Milos, "South Sudanese Communities and Australian Family Law: A Clash of Systems."

[31] Ibid.

[32] Cyndi Banks, "Protecting the Rights of the Child: Regulating Restorative Justice and Indigenous Practices in Southern Sudan and East Timor," *The International Journal of Children's Rights* 19, no. 2 (2011).

[33] Curt Taylor Griffiths and Ray Corrado, "Implementing Restorative Youth Justice: A Case Study in Community Justice and the Dynamics of Reform (Restorative Juvenile Justice: Repairing the Harm of Youth Crime, P 237-258, 1999, Gordon Bazemore and Lode Walgrave, Eds.--See Ncj-181924)," (1999).

including those relating to the family and children, remain rooted in custom and tradition. The post-conflict South Sudan has a pluralistic legal system comprising colonial law, statute law and custom and tradition as sources of law.[34] South Sudan has recently legislated a new law on juvenile justice which incorporates forms of restorative justice designed and practiced in some Western countries. The legislation is congruent with customary and traditional values and beliefs about the best interest of children.[35] With Jieng customary law, the aim of family dispute resolution is reconciliation, a fundamental principle is that disputes should be practically resolved out of court. Family disputes are ideally resoled within the family or at the lower levels of the family hierarchy out of the formal court.[36] Mediation initiative are normally taken by any of the parties to the dispute especially the aggrieved or the perpetrator who want to resolve the issue and be reconciled with the victim or perpetrator. Furthermore, the initiative may come from any member of the family or member of local community who is aware of the dispute.[37] This process takes several processes before the perpetrator and victim are brought together for a restorative meeting. This process is widely used in both major and minor conflicts across many ethnic groups within South Sudan. For instance; the Wunlit and Liliir reconciliation conferences held between Jieng (Dinka) and Nuer in 1999 and 2000, after series of ethnic targeted war that involved killings, raping and abduction of women and children from both side between 1991 and 1995.[38] In 1999 and 2000, two inter-communal peace conference were held in what is currently known as Jonglei state: the Jieng and Nuer west bank peace and reconciliation conference, and the east bank Nilotic People Peace and Reconciliation conference. The Wunlit and Liliir conferences brought together over 250 traditional and civil leaders from Anyuak, Jieng, Jie, Kachipo, Murle, and Duer ethnic groups, to resolve the deep division and conflict that have risen between them, especially as a result of South-North long civil war which has turned these communities against each other.[39] As a result of the reconciliation conference, the chiefs and other leaders agreed on access to

---

[34] Ibid.

[35] Ibid.

[36] Deng, *Customary Law in the Modern World: The Crossfire of Sudan's War of Identities*.

[37] Mennen, "Legal Pluralism in Southern Sudan: Can the Rest of Africa Show the Way?."

[38] Martina Santschi, "Traditional Authorities, Local Justice and Local Conflict Resolution Mechanisms in South Sudan," in *Is Local Beautiful?* (Springer, 2014).

[39] Kuyang Logo, "Exploring Linkages of Traditional and Formal Mechanism of Justice and Reconciliation in South Sudan," *Available at SSRN 3102242* (2018).

animal grazing areas and water points, to amnesty for prior offences, and to the return of all abducted women and children; these agreements were as a public covenant between the ethnic groups for peace and reconciliation and signed by all 129 representatives.

According to Deng, dispute resolution are overwhelmingly processed by employment local justice rather than statute law.[40] Family disputes in relation to marriage, divorce, adultery, child custody; criminal matters such as rape, murder, manslaughter, theft; some child protection issues; and property disputes are resolved through customary law's local justice instead of statutory law.[41] There is no distinction regarding issues that are criminal or civil, the underlying principles in local justice systems include the desire to resolve disputes, seek conciliation between the parties, and achieve satisfaction for as many parties as possible, in order to maintain the social cohesion and stability of the community.[42] Consequently, it is common for local justice to determine the compensation be paid in the form of livestock or agricultural goods to the injured party in order to restore what has been lost or damaged or to restore social equilibrium.[43]

In dispute resolution, chiefs play a central role having been given the power to preside disputes under local justice regarding customary rules and norms by the Chiefs' Courts Ordinance 1931.[44] Headmen, elders or the head of the sub-clan are usually the decision makers in dispute resolution. Parties only take their dispute to chief's court when they believe their dispute has not been dealt with to their satisfactory or when the headman believes that the dispute requires a formal hearing. The headman deals with cases informally whereas the Chief's court applies some formalities with flexible procedures that are inquisitorial in nature.[45]

---

[40] Deng, "Customary Law in the Cross-Fire of Sudan's War of Identities."
[41] William Twining and William Twining, "Human Rights: Southern Voices Francis Deng, Abdullahi an-Na'im, Yash Ghai and Upendra Baxi," *Law, Social Justice and Global Development Journal.*
[42] Deng, *Customary Law in the Modern World: The Crossfire of Sudan's War of Identities.*
[43] Jok, Leitch, and Vandewint, "A Study of Customary Law in Contemporary Southern Sudan."
[44] Sayyid Muhammad Abu Rannat, "The Relationship between Islamic and Customary Law in the Sudan 1," *Journal of African Law* 4, no. 1.
[45] Jok, Leitch, and Vandewint, "A Study of Customary Law in Contemporary Southern Sudan."

3.2.3. The Judiciary System: Statutory and Customary Courts

In South Sudan, the judiciary structure consists of formal government courts which are established by the Constitution and which apply statutory law. There are also customary courts which are presided over by traditional authorities and rule according to the customary laws of their respective ethnic groups.[46] A decision made in a customary court can be appealed by a statutory court, and therefore two different legal systems may be applied to a single dispute.[47] Generally, when customary cases are reviewed, deference is not given to the customary court due to the lack of adequate factual record.[48] The main legal texts establishing the judiciary and defining its jurisdiction and procedures are the Transitional Constitution of 2011,[49] *The Judiciary Act 2008,*[50] *The Code of Civil Procedure Act 2007, The Code of Criminal Procedure Act 2008,* and *The Local Government Act 2009.* The hierarchy and structure of South Sudan's judicial system are listed in the table below.

Table 4: Statutory Courts and Hierarchy

Court	Hierarchy	Description	Jurisdiction/Powers
Supreme Court	Highest	Statutory and the Supreme Court located in Juba, is the highest organ of the judiciary	National
Court of Appeals	2nd	Three regional Courts of Appeal (based in Juba, Rumbek and Malakal, for the Greater Equatoria, Greater Bahr-el-Ghazal and Greater Upper Nile regions respectively)	Regional

[46] Fadlalla, "Customary Laws in Southern Sudan: Customary Law of Dinka and Nuer."
[47] South Sudan Government, "South Sudan Judicary System," ed. Judiciary (South Sudan2011).
[48] Ibid.
[49] (ABS), "Culturally Diversity in Australia."
[50] South Sudan Government, "Judiciary Act," (2008).

High Court	3rd	Ten High Courts (one in each state capital) are the highest courts in South Sudan with original jurisdiction at the state level.	State
First Class Magistrate Court		The First-Class Magistrate Courts are courts of original jurisdiction that are responsible for a specific county within a state	County
Second Class Magistrate Court		The Third Class or Payam Court is the lowest government court	Payam

The highest organ of the judiciary is the Supreme Court located in Juba the capital city of South Sudan. It consists of seven judges (called Justices), one of whom is the Chief Justice of the Supreme Court and one is the Deputy President.[51] The court is able to form three different panels: The Constitutional Panel, the Criminal Panel, and the Civil Panel. The first consists of all justices and the latter of three justices. Generally, the Supreme Court decides whether cases are recorded but it can call litigants for oral argument if required.[52] The Supreme Court is also the highest appellate court in the country and takes appeals from the Court of Appeals. For constitutional law matters, the court is given original jurisdiction. The court must confirm any death penalty conviction.[53]

The Court of Appeal is the second in the hierarchy of the courts system whose functions and jurisdictions are discussed below. Across the country, there are three regional courts of appeals based in each of the regional

---

[51] Katharina Diehl, Ruben Madol Arol, and Simone Malz, "South Sudan: Linking the Chiefs' Judicial Authority and the Statutory Court System," in *Non-State Justice Institutions and the Law* (Springer, 2015).
[52] Mennen, "Legal Pluralism in Southern Sudan: Can the Rest of Africa Show the Way?."
[53] Government, "South Sudan Judicary System."

nominated cities.[54] The Court of Appeal for the Equatorial region is based at Juba; for Bahr-El-Ghazal the court is based at Rumbek; and for Upper Nile, it is based at Malakal.[55] The three regional bases of the court of appeal hear cases from the state-based high courts as intermediary appellate courts and they further fulfil an administrative function over the high courts in their jurisdiction.[56] Three judges sit on the bench, with one judge being the president as appointed by the Chief Justice of Supreme Court.[57]

As previously mentioned in this chapter, South Sudan has ten states with its own state government and judiciary system. The next in the hierarchy is the High Court, the highest court in the state jurisdiction system. There is a high court in each of the ten states.[58] The jurisdiction of the high courts is determined by *The Civil Procedure Act 2007* and *The Criminal Procedure Act 2008.*[59] The High Court hears appeals from all the lower courts. There is no internal appellate hierarchy among the lower courts.

After the High Court, there are the First-Class Magistrate Courts which are courts of original jurisdiction responsible for a specific county within a state. In the criminal cases, these courts can pass prison sentences of up seven years and fines of up to 5,000 South Sudanese Pounds (SSP). One of the results of the armed conflict is that many of the lower levels of statutory courts are not fully in place due, in part, to a lack of a sufficient number of judges. The judiciary has also been criticised for a lack of transparency and independence. These problems have meant that many people do not have sufficient access to justice.[60] Mobile courts have recently been deployed in response to the lack of access to the lower courts.[61]

The next statutory courts are the Second-Class Magistrate Courts, which are similar to the First-Class Magistrate courts but with less authority to pass

---

[54] Pimentel, "Rule of Law Reform without Cultural Imperialism? Reinforcing Customary Justice through Collateral Review in Southern Sudan."
[55] Ibid.
[56] Howell, *A Manual of Nuer Law: Being an Account of Customary Law, Its Evolution and Development in the Courts Established by the Sudan Government.*
[57] Leonardi et al., *Local Justice in Southern Sudan.*
[58] Government, "South Sudan Judicary System."
[59] Government of South Sudan, "Child Act 2008 and Penal Code 2008," (Ministry Justice and legal Affiars, 2008).
[60] International Commission of Jurists. South Sudan: Lack of Domestic Judicial Capacity and the Need for International Cooperation and Justice (2014).
[61] United Nations Peacekeeping, 'Mobile court delivers long-awaited justice in Western Lakes' (2019).

prison sentences (maximum of three years) and fines (maximum of 2,500 SSP). Finally, *The Judiciary Act* allows for Third-Class courts, however these courts have yet to be established. They are intended to occupy the lowest level of the court hierarchy, and would not be allowed to pass fines over 300 SSP.[62]

3.2.4. Customary Courts

In South Sudan, customary law is recognised in the Constitution, and there are a number of customary courts established across the ten states throughout the country.[63] These courts constitute part of the court hierarchy and are codified by *The Local Government Act (2009)*.[64] They are presided over by local chiefs or experienced chiefs who also act as judges at county and Payam court levels.[65] These courts are not formal but communal and are held in public, often outside with large numbers of community members observing, engaging in debate, and often offering contesting perspectives. Proceedings are not normally recorded.[66] In cases where the issue is not covered under the ethnic group's existing customary law, the chiefs or judges will often adopt, "customary norms of fairness" based on public opinion of the dispute at hand.[67] This means that customary law is flexible and amendable to the views of the community.[68] Customary courts can decide cases within their jurisdiction based on the customs, traditions, norms and ethnics of the communities.[69] *The Local Government Act (2009)* recommends general principles for decision-making within the customary courts, including the principle that courts should not be discriminatory, avoid needless delay, use mediation where possible, ensure appropriate

---

[62] Paul Mertenskoetter and Dong Samuel Luak, An Overview of the Legal System and Legal Research in the Republic of South Sudan (2012)

[63] Abu Rannat, "The Relationship between Islamic and Customary Law in the Sudan 1."

[64] South Sudan Government, "Local Government Act " (2009).

[65] Milos, "South Sudanese Communities and Australian Family Law: A Clash of Systems."

[66] Jok, Leitch, and Vandewint, "A Study of Customary Law in Contemporary Southern Sudan."

[67] Johnson, "Judicial Regulation and Administrative Control: Customary Law and the Nuer, 1898–1954."

[68] Pimentel, "Rule of Law Reform without Cultural Imperialism? Reinforcing Customary Justice through Collateral Review in Southern Sudan."

[69] Juuk, "South Sudanese Dinka Customary Law in Comparison with Australian Family Law: Legal Implications for Dinka Families."

compensation, and focus on substantive justice.[70] Statutory courts are not accessible to many people due to cost, unfamiliar procedures, and their use of English; and there are still many gaps where courts are not sitting due to the lack of judges.[71] As a consequence, customary courts are the preferred option and it is estimated that ninety percent of disputes in South Sudan are handled by these courts.[72]

Customary courts are not an indigenous institution but were set up as an interim arrangement that served a number of functions. From a political and ideological perspective, they provide a sense of identity within South Sudan and assist in maintaining social solidarity.[73] On a practical level, they hear the majority of cases in South Sudan. They were seen to be an inexpensive and undisruptive mechanism to support gradual change. This was to be achieved by bringing in local administrators who could change the substance of customary law. The use of existing customary courts also meant that new institutions did not need to be established in order to bring in reform. Chiefs serve a hybrid role that require them to serve both state and community, although their authority is based on the community's acceptance.[74] Procedures among customary courts vary between geographical regions, especially between rural and urban areas; however, there has been a shift towards using more formal proceedings.[75] The educational level of the chief and, if there is one, the court clerk also determines the formality of procedures. The laws used for adjudication in customary courts are a mix of traditional practice, the discretion of the chief, statutory provisions known to the chief, and negotiation between the parties.[76]

The way in which the customary courts run is invariably determined by a mix of tradition, the chief, and community involvement. Traditions are passed down orally and principles of binding precedent do not generally apply. The chief's personal view on the objectives of the court and, for instance, whether the chief views the court to be oriented towards education,

---

[70] Alexander P Danne, "Customary and Indigenous Law in Transitional Post-Conflict States: A South Sudanese Case Study," *Monash UL Rev.* 30 (2004).
[71] Jok, Leitch, and Vandewint, "A Study of Customary Law in Contemporary Southern Sudan."
[72] Ibid.
[73] Leonardi et al, op.cit. , 112; Danne, op.cit..
[74] Government, "South Sudan Judicary System."
[75] Ibid.
[76] Deng, "Customary Law in the Cross-Fire of Sudan's War of Identities."

restorative, or punitive objectives, can influence their decision-making.[77] Chiefs will also allow for the introduction of issues usually considered irrelevant or inadmissible in Western courts. Customary courts also often serve as a forum for negotiation and arbitration as well as adjudication, and this process can involve the entire community.[78] This means that the process of decision-making and its outcomes are highly contextual. The principle that like cases should be treated alike is not widely applied in South Sudan.[79]

South Sudan has several levels of administrative divisions. The ten states are divided into counties which are, in turn, divided into "Payams," and subordinate to them are "bomas." Customary courts are generally organised in two levels. The lower level B courts exist in every Payam, and their jurisdiction is limited by maximum penalties. Each county has a high-level C court. Some Bomas also have A courts, and urbanised areas often have town bench courts. The jurisdiction and hierarchy of the customary courts is shown in Table 5.

Table 5: Customary Courts and Hierarchy

Court	**Hierarchy**	**Jurisdiction**
County Court	Paramount Chief	County
B Court	Head Chief	Payam
A (Chief) Court	Executive Chief	Boma

The functions of the C courts are stipulated in the *Local Government Act (2009)*, the jurisdiction of the C courts comprised of criminal cases directed to them by the statutory courts. The C courts also presides over the cases relating to cross-ethnic disputes. The courts membership are the head chiefs from the county and Payam, and the county commissioner is the main supervisor of the court. The C courts are the final courts of appeal among the customary courts. A decision of the C court can be appealed to the statutory magistrate courts.[80]

The B courts have original jurisdiction over cases that involve large fines and prison sentences. They are presided over by the Payam's head chief, and are supervised by the county's paramount chief. The B courts hear appeals from the A courts, and decisions in the B court can be appealed to

[77] Ibid.
[78] Ibid.
[79] Ibid.
[80] Government, "Local Government Act ".

the C court. The A courts have the original jurisdiction over family and marriage cases, minor disputes, and local administrative cases. The courts are supervised by the Payam's head chief. Figure 6 below illustrates the chain of responsibility in South Sudan judiciary system.

Court Hierarchy in South Sudan

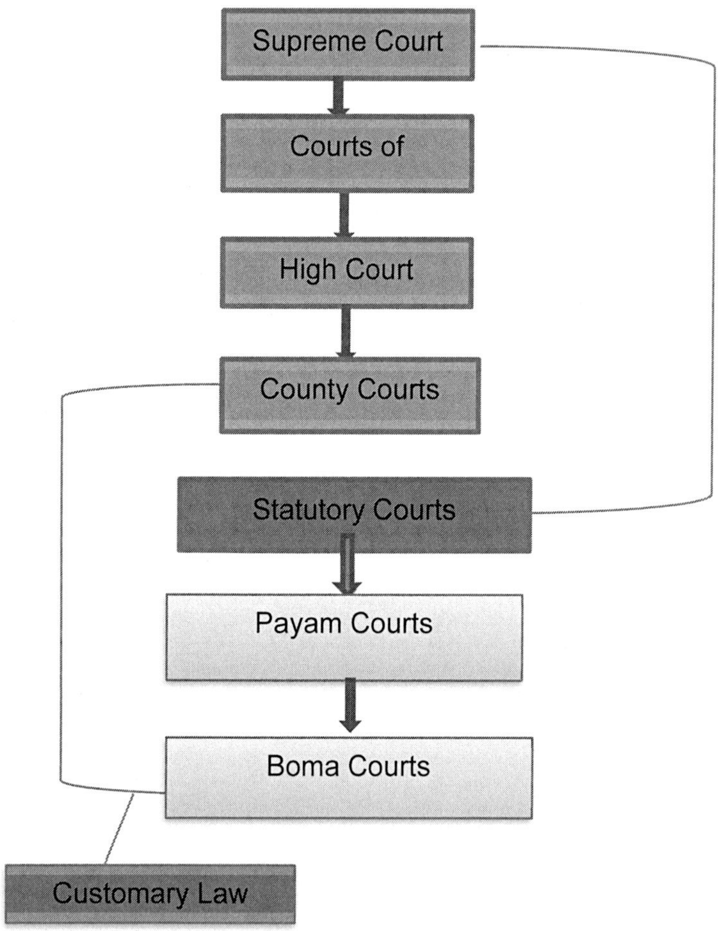

Figure 6: South Sudan Judiciary System - Hierarchy 1

3.2.5. Court Operations

Since the end of the civil war in 2005, statutory or "formal" laws have started to replace customary laws, primarily in urban areas.[81] In practice, most towns or cities have developed semi-parallel systems of statutory and customary law, however, these systems sometimes come into conflict. There have been efforts to define the types of issues that can be heard in each jurisdiction, although they have not been successful. Instead, individual chiefs apply their own personal discretion concerning how they adjudicate within their own customary courts and the processes that they will follow. For instance, individual chiefs often make their own personal decisions concerning jurisdictional limitations.[82] The statutory system has less influence in rural areas where chiefs resolve all types of issues.

The customary court system in South Sudan, despite decades of Sudan government oppression, has been relatively successful in terms of maintaining social order and a high level of community support.[83] South Sudanese people have been shown to perceive the customary courts as transparent and accountable,[84] and to believe that court decisions are generally fair.[85] This success is largely attributed to the high level of community participation and that fact that the courts are seen to be a reflection of community identity.[86]

Judgements are only passed down following arguments and debates that involve the individuals concerned, their family, community members, and the engagement of chiefs, who normally sit in a panel of a maximum of seven members.[87] The chiefs act as the community's advocate and arbiter, and consider community's views in the decision-making process. Chiefs are typically well-respected as the custodians of oral legal histories of ethnic groups. However, they are not immune from criticism. Chiefs who

---

[81] Susan Armstrong, "Good Practices with Culturally Diverse Families in Family Dispute Resolution," *Family Matters*, no. 92 (2013).
[82] Tiernan Mennen, "Lessons from Yambio: Legal Pluralism and Customary Justice Reform in Southern Sudan," *Hague Journal on the Rule of Law* 2, no. 02 (2010).
[83] "Legal Pluralism in Southern Sudan: Can the Rest of Africa Show the Way?."
[84] Jok, Leitch, and Vandewint, "A Study of Customary Law in Contemporary Southern Sudan."
[85] Ibid.
[86] Pimentel, "Rule of Law Reform without Cultural Imperialism? Reinforcing Customary Justice through Collateral Review in Southern Sudan."
[87] Milos, "South Sudanese Communities and Australian Family Law: A Clash of Systems."

repeatedly pass judgements that the community considers to be unfair risk losing their credibility and, in turn, will lose their reputation on the court panel. Chiefs who do not have the respect of their community also risk being relieved of their duties. [88]

The flexibility of the customary courts, especially in cross-jurisdictional matters, is best demonstrated in cases involving Internally Displaced People (IDPs) and returnees in South Sudan. Chiefs from different ethnic groups regularly convene in the same customary court to adjudicate cases between members of those different ethnic groups.[89] When a defendant appears from an ethnic group which is not represented on the panel, the case is suspended and a chief from the appropriate group is summoned to help adjudicate.[90] This example illustrates how South Sudanese are sensitive to getting disputes resolved in the manner which is directly relevant to their cultural norms.

Likewise, the jurisdiction in which matters can be heard has also developed considerable flexibility in the customary courts.[91] The high level of trust and accessibility of the customary courts means that they receive disputes in all areas of law, especially in rural areas. This is summarised by Jok et al.:

> While most customary law cases centre on family customary law or personal law in its many forms (including adultery, divorce, inheritance, and child custody), customary courts also adjudicate criminal, contract, land and property, and traditional disputes such as hexes.[92]

Even if a case is not directly covered under the ethnic group's customary law, chiefs will often adapt customary norms of fairness to the dispute at hand. The use of customary law justice is the most popular method for resolving disputes as customary courts are the entry point for the majority of South Sudanese citizens to dispute resolutions.[93]

---

[88] Jok, Leitch, and Vandewint, "A Study of Customary Law in Contemporary Southern Sudan."
[89] Mennen, "Lessons from Yambio: Legal Pluralism and Customary Justice Reform in Southern Sudan."
[90] Deng, "Customary Law in the Cross-Fire of Sudan's War of Identities."
[91] Mennen, "Lessons from Yambio: Legal Pluralism and Customary Justice Reform in Southern Sudan."
[92] Jok, Leitch, and Vandewint, "A Study of Customary Law in Contemporary Southern Sudan."
[93] Mennen, "Lessons from Yambio: Legal Pluralism and Customary Justice Reform in Southern Sudan."

3.3. Gaps in the Constitution

In South Sudan there are challenges related to the reconciliation of customary law that may be problematic for the legal instruments intended to protect people from harm. Customs can include practices that are discriminatory, harmful, and which violate human rights, especially those of women and children.[94] The transitional constitution clearly stipulates that all laws, whether customary or statutory, are subject to the South Sudan Bill of the Rights. Despite this, many concerns have been raised by Human Rights Watch in South Sudan that the rights of some vulnerable groups are not being protected by the Constitution.[95]

The transitional constitution also explicitly incorporates children's rights under Article 32(5) (Part 2 Bill of Rights), which states that: "The State shall protect the rights of the child as provided in the international and regional conventions ratified by the Sudan." South Sudan has ratified the 1989 UN Convention on the Rights of the Child (CRC). In addition, *The Child Act (2008)* protects, promotes and extends children's rights as defined under the CRC. *The Child Act (2008)* also explicitly allows for the application of customary practices, but only those practices that are not maximising harm to the best interests of the child. Regrettably, both the government and the courts have provided practice directions as to what constitutes the best interests of the child under the *Child Act (2008)*.[96]

Furthermore, marriage, divorce, child custody and other personal matters are handled through customary law as stipulated under the C*ode of Civil Procedure Act*.[97] In instances where customary law is in conflict with the principles of justice, equality, or good conscience, the Code makes it clear that customary law should not prevail.[98] The Code of Civil of Procedure, The Child Act, and the Transitional Constitute also all stipulate that customary law should not prevail over the consideration of human rights.[99] However, the way in which the Courts are meant to put these stipulations

---

[94] Government, "South Sudan Judicary System."
[95] Armstrong, "Good Practices with Culturally Diverse Families in Family Dispute Resolution."
[96] Government of South Sudan, "Child Act 2008 and Penal Code 2008," (Ministry Justice and legal Affiars 2008).
[97] Government of Southern Sudan, "Civil Procedure Act 2003," (South Sudan2003).
[98]

Elizabeth Lacey, "It Takes Two Hands to Clap Conflict, Peacebuilding, and Gender Justice in Jonglei, South Sudan," (2013).
[99] Sudan, "Child Act 2008 and Penal Code 2008."

into practice is unclear. No advice has been provided to the courts on how the provisions contained in the Transition Constitution requiring human rights considerations to be taken into account are to be put into effect.[100]

Generally, customary courts favour consensus solutions aimed at restoring community values rather than punishment. For instance, "homicide, adultery, theft, and injury may be resolved under customary law through awards of compensation, usually in the form of cows or other livestock from the perpetrator to the victim".[101] Even cases involving domestic homicide, where a wife has been murdered by her husband for having an extra-marital affair, are usually resolved by the customary courts following principles of restorative justice. One of the results of South Sudan's plural legal systems is that there is a culture of impunity which allows for the violation of rights of women and children.

Another legal challenge in the law relates to offences that do not exist in either the Penal Code or in any other written form. They include elopement, pregnancy, or having sexual intercourse. Girls and women may be arrested or imprisoned for attempting to marry without the consent of their families, for not accepting to marry the man chosen for them, or for running away after bride wealth has been paid.[102] According to the South Sudan branch of Human Rights Watch, women are being imprisoned upon requesting divorce from their husband and also for committing adultery.[103] These gaps in South Sudan's legal system create opportunities for families and husbands to intimidate women, and to coerce them into forced marriages or into continuing in marriages that they did not want, often with husbands who may be abusive.[104]

South Sudan has taken some action, since it gained autonomy from Sudan in 2005 and independence in 2011, to address women and children's rights which remain disadvantaged by customary practices. These include calls by

---

[100] Deal, "Torture by "Cieng": Ethical Theory Meets Social Practice among the Dinka Agaar of South Sudan."

[101] Jok, Leitch, and Vandewint, "A Study of Customary Law in Contemporary Southern Sudan."

[102] Lacey, "It Takes Two Hands to Clap Conflict, Peacebuilding, and Gender Justice in Jonglei, South Sudan."

[103] Armstrong, "Good Practices with Culturally Diverse Families in Family Dispute Resolution."

[104] Lacey, "It Takes Two Hands to Clap Conflict, Peacebuilding, and Gender Justice in Jonglei, South Sudan."

the President Salva Kiir Mayardit for women to participate in all spheres of life and a plea to eliminate harmful traditions that limit their progress. The government and development partners also promised to make gender equality a cornerstone of the country's development agenda.[105] This example demonstrates a government willingness to address the gaps between the formal and informal legal systems; however, lack of proper implementing instruments makes progress impossible.

The current transitional constitution of South Sudan has guaranteed women and girls the right to consent to marriage. Those rights are articulated in Penal Code provisions that criminalised kidnapping or abducting a woman and compelling her to marry. Furthermore, *The Child Act 2008* provisions also protect children younger than eighteen from early and forced marriages and guarantee them the right to non-discrimination in health, education, life, survival and development, and protection from torture, degrading treatment, and abuse.[106] For instance, Article 15[107] states that every individual who is over the age of eighteen is at liberty to marry a person of the opposite sex and this should be conducted in accordance to their respective family laws, provides all parties; a man and a woman entering into marriage with full consent and free-will.

Article 167 (1) (2)[108] provides for the role and establishment of Traditional Authority (TA) at the state level within the ten states of South Sudan. TA will be in accordance with customary law as recognised by the South Sudan constitution.[109] TA shall function in accordance with the constitution of the state under the direction of the nation's constitution. All the courts operating under TA will apply customary law subject to the national constitution. This move by the government illustrated the gaps that exist between the formal law and customary law; however, TA has not yet been established which means customary law remains parallel to statutory law.

As earlier indicated, this section has provided a general overview of South Sudanese customary law and its operations. The following section mainly focuses on Jieng customary law and how it resolves disputes related to marriage, divorce, and child custody in South Sudan. However, it is

---

105 (ABS), "Culturally Diversity in Australia."
106 Australian Bureau Statistics, "Canberra," *Australian Bureau of Statistics* (2011).
107 Fadlalla, *Customary Laws in Southern Sudan: Customary Laws of Dinka and Nuer*.
108 (ABS), "Culturally Diversity in Australia."
109 Statistics, "Canberra."

important to provide a brief background about who the Jieng people are and what their cultural outlook includes.

3.3.1. The Jieng (Dinka) People

The term "Dinka" was invented by outsiders, and no one precisely knows the origin of the word. The people now known as the “Dinka” actually call themselves “Muonyjang” or “Jieng”. The Jieng are the largest ethnic group in South Sudan numbering over three million in a country of around twelve million people.[110] Their culture is dominated by cattle and, to a lesser extent, sheep and goats to which they attach a social and moral significance far beyond their economic value.[111]

It is believed that the Jieng are the wealthiest in relation to cattle on the African continent. The average bride wealth (Hook ke Thieek) is around fifty cows, while daughters of prominent families are sometimes married with over a hundred cows.[112] They derive their distinctive socio-economic identity, cultural values, and institutions from their preoccupation with cattle. With the payment of bride wealth, cattle provide the foundation for the family and the continuation of the lineage.[113] The fundamental goal of every Jieng is to marry and produce children, especially sons, to keep the family lineage after death.

The Jieng believe in a creation God known as “Nhialic.” They communicate with Nhialic through spirits and institutions called “yath” or “jok,” and who is invoked by rituals. They believe that the spirits of their ancestors become part of the spiritual sphere of the current life. Cattle, which are the fundamental measure of Jieng wealth, also have religious significance. Cattle are the first-choice animal for sacrifice, although there may be occasions when sheep and goat may be sacrificed as a substitute.

Family and general social relations are primary values in the Jieng religion. Although Jieng traditional religion does not promise a heaven to come, they believe in some form of life after death; however, for them death is an end

---

[110] FM Deng, "The Cow and the Thing Calledwhat': Dinka Cultural Perspectives on Wealth and Poverty," *Journal of International Affairs* 52, no. 1 (1998).

[111] Francis M Deng, "The Cow and the Thing Called" What": Dinka Cultural Perspectives on Wealth and Poverty," ibid.

[112] Deng, *The Dinka of the Sudan.*

[113] Deng, "Customary Law in the Cross-Fire of Sudan’s War of Identities."

from which the only salvation is continuity through posterity.[114] What the Jieng worry most about is not death itself but dying without male progeny, in whom the survival of their individual identities and their source of immortality, are vested.[115]

The relatives of a man who dies unmarried assume a moral obligation to the deceased. One of the male relatives would marry a woman on his behalf, would live with her and would have children in his name. Equally, a man who dies leaving behind a widow of childbearing age bestows a moral obligation on kinsmen to have one of them cohabit with her to continue bearing children in his name.[116] This traditional marriage practice has remained even in present day South Sudan. Jieng customary law aims to create and reinforce a peaceful society. However, the overall cultural practice of the Jieng people revolves around the family; therefore, the following section discusses the ethnology of the Jieng ("Dinka") people and how their historical journey has influenced their current customary practice.

3.3.2. Family ("Kuaat")

Defining the term "family" in a Jieng customary law context is necessary. According to Jieng customary law, "family" includes all extended members such as grandparents, uncles, aunts, cousins, nephews, and nieces.[117] Values and solidarity within the family are extremely important as is hospitality and respect for elders. Men are the head of the family and the father or the oldest male within the household or the extended family resolves most family issues.[118]

In South Sudanese Jieng communities, a person is identified as a member of particular family from a particular clan, section, and ethnic group. Children of any marriage belong to the family or clan of the man. Families are patrilineal, meaning that names follow the male line.[119] In most African

---

[114] Deng, "The Cow and the Thing Calledwhat': Dinka Cultural Perspectives on Wealth and Poverty."

[115] Deng, "The Cow and the Thing Called" What": Dinka Cultural Perspectives on Wealth and Poverty."

[116] Deng, "The Cow and the Thing Calledwhat': Dinka Cultural Perspectives on Wealth and Poverty."

[117] Helen Chapin Metz, *Sudan, a Country Study*, ed. Congress Library Of and States United (Washington, D.C.: Headquarters, Dept. of the Army, 1992).

[118] Milos to be added

[119] Fadlalla, "Customary Laws in Southern Sudan: Customary Law of Dinka and Nuer."

customary family law systems, there are two main customary legal systems: matrilineal and patrilineal. Under the matrilineal system, children born in the marriage are affiliated to the clan of the wife.[120] In the patrilineal system, children born in marriage are affiliated to the clan of the husband, provided that all customary obligations are fully realised, especially the bride wealth for some ethnic groups.[121]

The Jieng customary family system is patrilineal and, therefore, Jieng children born in marriage are customarily affiliated to the husband's clan; they are not allowed to affiliate themselves with their maternal family. They can only refer to their maternal family as blood-related but are not affiliated to the wife's clan or ethnic group in any way.[122]

A multi-generational group of relatives who are linked by patrilineal descent consists of several related nuclear family members descended from the same man are considered as one clan ("Dhien"). People become dhien if they can trace descent to the same male ancestor. Both males and females inherit a patrilineal family membership but only males can pass it on to their descendants. This is also known as agnatic descent.[123] Figure 7 illustrates how patrilineal descent is practiced by Jieng.

---

[120] Lea Mwambene, "Divorce in Matrilineal Customary Law Marriage in Malawi: A Comparative Analysis with the Patrilineal Customary Law Marriage in South Africa" (University of the Western Cape, 2005).

[121] "Custody Disputes under African Customary Family Law in Malawi: Adaptability to Change?," *International Journal of Law, Policy and the Family* 26, no. 2 (2012).

[122] Jok, Leitch, and Vandewint, "A Study of Customary Law in Contemporary Southern Sudan."

[123] Ibid.

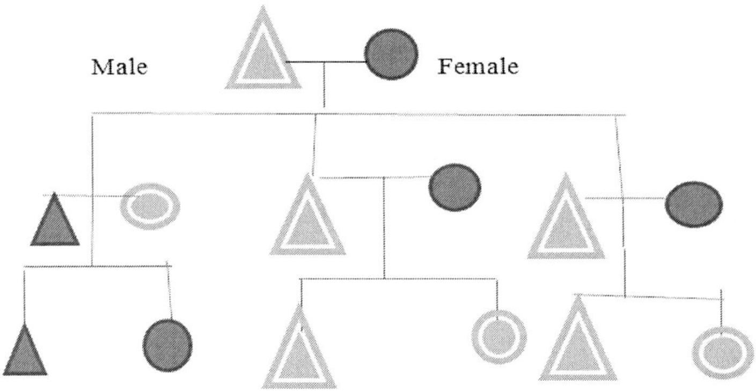

Figure 7: Patrilineal lineage

Kinship ties are enormously central to the Jieng people with family members providing an essential support network to their nuclear and extended relatives. Kinship is a communal connection among the Jieng that binds past, present, and future generations together.[124] One important family unit consisting of those who belong to the same sub-clan is defined as "all of those who come into contact with each other who know themselves to be agnatic descendants of an original ancestor."[125] This patrilineal structure theoretically allows everyone to trace his or her ancestors back to a single person. The closer the connection of the descent group, the more that is expected from one another in the way of alliances and mutual support.[126]

Traditionally, a marriage is arranged by the men of the families involved. Marriage brings together two extended families in a relationship that is established and sustained through payment of bride wealth. Bride wealth is paid by the extended family of the husband to the wife's extended family.[127] Historically, this system of marriage has provided stability during time of crisis, ensured that support is provided to all members of the entire extended family on both patrilineal and matrilineal sides as well as relatives

[124] Deng, *The Dinka of the Sudan.*

[125] Deng, "The Cow and the Thing Calledwhat': Dinka Cultural Perspectives on Wealth and Poverty."

[126] Beswick, "Islam and the Dinka of the Southern Sudan from the Pre-Colonial Period to Independence (1956)."

[127] *The Nature of Customary Law*, ed. Amanda Perreau-Saussine and James Bernard Murphy, Nature of Customary Law : Legal, Historical and Philosophical Perspectives (Cambridge: Cambridge : Cambridge University Press, 2007).

connected by marriage, and provided safety and security for women and children.

Bride wealth involves an exchange from the grooms' extended family to the extended family of the bride, and so is intended to strengthen the relationship between these families. It also allows the wife's extended family to intervene if the husband mistreats either his wife or their children.[128] This creates a strong incentive for the husband to ensure that he treats his wife with respect.[129]

A woman gains respect within the family when she produces many children, especially boys. Jieng parents and family love and value their children, and sons receive special attention as they are seen as essential to the continuity of the lineage. A man is considered truly dead when his death comes and he did not have sons to carry on his family name and lineage,[130] or to remember him. The past, present and future generations can only be linked through sons and, as a result, only sons are seen to be able to bring immortality to their fathers and the lineage.

The Jieng naming system significant in the family lineage. Children are named at birth using the name of one of their ancestors, and sons are given the name of their grandfather, great-father, and so on. Children are taught their families histories and are expected from a very young age to be able to recite their father's genealogy.[131] Being able to narrate family genealogies back to many generations ensures the honouring of the paternal lineage and connects families to their ancestors. The continuation of family lineage from generation to generation is maintained even when a man has no sons. If a man is married and dies without sons, or is away for some years because of war, the responsibility for ensuring that his name continues falls to his family. There are numerous ways a man's family can continue his name, all of which will be discussed in the following section.

---

[128] Makec, *The Customary Law of the Dinka People of Sudan: In Comparison with Aspects of Western and Islamic Laws*.
[129] Deng, "Customary Law in the Cross-Fire of Sudan's War of Identities."
[130] Deng, *The Dinka of the Sudan*.
[131] Deng, "Customary Law in the Cross-Fire of Sudan's War of Identities."

3.4. The Nature of Marriage ("Thieek")

In South Sudan, "marriage is considered the basis of forming a family, and in ethnic communities there is more than one definition of marriage".[132] According to Jieng customary law, "marriage is defined as a union between one man or his successor and one woman or more women for the purpose of sexual cohabitation."[133]

The further definition describes "marriage as a means of procreation and maintenance of the homestead." Marriage also encompasses the union between a childless woman and another woman. Further, marriage can be a union "between a deceased male person and one or more women through his successor."[134] Therefore, there are multiple forms of marriage within Jieng customary law. Marriage is not only between a man and a woman. It can also be between a barren woman and another woman, or women for the purpose of continuing the family line.

Furthermore, the definition also uses the term between a man and a woman or women. This implies that polygamous marriage is allowed according to Jieng customary law,[135] and there are no limits to the number of women a man can marry. In addition, the definition also uses the term "succession," which means one could enter marriage through "succession" in the event of death or infertility of the husband.

Marriage is divided into three categories: "single simple" marriage; polygamous marriage; and marriage by a deceased kinsman. In addition, there is another sub-category within this type of marriage which is the marriage between the barren woman and another woman.[136] As reflected in the above discussion it is important here to discuss how Jieng marriages acquire legal status.

---

132 Kok, "The Customary Law of the Dinka People of Sudan: In Comparison with Aspects of Western and Islamic Laws."
133 Fadlalla, "Customary Laws in Southern Sudan: Customary Law of Dinka and Nuer."
134 Abu Rannat, "The Relationship between Islamic and Customary Law in the Sudan 1."
135 Ibid.
136 Fadlalla, "Customary Laws in Southern Sudan: Customary Law of Dinka and Nuer."

3.4.1. Validity of Marriage

In Jieng tradition, marriage is a mutual agreement between two families and their relatives.[137] It is not an agreement between the potential husband and wife alone. According to Jieng customary law, marriage is valid or legal when all the processes of engagement, negotiation, acceptance (agam), and bride wealth are executed. Hence, the two parties can undergo the process to perform rituals to receive blessings through the ceremony. In Jieng customary law, there is no registration or issuing of certificates to validate the marriage, however, marriage is considered binding for life. Marriage can only be brought to an end if the wife dies. It is not the same case for men. Jieng customary law allows succession to take place making the woman property to be inherited by the next of kin or living brother, should the death of the first husband occur.

As discussed, it is important to look at the marriageable age at which Jieng girls are legally permitted to be married, as well as the implications between customary law's understanding of marriageable age and the statutory law definition of it.

3.4.2. Marriageable Age

According to Jieng customary law, no marriage should be consummated between a boy and a girl until both attain the maturity age known in Jieng as 'Dit'. Maturity in Jieng customary law is not stipulated by a minimum age; it is instead, determined by physical features.[138] The prerequisite of these features for the girl is marked by the first menstrual period, and for the boy it is marked by physical changes such as voice breaking, and growth of hair in the arm-pits or genital area.[139]

According to the Ministry of Gender and Child Affairs, forty-eight percent of South Sudanese girls between the ages of fifteen and nineteen years old are married, as well as some twelve-year-old girls. Despite South Sudan's

---

[137] Aldehaib, *Sudan's Comprehensive Peace Agreement Viewed through the Eyes of the Women of South Sudan.*

[138] Fadlalla, "Customary Laws in Southern Sudan: Customary Law of Dinka and Nuer."

[139] Ibid.

Child Act 2008 setting the minimum age for marriage at eighteen years of age, it is still the case that child marriage is prevalent in the country.[140]

However, early marriage is part of the customs of Jieng where once a girl reaches puberty, she is considered a woman and, consequently, many families do not hesitate to "give her away" in marriage in exchange for cows. Furthermore, the bride wealth payment is a key driver of child marriage in South Sudan, where families see their daughters as sources of wealth.[141] A marriage is sealed after a man and his family negotiate and pay a bride wealth to a woman's family in the form of cattle and which, more recently, may include money. Other families favour early marriage for fear that their daughters remain unmarried and get pregnant. This is a phenomenon condemned by Jieng culture and, after which, these girls are no longer wanted as wives or, if so, only in exchange for a few cows.[142] This example demonstrates that Jieng women and girls are particularly vulnerable members of society.[143]

Critics have argued that "the laws are not transcribed allows local leaders, mostly men, to interpret them to their liking."[144] The judicial system of South Sudan is meant to ensure that customary law, which comprises any oral and unrecorded laws, is applied in accordance with statutory law. However, child marriage and other contentious practices still occur.[145]

3.4.3. Forced Marriage

Forced marriage occurs "when one or both parties (usually the bride) are married without his or her free and full consent."[146] It is addressed in the Article 15 of the Transitional Constitution (The right to found a family) which states that: "no marriage shall be entered into without the free and

---

140 Tønnessen and Tønnessen, "Gendered Citizenship in Sudan: Competing Debates on Family Laws among Northern and Southern Elites in Khartoum."
141 Jok, Leitch, and Vandewint, "A Study of Customary Law in Contemporary Southern Sudan."
142 Lacey, "It Takes Two Hands to Clap Conflict, Peacebuilding, and Gender Justice in Jonglei, South Sudan."
143 Ibid.
144 Fozdar and Hartley, "Refugee Resettlement in Australia: What We Know and Need to Know."
145 Aldehaib, *Sudan's Comprehensive Peace Agreement Viewed through the Eyes of the Women of South Sudan.*
146 Makec, *The Customary Law of the Dinka People of Sudan: In Comparison with Aspects of Western and Islamic Laws.*

full consent of the man and woman intending to marry."[147] Nonetheless, force marriage often still takes place.

In South Sudan, early marriage is seen as a way to protect girls from sexual violence. This is done to ensure that in the future they do not bring shame on the family by getting pregnant out of marriage.[148] The widespread practice of child marriage exacerbates South Sudan's gender gaps in school enrolments, contributes to surging maternal mortality rates, and violates the right of girls to be free from violence. Despite the availability of legislation, there is a lack of protection for victims who try to resist forced marriage. A group of women activists who are part of a project known as Girls, Not Brides, is working hard to engage community leaders and traditional chiefs to end early and forced marriages. Human Rights Watch has also called for the South Sudan government to clearly set the age of eighteen as the minimum age for marriage. (Mohammed, 2014)[149]

3.4.4. Polygamy ("Thieek Diaar Juech")

Polygamy in any culture is marriage in which a spouse of either sex may possess a plurality of mates at the same time. Polygamy, as applied under Jieng customary law, is the practice of having more than one wife at one time.[150] Here, each wife and her children form an economic sub-unit with a separate kitchen, fields for food production, and cattle. Each extended family is embedded in a sociological structure characterised by networks of wider economic and political obligations based on kinship ties. Nonetheless, most households are self-sufficient economic units producing their own food, housing, and other necessities.[151]

Polygamy, as interpreted under Jieng customary practice, means a Jieng man has the right to enter into marriage with more than one woman. There are no legal limitations as to how many wives one can marry, and the only barrier is the financial status of the man. Polygamy is widespread, especially among the sixty-four ethnic groups of South Sudan and, to some extent,

---

[147] Government, "South Sudan Judicary System."

[148] Arifeen Mohammed, "Child Marriage and Problems," *Pakistan & Gulf Economist* 33, no. 20 (2014).

[149] Ibid.

[150] Kok, "The Customary Law of the Dinka People of Sudan: In Comparison with Aspects of Western and Islamic Laws."

[151] Abu Rannat, "The Relationship between Islamic and Customary Law in the Sudan 1."

across Africa, but it is also practiced in other legal systems like sharia whether in Africa, the Middle East, or other Islamic countries.[152]

In most cases, large families are well respected among African communities.[153] With Jieng ethnic group and other similar groups within African communities, the term "wife" has two essential meanings. First, it refers to a woman married to a given man (or woman). Second, it refers to a woman married into a given extended family and denotes her positions within a family lineage. Thus, this type of marital social organisation is communal rather than composed of nuclear family units.[154]

In addition to marrying more than one wife or polygamy, Jieng people also practice levirate marriage. According to the practice of levirate, should a married man die, the parents or family of the deceased man would nominate a male within the family to continue procreating with the widow on behalf of the deceased man. The nominated male is usually one of the deceased man's brothers, and the widow would still be recognised as the wife of the dead man.[155]

In Jieng society, a potential husband pays a bride wealth in cattle often through a competitive system controlled by the future father-in-law.[156] The highest bidder usually acquires the woman, and the bride wealth is made in a series of instalments over a lengthy period of time. Under the system of levirate marriage, if a man dies before having paid all the bride wealth, one of his brothers acquires the widow and continues making payments to the woman's family.[157] Thus, a woman's procreative capabilities are never "wasted," and she is never without a husband to care for her and her children.

Though most African families do not practice polygamy, and levirate marriage today as it has died out in many cultures, including a number in

---

[152] "The Relationship between Islamic and Customary Law in the Sudan 1."

[153] Twining, "Human Rights: Southern Voices Francis Deng, Abdullahi an-Na'im, Yash Ghai and Upendra Baxi."

[154] Abu Rannat, "The Relationship between Islamic and Customary Law in the Sudan 1."

[155] Deng, "Customary Law in the Cross-Fire of Sudan's War of Identities."

[156] Saeed Mohd Ahmed El Mahd, "Some General Principles of Acquisition of Ownership of and Rights over Land by Customary Prescription in the Sudan," *Journal of African Law* 20, no. 2 (1976).

[157] Deng, "Customary Law in the Cross-Fire of Sudan's War of Identities."

South Sudan,[158] Jieng and Nuer people continue to practice polygamy especially in the western Nilotic of Bhar El Ghazal region. This practice is important for the Jieng socio-economic lifestyle.[159] Until recently, there was a proverb which stated that: “many wives shall bring forth many daughters who shall be married with great numbers of cattle.”[160] Historically, polygamy has been critical to the successful economic, political, and ethnic expansion of the Jieng within the southern Sudan region.

Previous research has revealed that the Jieng people were not originally from the present South Sudan; rather they migrated from northern Sudan to their present regions some centuries ago.[161] (AKYEAMPONG, 1998) The expansion of Jieng ethnic into the South Sudan occurred over a few centuries. Historically, bride wealth within Jieng communities has been higher than that of their neighbouring ethnic groups. Consequently, inter-marriage between ethnic groups was not practiced due to the level of bride wealth paid. Over time, the Jieng population increased compare to their neighbouring ethnic groups and they continue to spread to many parts of South Sudan.

Before the division of the Sudan into two states, the Jieng was the largest single ethnic group, and currently they continue to be the largest population group within South Sudan. Thus, the practice of polygamous marriage customs among the Jieng communities were significant to their economic, political, and military power in the Sudan. When the British colonialists arrived within the region of South Sudan, followed by Christianity through missionaries, there were significant changes to the patterns of marriage among many other ethnic groups. The Jieng, however, have largely continued traditional patterns of marriage and family relations.[162]

---

[158] Ibid.
[159] Ibid.
[160] Danne, "Customary and Indigenous Law in Transitional Post-Conflict States: A South Sudanese Case Study."
[161] EMMANUEL AKYEAMPONG, "Social History Gender, Ethnicity and Social Change on the Upper Slave Coast: A History of the Anlo-Ewe. By Sandra E. Greene. Portsmouth Nh: Heinemann; Oxford: James Currey, 1996. Pp. Xiii+ 209.£ 40 (Isbn 0-85255-672-1);£ 14.95, Paperback (Isbn 0-85255-622-5)," *The Journal of African History* 39, no. 03 (1998).
[162] Deng, "Customary Law in the Cross-Fire of Sudan’s War of Identities."

3.4.5. Ghost Marriage ("kooc'')

"Kooc'', according to Jieng, means making a fallen object stand again or raising something to an upright position. When a Jieng man dies before being able to marry, his parents, siblings, or other close relatives are obliged to arrange a marriage for him in which one of his brothers or next of kin is nominated to be the candidate for marriage as his proxy. He would then procreate children in the name of his deceased brother or kinsman.[163] The wife in such marriages is referred to as ghost wife ("Ting Jook''). Children born to Ting-Jook recognise their biological father as uncle knowing that their "real" father is deceased and are culturally prohibited from calling him father. Some human rights activists[164] argue whether "kooc" could be considered as a violation of human rights particularly the rights of women and children. This kind of marriage denies woman the right to have someone she can call husband and instead compels her to consent to marry a deceased person through a successor; in addition, the children also are obliged to identify themselves with their deceased "father."

3.4.6. Levirate Marriage ("lohor")

When a Jieng man dies leaving behind his widow or widows, his parents or surviving close relatives meet and nominate his successor who continues to procreate with her, but no marriage ceremony takes place, nor is it necessary. It is expected that the widow continues to be legally recognised as the wife of the deceased man, since the death of a man in Jieng does not bring marriage to dissolution.

Death can only end the marriage when the woman in the marriage dies. A widow is expected to be loyal to her husband's family through the man who is cohabiting with her. A levirate marriage is a legal union, although it is considered as cohabiting with the widow in the name of deceased man, so any sexual intercourse outside the levirate union will be deemed as adultery and incurs the same consequences as adultery committed by a married couple. The critique of this practice argues that the institution of "Lohor'' is linked to the payment of bride wealth as it dictates the freedom of a widow to move on with her life after death of the husband.[165]

---

[163] Deng, *The Dinka of the Sudan.*

[164] Ibid.

[165] Tønnessen and Tønnessen, "Gendered Citizenship in Sudan: Competing Debates on Family Laws among Northern and Southern Elites in Khartoum."

3.4.7. Marriages of Barren or Son-Less Women

Marriages between barren or son-less women are marriages between one barren or son-less woman and another woman or women, and for whom male consorts are provided.[166] It is also referred to as woman-to-woman marriage and it has two categories. First, this marriage takes place when couples fail to bear children due to the woman's infertility or her husband is old or has passed away.[167] Given that in many African societies and in the South Sudanese in particular, a woman's traditional social obligation is to marry and procreate, a barren woman is considered a failure and is sometimes ostracised. Through woman-to-woman marriage, a barren woman is able to gain social prestige and her husband's favour, as she can opt to marry another woman and provide male companionship in the name of her (deceased) husband or imaginary son.[168] The male successor could be a close relative, for instance, a step-son, brother in-law, or a cousin's son.

The second category is where a woman bears only female children and there is no male to continue the family lineage. In this case, the woman will marry another woman and assume control over her and her offspring.[169] The wife will bear children in the name of the imaginary son, in the event that she has son who does not pass away at birth. All the ceremonial aspects of marriages are observed, bride wealth is paid to the girl's father, and all the rules of divorce in Jieng customs apply.

Furthermore, the female husband takes on the conceptual role of a male. She uses the institution of marriage as a way of achieving social prestige and increased economic security. The female husband usually has the same rights over the wife and her children as a man has over his wife and children. She must financially support them and is in charge of disciplining the children.[170]

---

[166] R. Jean Cadigan, "Woman-to-Woman Marriage: Practices and Benefits in Sub-Saharan Africa.(Special Issue: Comparative Perspectives on Black Family Life, Vol 1)," *Journal of Comparative Family Studies* 29, no. 1.

[167] Fadlalla, "Customary Laws in Southern Sudan: Customary Law of Dinka and Nuer."

[168] Cadigan, "Woman-to-Woman Marriage: Practices and Benefits in Sub-Saharan Africa.(Special Issue: Comparative Perspectives on Black Family Life, Vol 1)."

[169] Ibid.

[170] Ibid.

Several authors have argued that woman-to-woman marriage may involve lesbianism,[171] however, most researchers disagree with this idea. For example, Amadiume claims that interpretations of woman-to-woman marriage as lesbianism would be inapplicable, shocking, and offensive to those women, since the strong bonds and support between them do not imply lesbian sexual practices.[172]

After reviewing each type of marriage, it clear that no marriage is valid without payments of bride wealth. As a result, this section will explore in detail the concept of bride wealth and its significance among the Jieng families in South Sudan.

3.4.8. Bride Wealth ("Hocke-Thieek")

In Jieng cultural practice, a bride wealth which is negotiated and paid in the form of cattle to the woman's family by the man and his family, normally, seals the marriage. It is considered a gift paid by the groom to the family of the bride,[173] and is usually arranged before the couple come together as husband and wife. According to Fadlalla, bride wealth represents the compensation of services to the bride's family and relatives for the expenses incurred in raising her and also as a reimbursement for the costs incurred during the marriage of the bride's mother.[174]

The bride wealth also serves as an acknowledgement for services to be rendered by the bride to her husband and his family, and for the children she will bear. It is believed that a bride wealth brings stability to the marriage – in the form of economic benefits acquired by the bride's parents and relatives – as it is sought to supply a material symbol. This legalises the union between a man and a woman and establishes the legitimacy of its children and their lawful inheritance.[175]

---

[171] Peter Lubin and Dwight Duncan, "Follow the Footnote or the Advocate as Historian of Same-Sex Marriage," *Cath. UL Rev.* 47 (1997).

[172] Wairimu Ngaruiya Njambi and William E O'Brien, "Revisiting" Woman-Woman Marriage": Notes on Gikuyu Women," *NWSA Journal* 12, no. 1 (2000).

[173] Deng, *The Dinka of the Sudan.*

[174] Abu Rannat, "The Relationship between Islamic and Customary Law in the Sudan 1."

[175] Kok, "The Customary Law of the Dinka People of Sudan: In Comparison with Aspects of Western and Islamic Laws."

The bride wealth price is determined by the socio-economic status of the groom's family, and the personality, physical appearance, and temperament of the bride. It is widely believed that girls with approachable characteristics are preferred by many candidates. Nevertheless, the bride wealth is always followed by the marriage ceremony which starts immediately after settlement of the bride's price. The ceremony takes different forms and also depends on the status of the groom's family. It is not a requirement for marriage validation: just a ritual to dignify the concept of marriage. The payment of cattle as bride wealth accounts for the stability of marriage and the rarity of divorce.[176] Bride wealth is contributed to by a wide circle of a man's relatives and distributed among a correspondingly large circle of relatives on the bride's side.[177] In the event of a divorce, unless the marriage has resulted in having enough children (in which divorce may be more unlikely), bride wealth must be returned. This usually involves returning both the cattle which were given in the original bride wealth, as well as any calves. Some of the cattle that was paid as bride wealth would be needed to secure marriages of other relatives. The serious consequences of divorce for the whole extended family means that divorce should be avoided except if there are very compelling reasons.[178] The court can make an order for the repayment of bride wealth, however this can result in ongoing conflict between families.[179] This will be discussed in further detail in section 3.6 The Nature of Child Custody.

Bride wealth also makes separate and divorce especially difficult for women. Women who leave a marriage often forfeit all their possessions. The requirement to return bride wealth means that women may be forced to remain in violent marriages.[180] A woman who leaves her husband without obtaining a divorce faces the possibility of being accused of adultery. Accusations of adultery can also be extended to any man with whom she subsequently has a relationship. Adultery is an offence under South Sudan's

---

[176] Twining and Twining, "Human Rights: Southern Voices Francis Deng, Abdullahi an-Na'im, Yash Ghai and Upendra Baxi."

[177] Deng, "Customary Law in the Cross-Fire of Sudan's War of Identities."

[178] Juuk, "South Sudanese Dinka Customary Law in Comparison with Australian Family Law: Legal Implications for Dinka Families."

[179] Deng, *The Dinka of the Sudan.*

[180] Fozdar and Hartley, "Refugee Resettlement in Australia: What We Know and Need to Know."

penal code. Punishment for adultery include the payment of compensation, court fines, and up to two years imprisonment.[181]

As discussed, the bride wealth and how it operates among Jieng families in maintaining the bond between the families in marriage is critical. It is also worthwhile discussing how married women in Jieng are prohibited from having extra-marital affairs - another term for which is "adultery." This following section discusses how adultery is handled under Jieng customary law.

3.4.9. Adultery ("AKor")

According to section 266 of *The Penal Code Act* 2008,[182] whoever has consensual sexual intercourse with a man or woman who is, or who he or she has reason to believe is the spouse of another person, commits the offence of adultery and shall be addressed in accordance with the customs and tradition of the aggrieved party and in lieu of that and upon conviction, shall be sentenced to imprisonment for a term not exceeding two years or with a fine or with both.[183] In addition to this guidance from statutory law, Jieng customary law is very strict on adultery. Any Jieng female who is not a girl is presumed to be a married woman and any man who commits sexual intercourse with such a woman does so at his own risk.

There are two categories of risk. Firstly, if the man is found having sexual intercourse with someone's wife, he may be at risk of being killed or hurt by the husband or the male next of kin. In this instance, Jieng customary law would presume the killer innocent in the face of an act of self-defence or trespass. Secondly, he may face a fine of up to six head of cattle (Akor) and, if he has no cattle to pay, then he can be punished with imprisonment or a fine or both, in accordance with the provision of the South Sudan *Penal Code Act* 2008.[184] However, if the sexual intercourse results in the birth of a child, then the child also belongs to the husband of the woman who committed adultery. However, if the husband elects to divorce his wife, then

---

[181] Jok, Leitch, and Vandewint, "A Study of Customary Law in Contemporary Southern Sudan."
[182] Sudan, "Child Act 2008 and Penal Code 2008."
[183] Ibid.
[184] Ibid.

the child will return to live with the woman and her relatives. (Ebbeck and Cerna, 2007)[185]

There is no "Akor" payable if the adultery is committed for the second time by the same person. This is where the husband and the family file a case for divorce in customary court.[186] The adultery is exemplified by the following summary of the SPLM Court of Appeal Case at Rumbek on 11th May 2004:

The appellant in this case had cohabited with a woman for seventeen years and had five children with her. The woman was previously married and had one child. Her husband had been killed fighting for the SPLA, but Jieng (Dinka) custom of widow inheritance, she was still considered to be married to his family, and therefore her relationship with the appellant constituted adultery. Her first husband's brother had successfully sued for the return of the widow and all her children, in a series of local courts, and eventually the high court in Rumbek. The appeal court judges decided to reverse these judgements in favour of appellant by formally nullifying the marriage with her late husband and granting the paternity rights to her second husband for the children except the oldest child who was considered to belong to the first husband. Their recorded justifications were somewhat varied. One judge declared that in Jieng custom, if a wife had been left without care for two years or more, her legal husband's family could no longer claim rights over a child she produced with another man; also the length of an adulterous relationship validated it in terms of paternity rights. The other judge argued that in Jieng customary law the first marriage would never be invalidated unless formally divorced with the returning bride wealth, but that in this case the customary law should be set aside in order to consider the best interests of the woman and her children. As recorded in the court verdicts, in any case, Jieng customary law could have taken into account the impact of the impact of the national duty on the family of a soldier who goes to the war-front to liberate the country.[187]

Although these Jieng judges reached the same conclusions, their contexts were divergent regarding the best interest of women and children which is contrary to statutory law.

---

[185] Kok, "The Customary Law of the Dinka People of Sudan: In Comparison with Aspects of Western and Islamic Laws."
[186] Fadlalla, "Customary Laws in Southern Sudan: Customary Law of Dinka and Nuer."
[187] Government, "South Sudan Judicary System."

3.5. The Nature of Divorce ("Puoke-ruai/Thieek")

South Sudan Jieng communities address divorce matters in accordance with their customary law as stipulated in the transitional constitution of South Sudan.[188] Divorce, according to Jieng customary law, is the dissolution or end of marriage.[189] Marriage should be legally ended or granted by the court with the consent of all parties attached to the marriage contract. The court process and divorce are made more difficult rather than easier as a means of retaining family ties and relationships.[190]

Under Jieng customary law, divorce is not widely accepted and is only possible under extreme situations. One situation is when the bride's family is willing to repay some portion of the bride wealth to the husband's family when couples have children together. The requirement of repaying bride wealth always creates tensions, especially since the bride wealth is shared amongst the bride's extended family.[191] Consequently, families have an incentive to ensure that marriages remain intact. Even if girls face abuse and violence in their marriages, they may face pressure to reconcile despite risks to their safety and wellbeing.[192] For instance, the extended family has a stake in the marriage and will bring pressure to bear on the couple to manage a way to resolve their differences.

Continuity of the lineage through procreation is of vital importance to the Jieng and is the most important function of marriage. Marriage is only nullified by the court and the intention is to let everyone know that the relationship between these two families and their extended families has ended, specifically when adultery is involved.[193] In addition, the party to blame is publicised, making it difficult for him or her to remarry. It is particularly more challenging for a woman to remarry than the man, especially when misbehaviour or adultery was the cause of divorce.[194] A man can still marry whether in a relationship or not, however, the above-

---

188 Statistics, "Canberra."

189 Fadlalla, Mohamed, 'Customary Laws in Southern Sudan: Customary Law of Jieng and Nuer' (2009) New York: iUniverse

190 Fadlalla, "Customary Laws in Southern Sudan: Customary Law of Dinka and Nuer."

191 Ibid.

192 Twining, "Human Rights: Southern Voices Francis Deng, Abdullahi an-Na'im, Yash Ghai and Upendra Baxi."

193 Deng, "Customary Law in the Cross-Fire of Sudan's War of Identities."

194 Fadlalla, *Customary Laws in Southern Sudan: Customary Laws of Dinka and Nuer*.

mentioned misbehaviour is more important for women. Consequently, conflict arises in many cases during the recovery of the bride's wealth or property.[195] This is because the return of cattle usually includes its offspring and any cattle sold or which have died as a result of negligence or where death of cattle could not be proven. However, the proof of dead cattle includes the skin, or witnesses during the death and handovers take effect immediately after divorce.

Consequently, the major part of a dispute during the divorce is the custody of children. As discussed earlier, custody of children is associated with the conceptualisation of the family as well as payments of bride wealth by the man's family to that of the woman. Therefore, this section will discuss the approaches to child custody in Jieng customary law.

3.6. The Nature of Child Custody

The issue of child custody is unique, and Jieng customary law takes a patriarchal approach to it. According to Jieng family customary law, it is the right of the husband to take full custody of the children, unless *Aruok* has not yet been paid, therefore requiring the maternal family to live with the child or children until all dues are settled.[196] Furthermore, the man has the right to recover some of his bride wealth or property depending on the number of children from the marriage. In addition, he is allowed to take full custody of the children after the settlement is completed.

Jieng customary law scrutinises the rights granted by the custom patriarchy, giving males rights to full custody in the event of divorce.[197] The maternal family, however, has the right to be paid remedies before children are allowed to live with their paternal family. Therefore, it could be said that Jieng customary law does not consider the position of the children or the mother.

---

[195] Ahmed El Mahd, "Some General Principles of Acquisition of Ownership of and Rights over Land by Customary Prescription in the Sudan."
[196] Jok, Leitch, and Vandewint, "A Study of Customary Law in Contemporary Southern Sudan."
[197] Fadlalla, *Customary Laws in Southern Sudan: Customary Laws of Dinka and Nuer*.

3.7. Human Rights under Customary Law

Most of South Sudan's customary law reflects the values of a patriarchal society which means it is lacking when it comes to human rights protections of women and children. Those critics of human rights problems are mainly focused on Jieng customary law practices which are not reflective of all sixty-four ethnic groups in South Sudan. The foundation of Jieng society is the strength of the family and social cohesion.[198] The role of women in Jieng culture is that of strengthening family ties through bride wealth and producing children who will continue the family lineage. Women are thus seen as a means to an end: strengthening society and family bonds by producing children and necessitating bride wealth. However, they are profoundly valued for this role they play in society.[199]

Domestic violence is a family issue within Jieng communities; however, women are reluctant to report it. As a cultural norm, they are encouraged by their families and leaders to resolve it within the family with the aim of staying in the marriage for the sake of their family and children.[200] Women are encouraged not to seek external intervention from the authorities regarding domestic violence issues as it is considered as a family matter, and no one is allowed to intervene unless they are invited to do so. In serious cases of domestic violence where intervention is needed, women are encouraged to resolve the matter within their husband's family through elders who are next of kin.[201] Since the Jieng culture is patriarchal, all chiefs and leaders are male. There are no female chiefs in customary courts and women's voices are poorly represented throughout the Jieng communities.[202]

South Sudan has commenced building a modern judicial system. However, while customary law is somewhat different to statutory law and does not form a country wide legal system, it is a very important part of South Sudan and its culture, along with the justice system. It is argued that "judicial and legal policy continues to undermine and ignore the pre-existing, organic

---

198 Armstrong, "Good Practices with Culturally Diverse Families in Family Dispute Resolution."
199 Garcia, "The Future of South Sudanese Women: Restructuring Customary Law in South Sudan."
200 Mennen, "Lessons from Yambio: Legal Pluralism and Customary Justice Reform in Southern Sudan."
201 Ibid.
202 Ibid.

judiciaries while neglecting to consider the role customary law and courts are already playing."[203] Customary law in South Sudan survived decades of war, several changes in government and the statutory law legal system, as well as hundreds of years of culture. It is a system that is deeply embedded into the country and its people and a system that must be recognised and accepted as part of the legal system. However, it is also a system that is not formally recorded nor collectively adopted by all ethnic groups, and a system that favours men as head of household and families.[204] However, the practice of child marriage as discussed earlier in this chapter may be contrary to international human rights instruments. Local communities in South Sudan will often still perceive universal human rights standards as external imposition and threat to South Sudanese identity where they clash with customary practices. In many areas, customary law system is at odds with international human rights standards, especially where it takes on criminal justice matters.[205] Customary law system focus on restorative justice which often save perpetrators of less serious crimes from the inhumane reality of state current penitentiary system or corporal punishment. On the contrary, it can result in impunity for serious offenses, in particular sexual violence. For instance, rape cases the customary law authorities will often focus on arranging some kind of compensation and reconciliation agreement between families. Generally, the gap between international human rights and customary law is mostly common with regard to the position of women.[206] The majority of South Sudanese ethnic groups are generally patrilineal, polygamous and patriarchal in their social structure. Every leading and importance aspects are attached to a man passing on his name to a large number of children.[207] Moreover, in the event of divorce, custody of children is granted to the man unless enough bride wealth was not paid at the initial marriage. Additionally, many ethnic groups practice levirate marriage; which mean in case of death of the husband, another male next of kin from patrilineal line will inherit the wife.

---

[203] Ibid.

[204] Lacey, "It Takes Two Hands to Clap Conflict, Peacebuilding, and Gender Justice in Jonglei, South Sudan."

[205] Danne, "Customary and Indigenous Law in Transitional Post-Conflict States: A South Sudanese Case Study."

[206] Pimentel, "Rule of Law Reform without Cultural Imperialism? Reinforcing Customary Justice through Collateral Review in Southern Sudan."

[207] Malcolm MacLachlan et al., "Inclusion and Human Rights in Health Policies: Comparative and Benchmarking Analysis of 51 Policies from Malawi, Sudan, South Africa and Namibia," *PLoS ONE* 7, no. 5.

3.8. The Rights of the Child

The UN Convention on the Rights of the Child (CRC) was ratified by Sudan in August 1990. This occurred before South Sudan's succession although the nation acknowledges its obligations under the CRC. The CRC clearly states that every state must take appropriate measure to ensure that "all actions regarding children, whether assumed by the public or private social welfare institutions, courts of law, administrative authorities or legislative bodies, the best interest of the child be the primary consideration."[208]

Customary laws involving children often violate international conventions and charters to which South Sudan is signatory.[209] The tensions between the application of universal rights to protect children and local customs which may cause children harm are most clearly demonstrated in the example of child marriage. The African Charter on the Rights and Welfare of the Child (1990) urges states to outlaw child marriage and to implement legislation establishing the minimum age of marriage at eighteen years.[210] Similarly, the CRC also obligates states to adopt a minimum-age-of marriage law.[211] In South Sudan, the Child Act (2008) has set the minimum age of marriage to eighteen years.

Despite this, child marriage continues to be commonplace and to have community support. For instance, in 2019, UNICEF estimated that over forty percent of girls in South Sudan were married before they reached eighteen years.[212] In 2011, Judge Raimondo sentenced over sixty young men in Lake State, South Sudan, for impregnating girls under the age of eighteen years old.[213] However, the state is predominantly inhabited by Jieng ethnic groups who mostly rely on their customary law for family matters. This decision was so controversial that it led to the dismissal of the

---

208

Virginia Murphy-Berman, Helen L Levesque, and John J Berman, "Un Convention on the Rights of the Child: A Cross-Cultural View," *American Psychologist* 51, no. 12 (1996).

209 Mark Canavera et al., "'And Then They Left': Challenges to Child Protection Systems Strengthening in South Sudan," *Children & Society* 30, no. 5 (2016).

210 'Dejo Olowu, "Protecting Children's Rights in Africa: A Critique of the African Charter on the Rights and Welfare of the Child," *Int'l J. Child. Rts.* 10 (2002).

211 Losoncz, "Blocked Opportunity and Threatened Identity: Understanding Experiences of Disrespect in South Sudanese Australians."

212 UNICEF, 'World Children's Day' South Sudanese Children Calls for an End to Child Marriage' (20 November 2019).

213 Sudantribune, "High Court Judge to Lose Seat over Pregrancy Sentencing."

judge by the government by public demand who stated that he failed to incorporate the role of customary law.[214] This example illustrates the gap between the statutory laws and customary law where in most cases customary law would prevail over the state law.

Child marriage is clearly a violation of children's rights. It disregards the child's freewill and removes the child from her family without her consent. It also entrenches a pattern whereby girls and women are disempowered in other aspects of their lives. Child marriage can also result in a female child being denied the education that her brothers would most likely attain. For a child bride, it is likely that she will give birth before her body is fully developed.[215] This is not only harmful to her health and increases her chance of maternal mortality, but it also increases the likelihood that her child will also suffer from health problems.[216]

The issue of female children not receiving an adequate education compared to male children occurs more generally. Boys are more likely to receive an education while girls remain within the domestic household.[217] It is assumed in South Sudan society that a young girl will eventually grow up to be a wife and mother and that, therefore, a formal education is unnecessary. It is considered more important for the wellbeing of the family and her future that she remain at home, assist her mother with the younger children, and fetch drinking water and firewood at a distance away from home.[218]

This practice of keeping girls home arguably violates the CRC by denying a child the right to education based on gender. However, it has been argued that families, who live in extreme poverty, are dependent on their daughter's labour and that the bride wealth that the family receives in exchange for her marriage is an essential resource. Therefore, adhering to CRC has the potential to cause greater disadvantage to the child and her family.[219] Child marriage is most prevalent in very poor communities where families do not

---

[214] Ibid.

[215] Sharon Detrick, *A Commentary on the United Nations Convention on the Rights of the Child* (Martinus Nijhoff Publishers, 1999).

[216] Ibid.

[217] Tønnessen and Tønnessen, "Gendered Citizenship in Sudan: Competing Debates on Family Laws among Northern and Southern Elites in Khartoum."

[218] Nada Mustafa Ali, *Gender and Statebuilding in South Sudan* (US Institute of Peace, 2011).

[219] Tønnessen and Tønnessen, "Gendered Citizenship in Sudan: Competing Debates on Family Laws among Northern and Southern Elites in Khartoum."

have the resources to invest in alternative options for girls, largely seen as an economic burden to the family.[220]

The failure to extend legal protection to children in South Sudan is largely an outcome of the tension between respecting customary practices and the application of universal conceptions of human rights intended to protect children from harm. An extreme cultural relativist position would argue that local customs and culture are the sole source of norms, values and moral positions, and that the law needs to protect local customs regardless of their outcomes. While "the practice of cultural relativity was developed by anthropologists as a means of understanding another's culture or belief systems in an objective manner and without assuming that one is more acceptable than the other,"[221] it is argued that human rights violations are being progressed in the name of culture diversity. On the other hand, an extreme Universalist position would hold that context is not relevant, and that the law must protect fundamental human rights regardless of community views and local customary practice.[222] Universal human rights have been critiqued for privileging Western norms and for failing to consider the immense diversities that exist in the world.[223] Universal human rights can also be seen to be a luxury that people living in poverty cannot always afford. As demonstrated in the example of child marriage, what constitutes human rights violations amongst one group of people might be necessary for the survival of another.

Arguably, the transitional constitution and *The Child Act (2008)* have attempted to find a middle ground between cultural relativism and universalism by privileging the best interests of the child. However, Alston and Gilmour-Walsh argue that "it is impossible to define a child's best

---

[220] Jennifer Parsons et al, 'Economic impacts of child marriage: a review of the literature' (2015) 13(3) The Review of Faith & International Affairs, 12.
[221] Jane K Cowan, Marie-Bénédicte Dembour, and Richard A Wilson, *Culture and Rights: Anthropological Perspectives* (Cambridge University Press, 2001).
[222] Jack Donnelly, 'Cultural relativism and universal human rights' (1984) 6(4) Human Rights Quarterly, 400.
[223] Philip Alston and Bridget Gilmour-Walsh, "The Best Interests of the Child: Towards a Synthesis of Children's Rights and Cultural Values," (UNICEF Innocenti Research Centre, 1996).

interest under a set of universal guidelines."[224] What is in the child's best interests can differ according to who is making the determination.[225]

According to Eekelaar, "the best placed person to determine the child's best interest is the child."[226] He claims that a "child exposed to a wide range of influences as the child develops, it is encouraged to draw on these influences in such a way that the child itself contributed to the outcome."[227] Eekelaar's argument of dynamic self-determinism, however, has faced criticism that a child is not necessarily capable of deciding their own self-interests.[228] Eekelaar believes, however, that so long as the child possesses rationality and a foundation from where he or she can derive basic wisdoms, then they should be able to make decisions about their own lives.[229] The goal of self-determinism, according to Eekelaar, is to "ensure that the child develops into adult with the maximum opportunities to form and pursue life goals which reflect as closely as possible an autonomous choice."[230] Therefore, rather than have an international body or state determine the best interests of the child, Eekelaar believes that the child, with adequate competency, is capable of determining her/his own best interest.

Eekelaar's position contains a number of concepts that do not fit well within a South Sudanese context. Concepts such as rationality and autonomous individuality reflect Western values, which do not fit easily within the non-Western practices of the child being embedded within community relations.[231] The rights of women and children, which are often essential to their wellbeing, are not always recognised by some members of the society.[232] It is frequently claimed that international laws which are intended

---

[224] Ibid.

[225] Tønnessen and Tønnessen, "Gendered Citizenship in Sudan: Competing Debates on Family Laws among Northern and Southern Elites in Khartoum."

[226] John Eekelaar, "The Interests of the Child and the Child's Wishes: The Role of Dynamic Self-Determinism," *International Journal of Law, Policy and the Family* 8, no. 1 (1994).

[227] Ibid.

[228] Alston and Gilmour-Walsh, "The Best Interests of the Child: Towards a Synthesis of Children's Rights and Cultural Values."

[229] Eekelaar, "The Interests of the Child and the Child's Wishes: The Role of Dynamic Self-Determinism."

[230] Ibid.

[231] Ibid.

[232] Detrick, *A Commentary on the United Nations Convention on the Rights of the Child.*

to protect the rights of an individual, only follow the Western cultural values and did not to recognise cultural diversity. (Donnelly, 1984)[233]

Cultural and religious practices are occasionally based on rituals that violate human rights treaties.[234] For instance, some practices may allow a child to be left in the care of the father in the event of divorce even though the best interests of the child may be to leave the child in the care of the mother.[235] This may mean that the court's decision over who should care for the child may clash with social obligations and religious norms.

Alston and Gilmour-Walsh argue that the principle of the best interest of the child is ambiguous and open to interpretation. They warn that it is impossible to apply the same guidelines to different cases, and that the application of best interests of the child is unlikely to be universal. Depending of the cultural and religious context, traditional customs may be seen to be in the best interests of the child, whereas in another community the physical and emotional well-being of the child may be more important.[236]

In South Sudan, child marriage is seen by many to be harmful to the health and emotional wellbeing of the child. However, many South Sudanese people would argue that child marriage is an opportunity for the girl-child to take up some responsibility and to become independence.[237] Whilst child marriage may be seen (by others) to have particular benefits within Jieng society, it is not something that should be occurring to young girls. On the other hand, in case of Eekelaar's self-determinism, a child who chooses to reject traditional practices that he or she might find to be unacceptable could equally face exclusion in a society when conformity and submission to one's elder is demanded.

Kon K Madut, "Determinants of Early Marriage and Construction of Gender Roles in South Sudan," *SAGE Open* 10, no. 2 (2020).

[233] Jack Donnelly, "Cultural Relativism and Universal Human Rights," *Hum. Rts. Q.* 6 (1984).

[234] Edward, "South Sudanese Refugee Women: Questioning the Past, Imagining the Future."

[235] Fadlalla, "Customary Laws in Southern Sudan: Customary Law of Dinka and Nuer."

[236] Alston and Gilmour-Walsh, op.cit.

[237] Pavlish and Ho, "Human Rights Barriers for Displaced Persons in Southern Sudan.(World Health)."

3.8.1. Women's Rights

South Sudan's Bill of Rights recognises the rights of the women as equal to those of men.[238] However, in practice women are frequently exposed to gender discrimination that is supported by customary law which often supersedes civil and criminal law. One of the main impediments to gender equality is the lack of education for women. Figures from 2013 show that over ninety percent of women in South Sudan are illiterate, and this limits women's opportunities and ability to engage in decision-making.[239] While legislation now exists which places a greater emphasis on the rights of women, it is the customs and traditions that are upheld by society that enforce their marginalisation.[240] Therefore, it remains a strong argument that customary law must be addressed in an effort to recognise the rights of women under the international treaties on human rights and as a moral obligation to women as human beings.[241]

Many attempts have been made at different levels, including by the women of South Sudanese themselves, to gain acknowledgement of their rights and those of all the women and girls in South Sudan. According to Harris-Short, (Harris-Short, 2003)the state may expel harmful traditional practices in an effort to modernise and better assimilate with the West.[242] For example, the practice of Female Genital Mutilation (FGM) is outlawed by the state in several African countries. However, efforts to change customs in order gain support from the West are unlikely to gain community support. The practice of FGM was officially outlawed across the whole of the Sudan in 1925, and yet in the north Sudan it continues to be practiced primarily among the Muslims and in rural societies.[243] Furthermore, both criminal and civil laws have been modified to respect the rights of the people. These laws are not always accepted, and some people within those communities claim that their

---

[238] Susan M Armstrong, "Encouraging Conversations About Culture: Supporting Culturally Responsive Family Dispute Resolution1," *Journal of Family Studies* 17, no. 3 (2011).

[239] Gender Concerns International, 'Women in South Sudan: Predicament, challenge and hope'

[240] Deng, *Customary Law in the Modern World: The Crossfire of Sudan's War of Identities*.

[241] Sonia Harris-Short, "International Human Rights Law: Imperialist, Inept and Ineffective? Cultural Relativism and the Un Convention on the Rights of the Child," *Human rights quarterly* 25, no. 1 (2003).

[242] Ibid.

[243] Nahid Toubia, "Female Genital Mutilation," *Women's Rights, Human Rights: International Feminist Perspectives* (1995).

laws are overly influenced by Western laws and values. Consequently, many people rely on their customary laws as the only relevant form of law.[244] The effectiveness of law is always dependent on people's attitudes toward a particular practice, for example, many people accept the practice of FGM though it is illegal, and it is unlikely for anyone in the community to seek legal action from the state. Therefore, the elimination of customary practices that are harmful to some members of society cannot only be the responsibility of state, it requires collective efforts from both the state and the members of the society.[245]

Harris-Short also argues that the definition of human rights, as reflected in the conventions, are not essentially Western customs.[246] The drafting of the Human Rights Convention was primarily led by the Western countries, and some of the countries involved in drawing up the Convention do not consider the economic, social, and cultural rights to be essential rights or entitlements.[247] For example, the International Covenant on Civil and Political Rights was signed and ratified by the US. However, the US has declined to sign and ratify the International Covenant on Economic, Social, and Cultural Rights, arguing that human beings are not naturally entitled to such rights.[248] Harris-Short further argues that people do not adhere to some laws in some countries, simply because they feel their natural rights are being violated. This suggests that there cannot be universal rights that transcend cultures.[249]

With challenges that are facing women in South Sudan, women have been active in protesting against customary law practices that support gender inequality. Women in South Sudan have protested against girls being denied

---

[244] E Herieka and J Dhar, "Female Genital Mutilation in the Sudan: Survey of the Attitude of Khartoum University Students Towards This Practice," *Sexually Transmitted Infections* 79, no. 3 (2003).

[245] Paul Mkandawire et al., "Men's Perceptions of Women's Reproductive Health in South Sudan," *Health & place* 58 (2019).

[246] Harris-Short, "International Human Rights Law: Imperialist, Inept and Ineffective? Cultural Relativism and the Un Convention on the Rights of the Child."

[247] Sally Engle Merry, "Human Rights Law and the Demonization of Culture (and Anthropology Along the Way)," *PoLAR* 26 (2003).

[248] Jane Jenson, "Paradigms and Political Discourse: Protective Legislation in France and the United States before 1914," *Canadian journal of political science* 22, no. 02 (1989).

[249] Harris-Short, "International Human Rights Law: Imperialist, Inept and Ineffective? Cultural Relativism and the Un Convention on the Rights of the Child."

an education based on gender, and being forced into marriage.[250] If the concept of women's rights was limited to the West and did not transcend cultural boundaries, then women in many developing countries and states where they are considered second class citizens would accept their roles rather than demand recognition of rights.[251] The next section looks at the practice of customary law outside South Sudan in the refugee camps in neighbouring countries.

3.9. Practice of Customary Law in Refugee Camps and Australia

Despite over half a century of civil war in South Sudan during which physical and bureaucratic infrastructures have collapsed, the practices of customary marriage have survived particularly among South Sudanese Jieng communities, throughout their journey of displacement to refugee camps and resettlement in neighbouring countries.[252] While in neighbouring countries of Ethiopia, Kenya, and Uganda, South Sudanese refugees were living in refugee camps and were not subjected to local laws addressing their family-related issues like marriage, divorce and child custody, customary courts were established to litigate family disputes related to marriage, divorce, child custody and many other cultural conflicts without the interference of the host country jurisdiction.[253]

In the early 1990s, with the help of the United Nations High Commission for Refugees (UNHCR), many South Sudanese were resettled in Western countries mainly the United States, Canada, Norway, and Australia. Consequently, these countries' resettlement policies granted refugees permanent residency with the aims to integrate and become equal citizens of the host country after a certain period of time.[254] In Australia the South Sudanese and Jieng in particular were understandably keen to hold onto

---

[250] Pimentel, "Rule of Law Reform without Cultural Imperialism? Reinforcing Customary Justice through Collateral Review in Southern Sudan."

[251] Tim Brown, "South Sudan Education Emergency," *Forced Migration Review* 24 (2006).

[252] Riek Machar, "South Sudan: A History of Political Domination-a Case of Self-Determination," *Nairobi: November* (1995).

[253] Garcia, "The Future of South Sudanese Women: Restructuring Customary Law in South Sudan."

[254] Val Colic-Peisker and Iain Walker, "Human Capital, Acculturation and Social Identity: Bosnian Refugees in Australia," *Journal of Community & Applied Social Psychology* 13, no. 5 (2003).

their own customary practice and were reluctant to adapt to the laws of their new community. For instance, polygamy, arranged/forced, levirate, and ghost marriages continue to exist and pose potential clashes in Australia, as these practices are neither recognised nor allowed.[255]

Jieng girls and women are relatively powerless to determine their personal life including their choice of husband, which becomes a decision made by other members of her family.[256] If a woman refuses to marry the person their family has chosen, it is common for families to send her to jail until she changes her mind. This is not the case in Australia where marriage is not viewed as a binding agreement between the families; the decision to marry is within the sphere of the husband and wife. Furthermore, the use of bride wealth is not part of Australian custom. It is common practice that legal systems at all levels continue to rely on the interpretation of traditions and customary laws. This is especially the case in personal law, as customary law is recognised in the South Sudan transitional constitution.[257] Moreover, Jieng customary laws have mediators, leaders of formal and informal laws who come in various forms throughout South Sudan, depending on ethnic, religious and political factors.[258] Judicial courts are provided for both statute *and* customary law, while informal community practices also rely upon local chiefs known as "Bany-Alathith" (BA), to resolve disputes between community members. The judiciary relies greatly on popular justice for solving disputes through methods of reconciliation and the application of tradition.[259] Customary laws generally consist of non-state law systems that are usually based on local custom, traditional or tribal systems of justice. Nevertheless, the majority of Jieng marriages and family practices here in Australia clash with Australian family law.[260]

The concept of customary law is defined by Woodman as a set of customs and rules that reflect a certain community's beliefs, habits and values, also

255 Springvale, "Comparative Analysis of South Sudanese Customary Law and Victorian Law."
256 Jok, Leitch, and Vandewint, "A Study of Customary Law in Contemporary Southern Sudan."
257 Khawaja and Milner, "Acculturation Stress in South Sudanese Refugees: Impact on Marital Relationships."
258 Jok, Leitch, and Vandewint, "A Study of Customary Law in Contemporary Southern Sudan."
259 Khawaja and Milner, "Acculturation Stress in South Sudanese Refugees: Impact on Marital Relationships."
260 Terry Hutchinson, "Researching and Writting in Law."

referred to as a mirror of accepted usage.[261] Given this definition, the clashes of South Sudanese Jieng customary law with Australian family law have been experienced widely among the Jieng community in Australia. Jieng customary law aims to create and reinforce a peaceful society, as criminal and family issues are dealt with under the same body of law.[262]

Most Sudanese Australians are former refugees. As such, they experience social disadvantages and discrimination in their new homeland.[263] Research has shown that discrimination has a negative impact upon the health, economic success, and educational attainment of South Sudanese Australians. It also affects their relations with state authorities, most notably the criminal justice system. In addition, South Sudanese Australians who have faced discrimination are less likely to feel that they belong in Australia, and discrimination has negative impacts on well-being, mental health, civic participation, and social conduct.[264] A recent report of the Australian Human Rights Commission indicates that negative media representations of South Sudanese people also contribute to these negative outcomes.[265]

3.10. Customary Law during Civil Wars

The history of colonial rule in Sudan, ethnic conflict, and the struggle for identity greatly influences both customary laws and the desire to uphold such traditions.[266] Before the independence of Sudan from Colonial rule, Egypt was the dominant force in northern Sudan which has a predominantly Arab and Muslim population. Britain controlled the Southern part of the

---

[261] Simon Roberts, "Introduction: Some Notes on "African Customary Law"," *Journal of African Law* 28, no. 1-2 (1984).

[262] Helen Chapin Metz, *Republic of the Sudan: Country Studies*, ed. Congress Library Of (Washington, DC: Federal Research Division, Library of Congress, 2001).

[263] Yvonne Wohler and Jaya AR Dantas, "Barriers Accessing Mental Health Services among Culturally and Linguistically Diverse (Cald) Immigrant Women in Australia: Policy Implications," *Journal of Immigrant and Minority Health* 19, no. 3 (2017).

[264] Ignacio Correa-Velez, Sandra M Gifford, and Adrian G Barnett, "Longing to Belong: Social Inclusion and Wellbeing among Youth with Refugee Backgrounds in the First Three Years in Melbourne, Australia," *Social Science & Medicine* 71, no. 8 (2010).

[265] David Nolan et al., "Mediated Multiculturalism: Newspaper Representations of Sudanese Migrants in Australia," *Journal of Intercultural studies* 32, no. 6 (2011).

[266] Johnson, *The Root Causes of Sudan's Civil Wars.*

Sudan comprising a diverse ethnic African majority and a high proportion of Christians.[267]

As previous discussed, the beginning of the first stage of civil war in the Sudan started in 1955.[268] British-Egyptian divided the Sudan into two parts, north and South Sudan, attempting to barricade the south to maintain traditional African culture.[269] The creation of an independent government in the north to rule both the north and south sparked clashes that spiralled into a decade of bloody warfare. The Addis Ababa Peace Agreement signed in 1972 created an interval from conflict, however, clashes resumed in 1983 at the implementation of Sharia (Islamic law) across the country, imposing Islam rule over the largely Christian and ethnic African populations igniting what has become known as the second civil war in the Sudan. This second civil war was fought by the Sudan People's Liberation Army (SPLA) and its political wing the Sudan People's Liberation Movement (SPLM) against the Khartoum government with goal of creating a new secular Sudan where religion is separated from the state.[270]

While in their liberated and other marginalised areas in South Sudan, SPLM leaders confirmed in recent times that one of the key changes they were fighting for during the civil war was the right to practice customary laws, beliefs and traditions without coercion or undue interference from external parties.[271] Despite over four decode of civil war, during which the political and legal system collapsed, customary law survived. It has been the only source of social order and stability in South Sudan.[272] During the years of civil war in the SPLA/SPLM liberated areas, customary law was the only important mechanism and factor that was not affected by the war and was effectively utilise in bringing justice among the people in Southern Sudan then. In spite of this, customary law institutions were undermined regularly by the actions of SPLA commanders during the most recent periods of fighting. An example of this was the implementation of military tribunals to

---

[267] Anderson, *Sudan in Crisis: The Failure of Democracy*.

[268] Shadrack Wanjala Nasong'o and Godwin Rapando, "Lack of Consensus on Constitutive Fundamentals: Roots of the Sudanese Civil War and Prospects for Settlement," *African and Asian Studies* 4, no. 1 (2005).

[269] Ibid.

[270] Solomon A Dersso, "International Law and the Self-Determination of South Sudan," *Institute for Security Studies Papers* 2012, no. 231 (2012).

[271] Jok, Leitch, and Vandewint, "A Study of Customary Law in Contemporary Southern Sudan."

[272] Springvale, "Comparative Analysis of South Sudanese Customary Law and Victorian Law."

usurp customary courts throughout the civil war.[273] Even if this was in fact necessary, an unavoidable after-effect would be a significant weakening of traditional systems.

On the other hand, the genuineness of appeals for cultural sovereignty to be respected is confirmed by the fact that customary laws were recognised and given a legitimate central role in Southern Sudanese jurisprudence in the SPLM's statutory reforms of 2003. Earlier wartime actions on the part of the SPLM also confirmed the existence of an anticipated formalised role for customary law in South Sudan. One such example was the SPLMIA New Cush Civil Authority Conference in 1996 which resulted in significant restoration of customary law and justice through a formally recognised role for chiefs within the SPLM hierarchy and processes.[274]

The clash of military and customary laws also has a social interface exemplified by such events in the late 1990s when a local tribal youth was murdered by a SPLA soldier.[275] The SPLA Commander had the murderer executed for his action. However, for the youth's family, this was irrelevant and their demands for traditional remedying of the wrong by way of blood compensation payment in the form of cattle led to sporadic and increasing violence between them and the SPLA.[276] This brings us to the next section which examines legal consciousness and how it relates to South Sudanese former refugees in Australia.

3.11. Legal Consciousness

Legal consciousness refers to the way people think about law and understand how legal rules and regulations affect their daily lives. Although the law may not always directly influence peoples' lives or decisions, the previous chapters have shown how everyday problems between couples can

[273] Jok, Leitch, and Vandewint, "A Study of Customary Law in Contemporary Southern Sudan."
[274] BUILDING A NEW SUDAN, "The Sudan People's Liberation Movement/Army," *Rebel Rulers: Insurgent Governance and Civilian Life during War* (2011).
[275] Jok, Leitch, and Vandewint, "A Study of Customary Law in Contemporary Southern Sudan."
[276] Ibid.

be connected to, or result in, problems with the law.[277] According to Nielson, the "ideas about law, both conscious and unconscious, shape how people make sense of such interactions, what types of speech they consider problematic, and what remedies or responses they believe are possible."[278] Furthermore, legal consciousness also refers to what people do not think about the law and the presumptions they have about the law that sometimes get taken for granted.[279]

It is within legal consciousness research that the response to participants' problems can be situated. Legal consciousness research seeks to examine the role of law in constructing understandings, affecting actions, and shaping various aspects of social life.[280] The emphasis is on a subjective experience of law, rather than law and its effects on society.[281] Ethnographic studies of legal consciousness demonstrate that people interpret and respond to events in different, culturally specific ways. As Silbey argues, the issues that might give rise to disputes and legal claims are described as cultural events, evolving within a framework of rules about what is the normal or moral way to act, what kind of wrongs warrant action, and what kinds of remedies are acceptable and appropriate.[282]

On the other hand, Von Benda-Beckmann and Griffiths(von Benda-Beckmann et al., 2017)[283] argue that migrants take their law to the new country of domicile. That is, the customary or religious law of their place of origin, but to some extent their national law as well, do not lose their relevance for migrants after they arrive in their adopted country.[284] These laws are usually seen as opposing the law of the receiving national state, creating a host of problems for politicians, lawyers, and migrants.[285]

---

277 Laura Beth Nielson and Robert L Nelson, "Rights Realized-an Empirical Analysis of Employment Discrimination Litigation as a Claiming System," *Wis. L. Rev.* (2005).
278 Ibid.
279 Ibid.
280 Susan S Silbey, "After Legal Consciousness," *Annu. Rev. Law Soc. Sci.* 1 (2005).
281 Ibid.
282 Ibid.
283 Franz von Benda-Beckmann, Keebet von Benda-Beckmann, and Anne Griffiths, "Mobile People, Mobile Law: An Introduction," in *Mobile People, Mobile Law* (Routledge, 2017).
284 Ibid.
285 Ibid.

When examining legal consciousness, Ewick and Silbey locate people as either before the law, with the law, or against the law. These categories are used as a cultural paradigm from which people's understandings of law are constructed.[286] People "before the law" view the law as a distinctive, authoritative, and formal hierarchical system that is separate and superior to everyday social life. People "with the law" view the law as a system of rules that are part of everyday life, which can be changed and manipulated to benefit them if the game is played correctly. Finally, people "against the law" view the law as opposed to their interests, often finding themselves up against the law, wanting to resist or fight it.[287] These positions influence the way people understand and respond to legal problems. For example, a person who is "with the law" is more likely to seek legal assistance than a person "before the law," as they feel more empowered and connected to it.[288]

The response to some groups of parents' concerns, particularly on how parenting issues were handled by the court, resulted in the introduction of mandatory pre-filing of family dispute resolution in 2006. The literature in Chapters Two and Three have indicated that South Sudanese handle family law disputes in accordance with their customary law, and that, in Australia, they face challenges in trying to reconcile the two legal systems. The next chapter analyses and discusses family dispute resolution, and how it is accessible or not to south Sudanese Jieng families in Australia.

3.12. Conclusion

This chapter has provided an overview of customary law in South Sudan, particularly how disputes related to marriage, divorce, and care arrangements for the children are resolved among Jieng communities. The chapter has discussed and defined what customary law is, and examined the extent of the pluralistic legal system in South Sudan. It has described how customary law co-operates alongside the statutory laws among the diverse sixty-four ethnic groups where each has an individual and distinct body of functioning customary law. It is clear in the discussion that ninety percent

---

[286] Silbey, "After Legal Consciousness."

[287] Ibid.

[288] Lindsey Webb, "Legal Consciousness as Race Consciousness: Expansion of the Fourth Amendment Seizure Analysis through Objective Knowledge of Police Impunity," *Seton Hall L. Rev.* 48 (2017).

of cases including some criminal offences are resolved through customary law courts.

The chapter has outlined the judiciary structure and the operations of customary and statutory courts in the country and has highlighted the importance of a communal approach in resolving disputes within the families, clans, and throughout the hierarchy of various customary courts from the bottom to the top. It further explored the concept of family and how that influences the resolution of disputes related to marriage, divorce and child custody as practiced among Jieng communities. It was argued that Jieng customary law maintains practices which are not being followed in other cultures outside South Sudan. For instance, polygamy, arranged/ forced, levirate, and ghost marriages are not commonly practiced and may clash with the legal systems of other countries like Australia where Jieng communities have settled in the last few years. However, the definition of marriage and its validity were classified into three different categories in Jieng custom.

It was noted that in Jieng customary law, marriage was the agreement between two families and their relatives. Therefore, it can be concluded that South Sudanese Jieng communities are likely to continue to utilise their traditional marriage practices by resolving their marriage and other related disputes within their communities wherever they reside outside South Sudan and including in Australia.[289]

It is clear through the discussion that divorce under customary law is made difficult as it does require the consensus of the both families because marriage is an agreement between two families and not between individual couples. Furthermore, child custody was discussed from the Jieng communities prospective and it was evident that children are traditionally affiliated to their paternal parents and can be taken after divorce once all "Hocke Thieek" or "Aruok" are paid.

Finally, this chapter examined and critiqued the role of international human rights instruments under customary law in South Sudan. It argued that the rights of women and children are and continue to be violated despite the relevant legislations in place. The chapter also addressed legal consciousness with South Sudanese former refugees and concluded that most refugees including the South Sudanese struggle to understand the

---

[289] Hutchinson, "Researching and Writting in Law."

Australian legal system and may be underrepresented within the family law sector which is discussed in the next chapter.

CHAPTER FOUR

FAMILY LAW IN AUSTRALIA

4.1. Introduction

Australia has approximately over 30,000 former refugees from South Sudan, and the number continues to grow.[1] This massive resettlement was due to over half a century of civil war, during which massive displacement occurred inside South Sudan and to refugee camps in the neighbouring countries. Consequently, many South Sudanese people were resettled in different and distant countries such as Australia, USA and Canada. In their adopted countries, they became exposed to different cultures, customs, and formal legal systems, which were significantly different from the customary law with which they were more familiar. As explained in Chapter Two, family law disputes in South Sudan are traditionally resolved within families or the community and have relied on customary legal practices,[2] rather than by government statutory authorities.

In Chapters Two and Three, the book provided an overview of customary law in South Sudan, in particular, through examining how Jieng communities resolve family customary law disputes. It also offers a brief discussion on the evolution of Jieng custom and cultures in the refugee camps and in their adopted countries like Australia. This discussion is crucial to examine the changes that Jieng customs and culture have undergone in South Sudan. This provides an essential context to this chapter which examines the legal consciousness of Jieng families in Australia, especially those who continue to apply customary law and may come into conflict with the formal family law system.

Thus, this chapter provides a brief account of Australian family law and its progression from its English heritage to its application in contemporary multicultural Australia. The chapter will give a historical narrative of the

---

1 Robinson, "Sudanese Heritage and Living in Australia: Implications of Demography for Individual and Community Resilience."

2 Fadlalla, "Customary Laws in Southern Sudan: Customary Law of Dinka and Nuer."

major changes to family law in Australia and offer a brief overview of the progress toward the rights of the child and the recognition of non-traditional families. It focuses on the ways in which family disputes are resolved. It then examines the published research on the experiences, challenges and opportunities encountered by South Sudanese former refugees in relation to the resolution of family disputes within the family law system in Australia. To do this, this chapter will examine how Australian law operates or does not operate within the context of legal pluralism.

While this chapter provides essential background to the following chapters which present an original empirical analysis of the experiences of Jieng former refugees living in Australia, it also provides a significant contribution in its own right. There have been many amendments to the *Family Law Act 1975*, including recent changes which recognised same sex marriage. However, little attention has been paid to the existence of legal pluralism within Australia, including the way in which refugee, migrant and Indigenous social groups need to interact with both formal and customary legal systems.

4.2. History of Major Family Law Changes in Relation to Marriage, Divorce, and Co-Parenting

Australian family law owes much to its English colonial heritage.[3] The family has for many years been regarded as one of the foundations of English society. In Australia, family means different things to different people. Many people in Australia perceive the modern family as being the nuclear family; that is, formed by a man and a woman living together and bringing into the world and rearing one or more children to adolescence or adulthood.[4] Traditionally, the family unit was based on marriage, and so family law has largely developed to protect the traditional nuclear family unit and the institute of marriage.[5]

On the other hand, Aboriginal and many other cultural groups regard the family unit as comprising an extended group of people who are related through marriage, blood, or adoption. Individuals within the extended family are involved with one another in their designated roles of husband,

[3] HL Finlay, MFA Otlowski, and R Bailey-Harris, "Family Law in Australia," (1997).
[4] Eithne Mills and Marlene, *Family Law* (Chatswood, N.S.W.: Chatswood, N.S.W. : LexisNexis Butterworths, 2012).
[5] Ibid.

wife, father, mother, son, daughter, brother, sister, uncle, aunt, cousin, grandparent, etc., and create and maintain a common sub-culture.[6] The distinction between the nuclear and extended family units come with diverse views and values in relation to legal expectations.

Australia family law neither defines the family, nor gives the "family'' a special legal status. The law focuses on the individual member of the family and their respective rights and obligations.[7] Australian family law exalts the values of individual freedom over obligations to family and community. However, despite the lack of the definition of the word "family,'' the law largely assumes the nuclear family as the focus of its consideration. However, the majority of ethnic minorities within Australian society emphasise the importance of collective values.[8] Therefore, marriages, divorce, and care of the children after separation are not merely alliances of individuals.

4.2.1. Marriage and Divorce in Colonial Australia and after the 1900s

In 1788, the British Empire established Australia as a penal colony.[9] When convicts arrived in Australia soon after, there were not many husbands and wives who were able to follow their spouse from the United Kingdom to Australia.[10] Proper records were not regularly kept, which meant that the original details of convicts' marriages were usually not accessible. Consequently, convicts who came to Australia without their spouses often entered into another marriage.[11] Many early settlers avoided formal marriage and only lived together.

---

[6] Khawaja and Milner, "Acculturation Stress in South Sudanese Refugees: Impact on Marital Relationships."
[7] Patrick Parkinson and Patrick Parkinson, *Australian Family Law in Context : Commentary and Materials* (Pyrmont, N.S.W.: Pyrmont, N.S.W. : Thomson Reuters Professional Australia, 2012).
[8] Malcolm Voyce and Adam Possamai, "Legal Pluralism, Family Personal Laws, and the Rejection of Shari'a in Australia: A Case of Multiple or "Clashing" Modernities?," *Democracy and Security* 7, no. 4 (2011).
[9] Neal M Ashkanasy, Edwin Trevor-Roberts, and Louise Earnshaw, "The Anglo Cluster: Legacy of the British Empire," *Journal of World Business* 37, no. 1 (2002).
[10] Lisa Young et al., *Family Law in Australia* (LexisNexis Butterworths, 2012).
[11] Ibid.

Generally, divorce was not available and rarely accessible to women in England until 1857, except through an Act of Parliament.[12] This was to protect a man's lands and titles for his inheritors. This double standard meant that women were seen as the property of men. If a wife committed one single act of adultery, then the husband could apply for a divorce.[13] Wives could only apply for divorce if her husband committed adultery with aggravating circumstances such as desertion, cruelty, sodomy or bestiality, bigamy or incest.[14]

Australia and other British colonies were able to enact their own legislation after the British Parliament passed the *English Divorce Act*, in 1857. The Tasmanian Legislative Council introduced a Divorce Act in 1858, although it was opposed on the grounds of immorality. A subsequent attempt in 1860 was successful, and consequently the focus of family law shifted away from protecting the rights of men, towards protecting wives and children of husbands who had deserted their family.[15] This shift is also evident in subsequent legislation.

Australia gained its independence in 1901. From 1901 until 1959, marriage and divorce were regulated by the State. The implementation of the *Matrimonial Causes Act (1959)* and the *Commonwealth Marriage Act (1961)* bought marriage and divorce under federal jurisdiction.[16]

The Matrimonial Causes Act 1959 introduced "fault-based divorce." For a spouse to obtain a divorce, they needed to prove marital fault. The Act listed reasons for divorce; the most common being adultery, drunkenness, desertion, habitual, imprisonment and insanity.[17] A private detective or a solicitor were hired to gather evidence to prove marital fault, which made the process of applying for a divorce costly and slow. Couples also needed to be separated for at last five years before they had grounds to apply for a divorce. In addition, except with leave of the court, a spouse could not apply for a divorce unless the couple had been married for at least three years.

---

[12] Finlay, Otlowski, and Bailey-Harris, "Family Law in Australia."

[13] André Renzaho et al., "Parenting, Family Functioning and Lifestyle in a New Culture: The Case of African Migrants in Melbourne, Victoria, Australia," *Child & family social work* 16, no. 2 (2011).

[14] Parkinson and Parkinson, *Australian Family Law in Context : Commentary and Materials*.

[15] Ibid.

[16] Garfield Barwick, "The Commonwealth Marriage Act 1961," *Melb. UL Rev.* 3 (1961).

[17] Ibid.

During this era, family law also mostly protected the rights of men and took little consideration of women and children, as they were largely conceived of as property. This continued until 1975 when no-fault divorce was introduced.

In 1975, *the Family Law Act* was enacted by the Australian Government and is arguably the most significant change in family law in Australia. It dramatically shifted gender relations and enabled much more recognition of women's rights. Its most significant impact was to introduce no-fault divorce.[18] In a no-fault divorce, it is not necessary for a husband or wife to prove that the other spouse did something wrong in order to obtain a divorce.[19] One spouse must simply show that their relationship has suffered an irreconcilable breakdown.[20] *The Family Law Act (1975)* also reduced the amount of time a divorce came into effect from three months to one month. This resulted in a large number of divorces recorded in 1976.[21]

4.2.2. The Rise of Children's Rights

In 1983, the *Family Law Amendment Act 1983* was amended in an effort to reduce the formal and antagonistic nature of family law disputes by clarifying the concepts of "custody" and "guardianship of children."[22] The goal of this change was to remove the idea that a spouse had to "win" a family law case. Consequently, children were no longer seen as property and their rights started to come to the fore. The rights of the child became an even stronger force within family law in 1990, when Australia signed the UN Convention on the Rights of the Child (UNCROC). This continued Australia's shift towards protecting children and resulted in the *Family Law Reform Act (1995)*.[23]

The Family Law Reform Act 1995 changed the language of the act to reflect a significant shift towards a perception of children as independent beings, not owned by parents but for whom parents had responsibility. Any

[18] Ruth M Ferrell, "No-Fault Divorce," *Women Law. J.* 62 (1976).
[19] Finlay, Otlowski, and Bailey-Harris, "Family Law in Australia."
[20] Ferrell, "No-Fault Divorce."
[21] Barwick, "The Commonwealth Marriage Act 1961."
[22] Brooke Wilmsen, "Family Separation: The Policies, Procedures, and Consequences for Refugee Background Families," *Refugee Survey Quarterly* 30, no. 1 (2011).
[23] Alastair Nicholson and Margaret Harrison, "Family Law and the Family Court of Australia: Experiences of the First 25 Years," *Melb. UL Rev.* 24 (2000).

consideration of "custody" was now inappropriate, irrelevant, and incorrect at law.[24] The language of "custody" was changed to "residence," and "access" to "contact." However, the change was intended to support deeper social change. The Act focused on the duties and responsibilities of parents rather than parental rights. It also implied that both parents had the same legal parental responsibilities for their children.[25] The Act also stressed after separation or divorce that the best interests of the child usually involved the presence of both parents in the child's life. To this end, the Act introduced "shared parental responsibility" which recognised that parents have a joint duty to care for a child and that parenting should be co-operative.[26] More changes were also introduced to increase a child's rights and protection from violence, with the focus shifting even further towards the child's best interest.[27]

In 1996, there was a clear move away from litigation towards alternative dispute resolution and mediation. This change followed increasing concern about the cost of lengthy family law court cases. Separating parents were supported to reach agreements outside of the courts, and the introduction of simplified procedures were found to reduce the psychological and emotional effects of divorce, resulting in better decisions especially for children. In the early 2000s, there was a move to reduce delays for separating parents to access services to support early resolution of family law cases without the need to go to court, and to also allow families to attend voluntary counselling.[28]

This shift towards the use of mediation and other forms of Alternative Dispute Resolution (ADR) has continued and included the opening of Family Relationship Centres in 2006. Couples were now required to attend compulsory mediation before they made any application to the court regarding children.[29] Other changes also came about in 2006. *The Family*

---

[24] Parkinson and Parkinson, *Australian Family Law in Context : Commentary and Materials*.
[25] Young et al., *Family Law in Australia*.
[26] Andrew Bainham, *Children, the Modern Law*, ed. Stephen Michael Cretney (Bristol, England: Bristol, England : Family Law, 1993).
[27] Nicholson and Harrison, "Family Law and the Family Court of Australia: Experiences of the First 25 Years."
[28] Linda Fisher, *Mediating with Families*, ed. Mieke Brandon (Pyrmont, N.S.W.: Pyrmont, N.S.W. : Lawbook, 2009).
[29] Richard Chisholm, "Making It Work: The Family Law Amendment (Shared Parental Responsibility) Act 2006," *Australian Journal of Family Law* 21, no. 2 (2007).

Law Act previously only covered situations concerning children born or adopted into a marriage. It was only in 2006 that *The Family Law Act* was changed so that the Commonwealth was able to handle circumstances related to children born outside of the marriage.[30] In 2009, the Australia Government included all de facto couples (including same sex couples) under the Family Law Act.[31] This granted de facto and same-sex couples the same property rights as married couples. It also meant that unmarried parents had the same parental responsibilities and duties and could seek the same orders for residence and contact as married parents. Clearly, marriage and divorce have changed significantly since colonial days. Even today, there is a push towards equity for all types of family units, regardless of its composition.[32]

4.3. Family Dispute Resolution (FDR)

This section briefly discussed family dispute resolution and how Jieng families accessed or did not access services to resolve family law problems currently faced in Australia. Australia is one of the world's leaders in establishing family dispute resolution in a usable and affordable way. It has been practiced in Australia since the 1980s, with a statutory basis for it provided in 1991.

Since July 2006, the Family law Amendment (Shared Parental Responsibility) Act 2006 amended the Family Law Act to execute a number of important changes aimed to shift the way disputes over the care of children are resolved. Consequently, it became a requirement for the parties to attempt family dispute resolution before applying for a parenting order, with certain exceptions,[33] a legal presumption of equal shared parental responsibility and, where an order is made for equal shared parental responsibility, consideration of equal parenting time or substantial and

---

[30] Ibid.

[31] Ibid.

[32] La Trobe University. National Centre for Socio-Legal Studies and Lawrence Moloney, *Managing Differences: Federally-Funded Family Mediation in Sydney: Outcomes, Costs and Client Satisfaction* (Attorney-General's Department, 1996).

[33] Australian Government, *Family Law Handbook : Containing Family Law Act 1975 and Family Law Regulations Together with an Explanatory Summary and an Index to the Act and Regulations*, ed. statutes etc Family Law Act Australia. Laws and Australia (Canb.
Canberra: Canb. : Aust. Govt. Pub. Serv., 1975).

significant time with both parents.[34] The resumption does not apply where there are reasonable grounds to believe there has been family violence or child abuse.[35]

Family dispute resolution (FDR) is a form of family mediation that aims to help separated parents manage and resolve disagreements about their children's care.[36] Some of family dispute resolution processes include facilitation, mediation, conciliation and negotiation. These process are conducted by an accredited independent practitioner or practitioners to help families affected or about to be affected, by separation or divorce, to resolve their disputes with one another.[37] Since the introduction of mandatory pre-filing family dispute resolution in 2006,[38] people are not able to file a court application to resolve a parenting dispute regarding their children unless they have first made a genuine effort at FDR, with some exceptions.[39] FDR practitioners are required to advise disputing parents that any agreement they reach should be in their children's best interests and to encourage them to consider a range of shared parenting options. Australian FDR is premised on the assumption that parents are best placed to make decisions about their children,[40] and so affirms parental self-determination, whilst also facilitating a child focus in process and outcomes, with FDR practitioners often assuming an advocacy role in relation to children's interests.

Available data indicate that families from minority cultural backgrounds do not use FDR at a rate proportionate to their representation in the community.[41] A number of reviews have concluded that the family law system does not meet the needs of people from culturally and linguistically diverse (CALD) backgrounds, and that a range of personal and systemic

---

[34] Chisholm, "Making It Work: The Family Law Amendment (Shared Parental Responsibility) Act 2006."

[35] Gráinne Dennison, "Is Mediation Compatible with Children's Rights?," *Journal of Social Welfare & Family Law* 32, no. 2 (2010).

[36] Fisher, *Mediating with Families*.

[37] Family Law Council, *Improving the Family Law System for Clients from Culturally and Linguistically Diverse Backgrounds: A Report to the Attorney-General* (Attorney-General's Department, 2012).

[38] Armstrong, "Good Practices with Culturally Diverse Families in Family Dispute Resolution."

[39] Lisa Young & Geoff Monahan, *Family Law in Australia* (Sydney: Ligar Pity Ltd, 2009).

[40] Ibid.

[41] Armstrong, "Encouraging Conversations About Culture: Supporting Culturally Responsive Family Dispute Resolution1."

factors limit the ability of people from minority cultural backgrounds to access family law services.[42] In addition, people born in a country where a language other than English is spoken are less likely to recognise family problems as legal issues and, thus, less likely to seek assistance from professionals to address them.[43] It is important to understand the needs of separating families, including children, from CALD and faith backgrounds so that processes are developed to facilitate access to family mediation and to support minority parents to make informed decisions in mediation that are in their children's best interests.

While the proportion of separated couples from minority cultural contexts involved in family mediation is disproportionately small,[44] many have no choice but to participate in FDR. Children of these couples generally have no direct involvement in FDR at all, but it is their futures that are decided in such mediations.[45] The relationship between the parties and with the mediator will often be unequal, but unless the mediator recognises the possible effects of the parties' minority backgrounds on their capacity to access to FDR, on the dynamics of the mediation and the negotiations between the parties, and particularly on their absent children, these inequalities may be exacerbated.

As previously stated, research suggests that involvement of family law with culturally diverse populations is proportionally over-represented in litigated disputes concerning children, but under-represented with family mediation.[46] This under-representation in help seeking, could suggest a lack of trust, fear, knowledge and understanding of the Australian family legal system. On the other hand, some literature suggests that, minorities such as Indigenous, CALD and religious groups may be trying to resolve family disputes outside the court which brings us to the next section: the examination of legal pluralism, its recommendation in the past, and the lack of action taken by the federal government to address it.

---

[42] Ibid.
[43] Susan Armstrong and Australian Family Relationships Clearinghouse, *Enhancing Access to Family Dispute Resolution for Families from Culturally and Linguistically Diverse Backgrounds* (Australian Institute of Family Studies, 2010).
[44] Ibid.
[45] Armstrong, "Good Practices with Culturally Diverse Families in Family Dispute Resolution."
[46] Khawaja and Milner, "Acculturation Stress in South Sudanese Refugees: Impact on Marital Relationships."

4.4. Legal Pluralism

This section addresses legal pluralism and the fact that it is not been recognised in the Australian legal system. Legal pluralism is the system of law that allows for more than one legal system to operate simultaneously within one jurisdiction.[47] The expression of legal pluralism conceives that separate personal law may operate in the area of family law. Historically, legal pluralism has expanded from a concept that refers to the relations between the colonised and coloniser to relations between dominant and subordinate groups, such as religious, ethnic, or cultural minorities, immigrant groups and unofficial forms of ordering located in the societal networks or institutions.[48]

The Australian legal system, despite having white, middle-class Anglo-Celtic origins, now operates in the context of a multicultural society.[49] Laws, which successfully encapsulate the concept of cultural diversity, recognise the multiplicity of "Australian" values, regardless of whether they are derived from cultural, linguistic, racial, religious or political backgrounds, and seek to protect this diversity against discrimination and intolerance.[50] As interpreters of law, the courts have significant influence in the promotion of awareness of and respect for other cultures in the wider community.

The debate over the recognition of legal pluralism and, in particular, customary law has to be understood in the context of the wider function of family law – that is, maintaining the hegemony of the self-understanding of Australia as a modern, liberal society.[51] Legal pluralism is achievable if it remains the responsibility of everyone to ensure that the resulting legal arrangements are fair and non-discriminatory for all members of society.

The expression of legal pluralism conceives that separate personal laws may operate in the areas of family law.[52] A personal law system is defined as a

---

[47] Brian Z Tamanaha, "Understanding Legal Pluralism: Past to Present, Local to Global," *Sydney L. Rev.* 30 (2008).
[48] Archana Parashar, "Australian Muslims and Family Law: Diversity and Gender Justice," *Journal of Intercultural Studies* 33, no. 5 (2012).
[49] Voyce and Possamai, "Legal Pluralism, Family Personal Laws, and the Rejection of Shari'a in Australia: A Case of Multiple or "Clashing" Modernities?."
[50] Anne Griffiths, "Pursuing Legal Pluralism: The Power of Paradigms in a Global World," *The Journal of Legal Pluralism and Unofficial Law* 43, no. 64 (2011).
[51] Parashar, "Australian Muslims and Family Law: Diversity and Gender Justice."
[52] Griffiths, "Pursuing Legal Pluralism: The Power of Paradigms in a Global World."

system in which each individual is subject to jurisdiction of her/his own religio-legal norms and institutions with regard to matters of marriage, maintenance, living arrangement for children, and inheritance.[53] In such systems, an African may be subject to customary law or a Jewish person subject to Halakhah. Historically, legal pluralism can be seen to stalk from the implications of colonisation. In the fifteenth century, legally pluralistic societies around the world were produced as a result of European colonisation.[54] During colonisation, a new set of laws, rules and a new system of governance emerged. However, the traditions and customs of the colonised country remained. Consequently, the indigenous peoples were left to apply their traditional laws while colonial laws were applicable to the colonisers.[55] Both colonial laws and the customary law were markedly different and were further separated by law barriers and the effective reach of the legal system which was limited to urban areas.[56]

In Australia, there is one nationwide system of law and no form of legal pluralism in the area of personal law.[57] The Australian Law Reform Commission[58] issued a report that recommended that Indigenous law be recognised in the family law area but stopped short of recommending separate Indigenous legal mechanisms for those communities. However, this report has not been acted upon and its recommendation have not been implemented. A later report from Western Australia on the recognition of customary law warned against the recognition,[59] concluding that the operation of two separate systems of law would have a divisive outcome.[60]

---

[53] John Griffiths, "What Is Legal Pluralism?," *The journal of legal pluralism and unofficial law* 18, no. 24 (1986).
[54] Ibid.
[55] Tamanaha, "Understanding Legal Pluralism: Past to Present, Local to Global."
[56] Ibid.
[57] Voyce and Possamai, "Legal Pluralism, Family Personal Laws, and the Rejection of Shari'a in Australia: A Case of Multiple or "Clashing" Modernities?."
[58] Australia. Law Reform Commission and Australian Law Reform Commission, *The Recognition of Aboriginal Customary Laws: Summary Report* (Australian Government Publishing Service, 1986).
[59] Mark Horstman and Glenn Wightman, "Karparti Ecology: Recognition of Aboriginal Ecological Knowledge and Its Application to Management in North-Western Australia," *Ecological Management & Restoration* 2, no. 2 (2001).
[60] Ibid.

4.5. Family Law Challenges with South Sudanese and Other Minority Groups

Many studies investigating the experiences of South Sudanese families in Australia focus largely on the experiences of early settlement, exploring participation in labour markets, housing, and education.[61] Many others look at mental health and the correlations between resettlement issues and psycho-social well-bcing.[62] Nonetheless, these studies fail to explore the challenges encountered in how family law disputes are resolved or not resolved among their families in Australia.

This lack of literature documenting the experiences of these individuals with the family law sector, reveals the need to build a knowledge base to assist service providers, develop and implement appropriate programs to assist families from South Sudan and other cultural groups, as they experience challenges in adapting or navigating the family law system.

In 2011, the Attorney General asked the Law Council of Australia to investigate how the family law system meets the needs of parties from culturally and linguistically diverse backgrounds and suggest strategies for improvement in this area. The LCA acknowledged that much focus had been on the provision of access to a range of government services, particularly in the areas of health, employment, housing, education, family, and child support.[63] Conversely, less attention was paid to ensuring access to the civil justice system for people from CALD backgrounds. The final report revealed that the family law system is systemically not meeting the needs of people from CALD communities. This, in turn, leads to a lack of access to services within family law and the civil justice system.

In response to this gap, the Federal government-initiated strategies to enhance and promote access to justice within civil justice system. This provided a platform for change intended to enhance access to justice for every Australian while recognising the cultural diversity of individuals

[61] Bishop, *To Be a Family: Changes Experienced within South Sudanese Families in Australia*.
[62] Lejukole, "" We Will Do It Our Own Ways": A Perspective of Southern Sudanese Refugees Resettlement Experiences in Australian Society."
[63] Helen L. Rhoades, "Improving the Family Law System for Clients from Culturally and Linguistically Diverse Backgrounds. (Australia). Australian Journal of Family Law,," *Australian Journal of Family Law*, no. 3 (2012).

looking for help from the legal system.[64] Despite these initiatives, recent research suggests that culturally appropriate family law services are still lacking. Research shows that there are significant settlement challenges facing newly arrived families, which then places strain on relationships and increases the likelihood of family breakdown and the need for legal and family support services. Further studies also indicate growing concerns about family violence within new and emerging communities, as changing gender roles within families after settlement in Australia threaten traditional power relations and family stability. This research acknowledges that there is little investigation to date of the barriers that people face from new and emerging communities in accessing the family law system, and there is limited knowledge of how services in the system are attempting to respond to the needs of families from CALD backgrounds and the challenges they face in doing so.[65]

Instead, studies of South Sudanese-born settlement focus largely on employment experience,[66] language and communication skills,[67] experience in pursuing education[68] and child rearing practices of South Sudanese former refugees.[69] Others explore experiences of young people, including challenges of acculturating into new social environments, navigating education systems, social and peer groups, and discrimination.[70] These studies reveal the challenges in achieving integration goals. Khawaja and colleagues found settlement challenges amongst South Sudanese families in Australia were acquiring skills to navigate and understand host society.[71]

---

[64] Hazel Genn, "What Is Civil Justice for-Reform, Adr, and Access to Justice," *Yale JL & Human.* 24 (2012).
[65] Milos, "South Sudanese Communities and Australian Family Law: A Clash of Systems."
[66] Chisholm, "Making It Work: The Family Law Amendment (Shared Parental Responsibility) Act 2006."
[67] Alese Wooditch, "Human Trafficking Law and Social Structures," *International Journal of Offender Therapy and Comparative Criminology* 56, no. 5 (2012).
[68] Ibid.
[69] Marjory Anne Ebbeck and Carmencita H Dela Cerna, "A Study of Child Rearing Practices Amongst Selected, Sudanese Families in South Australia: Implications for Child Care Service Selection," *Early Childhood Education Journal* 34, no. 5 (2007).
[70] Noah T Mbano, *The Perceptions of African Refugee Background Students: Their Schooling in Wa and Their Adjustment to the Australian Cultural Context* (Curtin University., 2012).
[71] Khawaja and Milner, "Acculturation Stress in South Sudanese Refugees: Impact on Marital Relationships."

Thus, it is likely that South Sudanese refugees will also face settlement challenges when navigating the family law system in Australia.

Migrant and refugees living in Australia and other countries experience widespread racism, ranging from social and economic exclusion to explicit abuse.[72] Even being described as a “refugee” can have negative implications on newcomers.[73] The racism faced by former refugees is deeply embedded into the Australian political system, as evidenced when Australian Immigration Minister Kevin Andrews publicly declared that individuals from Africa and particularly Sudan were not adjusting to the Australian way of life.[74] Similar claims have been made by the Minister of Home Affairs and Border Protection, Peter Dutton, in response to alleged Sudanese gangs in Melbourne: “Victorians are scared to go out to restaurants” because of “African gang violence.” Dutton claims that Sudanese people are over-represented in crime statistics, although in reality, the crime rates have actually been decreasing.[75] Dutton also stated that “the federal government needed to weed out the people who have done the wrong thing, including deporting people who are not Australian citizens”.[76] Such experiences can lead to feelings of social exclusion. Shakespeare-Finch and Wickham stated Sudanese families in Australian faced difficulties finding work, appropriate housing, and dealing with the education system, and that these difficulties were a significant source of stress.[77] Some Sudanese people viewed these problems as arising from the discrimination by Australian government against refugees.

Former refugees from South Sudan experience may experience resettlement problems due to the lack of fit between Australian social institutions and

---

[72] Bishop, *To Be a Family: Changes Experienced within South Sudanese Families in Australia.*

[73] Colic-Peisker and Walker, "Human Capital, Acculturation and Social Identity: Bosnian Refugees in Australia."

[74] Joel Windle, "The Racialisation of African Youth in Australia," *Social identities* 14, no. 5 (2008).

[75] Mandisi Majavu, "The ‘African Gangs’ Narrative: Associating Blackness with Criminality and Other Anti-Black Racist Tropes in Australia," *African and Black Diaspora: An International Journal* 13, no. 1 (2020).

[76] Nino Bucci. (2018, January 16). Dutton, PM 'legitimising' vigilantes. The Age (Melbourne, Australia), p. 12.

[77] Shakespeare-Finch and Wickham, "Adaptation of Sudanese Refugees in an Australian Context: Investigating Helps and Hindrances."

their communities' norms and values.[78] According to the Refugee Council of Australia "one of the greatest settlement challenges amongst refugee groups was the significant impact of change in family power dynamics." Studies repeatedly revealed that family tension can arise when the breadwinner role changes after women gain employment and men as traditional breadwinners do not find work. These tensions may result in separation or divorce.[79]

Research undertaken by the Footscray Community Legal Centre concluded that, many women remain in abusive relationships simply because they believe that it is not possible to obtain a divorce. These women lack knowledge of family law and their legal rights in relationships.[80] Armstrong's research similarly found that a lack of knowledge of the law meant that women from culturally and linguistically diverse communities were often scared to divorce or separate from their husbands because they feared the husband would take their children.[81] Studies also highlighted the controversial issues that South Sudanese Australians face included many difficulties in understanding Australian Family Law as their practices of customary law are contrary in many ways. (Fadlalla, 2009a, Wooditch, 2012) [82]

A study investigating the role of institution and practice of bride wealth – a term that is also used among South Sudanese in refugees camps and here in Australia[83] – highlighted that bride wealth paid to the family of the bride reflects the conflicts between international human rights and the rights granted to women and children under customary law systems. The research further claimed that the role of women within the institution of marriage was to cement family ties through bride wealth and childbearing. It also revealed that bride wealth had been practiced by Sudanese refugees in

---

78 Elizabeth Heger Boyle and Ahmed Ali, "Culture, Structure, and the Refugee Experience in Somali Immigrant Family Transformation," *International Migration* 48, no. 1 (2010).

79 Ramón Spaaij, "Cultural Diversity in Community Sport: An Ethnographic Inquiry of Somali Australians' Experiences," *Sport Management Review* 16, no. 1 (2013).

80 Armstrong and Clearinghouse, *Enhancing Access to Family Dispute Resolution for Families from Culturally and Linguistically Diverse Backgrounds*.

81 Armstrong, "Good Practices with Culturally Diverse Families in Family Dispute Resolution."

82 Fadlalla, "Customary Laws in Southern Sudan: Customary Law of Dinka and Nuer."

83 Sarah Shteir, "The Institution & Practice of 'Bride Wealth' in Southern Sudan," *Refuge: Canada's Journal on Refugees* 26, no. 2 (2007).

refugee camps in Uganda and Kenya and Australia respectively. However, the study did not further investigate how bride wealth paid to the bride's family and close relatives influenced the nature of marriage, divorce, and the child custody outcome.

Further research investigating access to justice with South Sudanese community in Australia found that the differences between South Sudanese customary law and the Australian legal system led to misunderstandings with the law and a lack of access to services and legal injustices.[84] The study revealed that South Sudanese communities in Australia faced difficulties in understanding, following and applying Australian law in addition to their customary law. This is due to a lack of school-based education and provision of general information about Australia prior to arrival and to difficulties with the language. The study concluded that service delivery could be more effective among South Sudanese if service providers in Australia take a holistic approach to understanding the functions and the role of South Sudanese customary law in their daily dealings with clients.

Nevertheless, a study comparing South Sudanese customary law with Victorian law in Melbourne found that many South Sudanese Victorians have difficulty understanding, complying with, or adapting to specific categories of Victorian law.[85] These include laws related to the family law and family violence, regulation of road, traffic, and public transport, and consumer law. The study concluded that the problems experienced were mostly a result of a lack of understanding, a lack of respect for or willingness to comply with the law or differing social and cultural norms in the South Sudanese and Australia.

Further studies investigating the sense of disrespect brought about by blocked employment opportunities among Sudanese Australians revealed that the lack of employment opportunities was a threat to their cultural identity and traditions. This was provoked by the intervention of regulating authorities such as police in the case of domestic violence incidents and child protection services.[86] In South Sudanese customs, men are the heads of the family with a responsibility to care and discipline their wives and

[84] Milos, "South Sudanese Communities and Australian Family Law: A Clash of Systems."

[85] Springvale, "Comparative Analysis of South Sudanese Customary Law and Victorian Law."

[86] Losoncz, "Blocked Opportunity and Threatened Identity: Understanding Experiences of Disrespect in South Sudanese Australians."

children. However, in Australia, South Sudanese discipline practices such as physical discipline are not permitted by law. Those men who are involved in the physical discipline of their wives or children may be removed from their home by the relevant authorities.

All male participants of this study revealed that Australian domestic violence laws undermined the role of husbands in their community and were a threat to their own family and culture. Furthermore, all participants in the study, including young adults were genuinely concerned that too much freedom given to children and youth in their community had harmful consequences as Australian child protection laws undermined the role of parents, and made it difficult for parents and communities to care for their families.[87] The study further found that the legitimacy of Australian family laws, as they believed agencies were interfering in what is seen by the community as a family matter.

In South Sudan, parents have ultimate authority over their children. Similarly, quarrels between husband and wife are considered to be a private matter into which authorities should not intervene. One participant was quoted saying:

> the legal system here in Australia has clearly damaged our families. For instance, the law enforcement agents, they have no right to come into our families; parents have the right to bring their kids up the way they want them to. What you call domestic violence laws they cause all the divorces and are destroying our families. Our community has many divorces in here.[88]

Jensen and Westoby's study exploring restorative justice for Sudanese youth also highlights several issues for the community with navigating the legal system. They explore the restorative justice model applied to Sudanese youth in Toowoomba, focusing on "the socio-psychological and the socio-structural dimensions of protection and risk for young people from a Sudanese background."[89] The purpose of this model was to assist with the cultural transitioning and youth crime and to build capacity of the community leaders to manage criminal offences within the community.[90] The study found a number of issues specific to Sudanese youth, including

---

[87] Ibid.
[88] Ibid.
[89] Peter Westoby, "Developing a Community-Development Approach through Engaging Resettling Southern Sudanese Refugees within Australia," *Community development journal* 43, no. 4 (2008).
[90] Ibid.

inter-generational strain: young people attempting to adapt to their new culture while older people see this as a rejection of their old culture and customs. As a consequence, family and community disputes within the Sudanese community arise and the "Southern Sudanese community often feel disrespected in their conversations with youth, experience shame in the increasing level of youth criminal avidity and domestic violence and are somewhat unsure about how to respond."[91]

Furthermore, the Sudanese community often do not access counselling or mediation services when they experience legal problems, but rather try to resolve their problems "in-house" wherever possible as these services are often not culturally tailored. Jensen and Westoby believe that in order to deal with these issues and empower the Sudanese community, the community needs to be involved in the legal processes. They argue that, "both the formal judicial processes and the traditional alternative dispute resolution processes are required to serve the interests of justice and community stability within both re-settled refugee communities and the broader community." While Sudanese elders do not have the power to mediate offences, Jensen and Westoby argue that they need to reconstruct their role as community leaders and work together with authorities and their communities to develop a "restorative justice plan for cultural change and based on 'informal' restorative justice principles and practices."

In order to deal with some of the challenges facing Sudanese refugees and the law, and to foster an understanding and promote trusting relationships between the community and police, Victoria Police developed a cross-cultural training package. Consultations with the Sudanese community, community leaders and the police were held in the initial design phase of the training package to raise awareness of the issues experienced by the Sudanese community.

Furthermore, Westoby concludes that in order to engage the South Sudanese community and provide services which will be of benefit to them, one needs to "understand how refugees have experienced the loss of their social world, practitioners need to critically evaluate their own assumptions and listen carefully."[92] Further, he argues a dialogical methodology of intervention must be applied, creating a safe space for dialogue and foster understanding.

---

[91] Ibid.
[92] Ibid.

Finally, Westoby argues that there should be a journey of discovery between the community development officer and the refugee community. This approach empowers the refugee community and helps rebuild a new social world that optimises refugee recovery within a resettlement context.

4.6. Conclusion

This chapter has discussed the historical background of family law in Australia and the progressive changes and amendments which took place over the years. Despite the diversity in Australian society, family law does not in any way consider the recognition of customary law or legal pluralism. Family Dispute Resolution may be the alternative avenue to address CALD and Indigenous family law disputes. The literature, nevertheless, suggested under-representation of those groups in family dispute resolution services which may indicate that they may be using other means such as family and community to resolve family disputes including the care of children after separation.

The chapter also analysed the available literature which suggests that, there are many family law issues faced by the South Sudanese community and other similar groups in Australia. It is unlikely these problems will have any policy impact in the Australian family law system, hence, the need to undertake empirical research to understand from the South Sudanese families' perspective their experiences with those issues.

CHAPTER FIVE

FAMILY LAW PROBLEMS EXPERIENCED BY JIENG FAMILIES IN AUSTRALIA

5.1. Introduction

Chapters Three and Four suggested that South Sudanese Jieng families in Australia would face challenges regarding the resolution of family disputes related to marriage, divorce and co-parenting after separation. However, as there has been no previous research on how South Sudanese former refugees experience family law problems in Australia, the exact nature of these challenges is unclear. It is also evident that South Sudanese Jieng and other similar groups rarely access formal family law services to resolve their family disputes. Previous research, however, has also been unable to account for this, and has not explored the ways in which former refugees attempt to resolve family law problems outside the formal legal system.

This chapter presents original and significant analysis of the problems that Jieng families face with formal family dispute resolution using the themes emerging from the interviews and focus groups. As explained in the methodology chapter, participants were given pseudonyms to ensure anonymity; any interview participant name referred to here is not their real name.[1] The chapter illustrates that participants experience several problems that can be defined as family law disputes. The most common type of problem experienced were disputes over who should take care of the children after separation. The majority of participants in this study were male, and the findings highlight in particular the problems resolving family law problems from a male point of view. For many participants, the source of the dispute laid with the misuse of freedom, rights and protection of women by the courts. Participants were often involved in both the family and the criminal legal system, and their concern with regards to the use of intervention orders and police involvement in family matters resulted in a

[1] As stated in the methodology chapter, participants were given pseudonyms to ensure anonymity and any name refer to here with the interview participant is not their real name.

reluctance to use the formal legal system to resolve family problems. Instead, participants turned to family members and elders to reach a resolution. Furthermore, participants revealed that they did not trust government agencies to resolve their family matters. Most participants believed that the Department of Child Protection and domestic violence services were created to separate families and take children away to create employment for people seeking jobs in the sector.

In Australia, most couples try to resolve the living arrangements for the children without external assistance or through formal family dispute resolution services offered by Family Relationship Centres (FRCs) across Australia.[2] However, if informal methods for resolving disputes do not work, then couples will turn to the formal legal system for resolution. For most couples, this means going to Family Law Mediation and if that fails or is inappropriate, to court. In contrast, the literature indicates that families of CALD background are underrepresented within the family law sector, particularly, family dispute resolution. Instead, the majority of couples within multicultural communities would normally try to resolve issues on their own or involve religious leaders and family members.[3] The way in which Jieng couples attempt to resolve problems does not usually involve formal family law processes either.

5.2. The Involvement of Police and Use of Intervention Orders

Another part of the formal legal system is the involvement of police and the use of Intervention Orders to deal with domestic violence. Domestic violence refers to violence, abuse, and intimidation between people who are currently or have previously been in an intimate relationship. The perpetrator uses violence to control and dominate the other person. This causes fear, physical harm and/or psychological harm.[4]

Previous research indicates that cultural values and immigration status enhance the complexities normally involved in domestic violence cases and women from CALD backgrounds are generally less likely than other groups

---

[2] Parkinson and Parkinson, *Australian Family Law in Context : Commentary and Materials*.

[3] Armstrong and Clearinghouse, *Enhancing Access to Family Dispute Resolution for Families from Culturally and Linguistically Diverse Backgrounds*.

[4] Mason and Pulvirenti, "Former Refugees and Community Resilience 'Papering Over'domestic Violence."

of women to report cases of domestic violence.[5] It was also very clear from this study that members of the Jieng community are reluctant to involve the police or apply for intervention orders to tackle domestic violence.

There appeared to be several reasons for this reluctance. For female victims of domestic violence, the involvement of the police can result in their exclusion from the community. A female Interview participant, referred to here as Akon (not her real name), explains:

> *My ex-husband was controlling and violent, we were regularly fighting, and when I tell my mum what happened, she always tells me to report the issue to my in-laws. When I talk to his uncle, he would come and talk to us or come with another cousin and they would warn him not to repeat the fight, but unfortunately, he was not listening until I involved the Police, and he was arrested and charged with assaults. Now they are blaming me for the divorce. (Akon)*

The narrative from Akon revealed that families from the South Sudanese and other similar cultural backgrounds try to resolve their own problems despite domestic and family violence problems, before seeking help with law enforcement agencies. Factors which may influence this behaviour include: limited availability of and access to support services; a lack of support networks and reluctance to confide in others; isolation on the part of the victim; lack of awareness about legal rights; continued abuse from the immediate family; cultural and/or religious shame; and religious beliefs about divorce.[6] Studies with former refugees from Iraq, Sudan, Ethiopia, Bosnia, Serbia and Croatia have shown that men see government intervention intended to address family conflict as undermining their authority and family cohesiveness. Both men and women felt that women who seek help for domestic violence usually have a negative experience. Women felt that the mainstream community would not believe their claims and thus believed that they would not provide assistance.[7]

The Footscray Legal Service's Out of Africa Report also states that "clients of its African Legal Service were often reluctant to report family violence to police as they believed domestic arguments were private matters which

---

[5] Ibid.

[6] *The Multi-Cultural Family*, ed. Ann Laquer Estin (Aldershot, England: Aldershot, England : Ashgate, 2008).

[7] Mason and Pulvirenti, "Former Refugees and Community Resilience 'Papering Over'domestic Violence."

should be resolved by extended family members and community elders."[8] This concern is supported by the Australian Human Rights Commission's recent consultations with African Australian communities, which noted that women from these communities may be reluctant to report domestic violence to male police officers as it "might be culturally inappropriate for her to share that kind of information with a man."[9]

Many families are usually reluctant to engage with family law system, including using the legal system to resolve family disputes and to address domestic violence due to cultural perceptions of family pride. Family law problems are traditionally dealt with within the privacy of the family unit, and it is often considered culturally inappropriate to involve non-family members, especially state agencies; to do so can bring a sense of shame onto the family and undermine family and community cohesion. This is stated below by the one of interview participants referred to here as Deng (not his real name):

> *We have language and communication difficulties with the government agencies and other service providers. I don't think taking family issues to strangers was useful. I decided to leave my children in the care of their mother because I don't want to have trouble with police. If my wife understands the benefit of our children having their father around them, then, she will allow me to come back and live with my children again as family (Deng).*

Despite family and domestic violence concerns, Jieng families would normally try to resolve the dispute between the couple with the aim of reuniting the family using a restorative approach. If the restoration of the family unit fails, then the community does not play a role in resolving the living arrangements for the children due to its complexities and impact on both parents and the children. Participant Anyang from the focus group summed it up:

> *The issue of the Intervention Order is tearing families apart, IO does not work for us, we have social intervention order, where a person who is at wrong is warned and sanction to reframe from their wrong. This is the only effective way of keeping the level of conflict down and manageable. IO create isolation for the protected person because the community would view*

---

[8] SALLY Aplin, "Analysis of the Legal Needs of Horn of Africa People in Melbourne," (2002).

[9] Ronald Sackville, "Access to Justice: Towards an Integrated Approach" (paper presented at the Judicial Review: Selected Conference Papers: Journal of the Judicial Commission of New South Wales, The, 2011).

that person as someone who misused law and order because paper by itself cannot protect a person, but community do play a role in ensuring that someone is not left at a disadvantage situation. IO breach the role of elders to resolve the dispute in most case. (Anyang)

Anyang highlighted that the majority of Jieng families do not see family matters as legal issues and they would rather give up the contact with the children than proceeding into unknown territory. The majority of participants interviewed were concerned with the involvement of the police stressing that family matters were not supposed to be dealt with outside the family. Atem stated the following:

It is a normal process in Jieng culture, "when issues arise within the families, you usually called your relatives to intervene, but now when you have small issues nowadays things have changed, and you no longer have the privilege of having your relatives coming to resolve your problems instead women go straight to police for any small issues and do not value the traditional ways of resolving family matters. Police have become the family, relatives and elders, uncles and aunties. It is so embarrassing (Atem).

Participants in both interviews and focus groups have claimed that the role of elders (uncles and aunties) is no longer effective in Australia. For instance, at the focus group held in Melbourne, Adeng stated that:

We the elders are helpless nowadays, this generation is different to ours, and we used to listen to our elders. We now know in this country everything is about the law and our wish is to keep families together. Unfortunately, we have no power to make that happen. Our culture respect and value family unity but due to freedom and love of money, everything is falling apart (Adeng).

For some participants, the police have replaced the role of elders, and this was causing considerable tension within Jieng communities. In some instances, the police were seen as the cause of family conflict. This was explained by participant Malual during one of the focus groups:

Police are big contributors of family breakdown, family relationship in South Sudan was not a government business, it used to be family matter which was a very effective way of dealing with family matters but now police have replaced the elders, aunties and all the extended family who know in and out of issues affecting a family. If Intervention Orders and police involvement are removed, I think our families will be strong again. Care of children should be left to their families and communities to resolve it among themselves instead of the government and its agents as they do not understand the important of the family to different communities (*Malual*).

Malual has highlighted the concerns of the families regarding the changing dynamic in dispute resolution process in Australia. The role of police and domestic violence services are not appreciated within Jieng communities. The majority of participants stated clearly that the involvement of government agencies in family matters is breaking their families apart and have taken over the role of uncles, aunties and the next of kin in the dispute resolution process.

The concerns of the police's role in community affairs are so common particularly among the men, that they feel vulnerable when dealing with family issues. One party to the dispute who believed they had not been heard during the dispute resolution process would threaten the mediating team with police. This notion was repeatedly mentioned by most of the participants. There is a fear among the elders and religious leaders when trying to resolve the dispute in their customary ways, that the disagreeing party may report them to the authorities.

5.3. Barriers to accessing help government 's institutions

Research participants' negative interactions with the police were also extended to their experiences of dealing with other state agencies and institutions. These interactions, although not necessarily part of the formal legal system for resolving family law disputes, nevertheless shape the legal consciousness of the Jieng community. The majority of the focus group participants stated clearly that they did not trust government agencies with family matters. They also disclosed that they feared being reported to the Department of Child Protection and other agencies and that their children may be removed. This fear was also due to the fact that the revelation of these family secrets was seen by many as a breach of family taboos.

Most government agencies and institutions' policies and procedures are based on mainstream Western values and practice. Though there is a progressive agenda of multiculturalism in Australia, there is less progress within the legal system and, as a result, a new emerging community like the South Sudanese find it hard to navigate the legal system. During the interviews and focus groups, some of these complexities emerged. One of the interview participants, Manute (not his real name), explained the frustration he experienced when he arrived in Australia with his brother's widow whom he inherited after his brother died during the war in South

Sudan. After arrival in Australia, they had four more children who are known in the community as his late brother's children. However, they then had difficulties when applying for Family Tax Benefit through Centrelink, part of the federal Department known as Services Australia. He was assumed to be the father of the children and almost clashed with Centrelink as he was being questioned about why he continued producing children with her while simultaneously declaring that they were not partners. Manute tried to explain but felt that no-one listened; as a result, he moved out and accepted child support which put him in the position of shame before the community. Here he points out that:

> *It became difficult to continue helping my brother's family who the government assumed was my wife. They thought, I was cheating the system. I feel bad having moved out from my brother's widow to avoid persecution. If I did take her as my wife and forsake the respect for my brother and the family values, I would have been in trouble with the family and the community. It could have been difficult for me to marry my current wife. Australia is good with lots of opportunities but not for the wellbeing of our family's circumstance (Manute).*

Manute's situation is what Makec described in his book,[10] when a Jieng man dies leaving behind his widow or widows. When this occurs, his parents, or surviving close relatives meet and nominate his successor who continues to procreate with her although no marriage ceremony takes place nor is it necessary.[11] It is expected that the widow is still legally recognised as the wife of the deceased man, as the death of a man in Jieng does not bring marriage to dissolution.[12] This kind of practice is incomprehensible within Australian society and is not considered within the formal family law system. Some South Sudanese Jieng families moved to Australia with "Ting-jok" (ghost wife) or inherited widows of a brother or uncle. In the community, it is known that such relationships are not official marriages but are only for procreating with Ting-jok or the inherited widow. The children from that relationship are the biological children of the successor but socially they are not his children. The children are not allowed to refer to him as father; they can only refer to him as an uncle. According to Centrelink, the interviewed participant Manute was the father therefore, when he works, the brother's widow payments were affected. In addition,

---

[10] Makec, *The Customary Law of the Dinka People of Sudan: In Comparison with Aspects of Western and Islamic Laws*.

[11] Ibid.

[12] Kok, "The Customary Law of the Dinka People of Sudan: In Comparison with Aspects of Western and Islamic Laws."

when they have children, he is required to sign the birth certificate as the father and there is no room for his deceased brother or uncle's name to appear on the form. Another challenge is that children may be confused with their identity when talking to peers at schools or at social events. Manute further stated:

> *One of the children privately asked me, why do we keep calling you uncle and I heard that the person being refer to as our father died many years ago in South Sudan but four of us were born here in Australia, how did this happen. I told him that it is true the person known as your father died many years ago. I said, biologically I am your father, but our culture only recognised him as the father because he was the one who married your mother, then he replied should we be calling you dad instead! I replied no; it is culturally inappropriate (Manute).*

Some children may experience difficulties explaining themselves to their peers as their peers may lack a cultural context to understand the circumstance facing Jieng children.

Secondly, when the same man wants to marry his own wife, he is faced with legal question of whether he should divorce his brother's widow or Ting-jok, as it is illegal to have more than one wife in Australia. When Manute came to Australia with his brother's widow, he assumed the role of the husband. As there was no option for any other type of relationship that better described his circumstance, Manute ticked yes to husband on the Centrelink form.

5.4. Family Dispute Resolution

As previously discussed in chapter four of this book, Family dispute resolution (FDR) is a form of family mediation that aims to help separated parents manage and resolve disagreements about their children's care.[13] Since the introduction of mandatory pre-filing family dispute resolution in 2006,[14] people are not able to file a court application to resolve a parenting dispute regarding their children unless they have first made a genuine effort at FDR, with some exceptions.[15] FDR practitioners are required to advise disputing parents that any agreement they reach should be in their children's

---

[13] Fisher, *Mediating with Families.*

[14] Armstrong, "Good Practices with Culturally Diverse Families in Family Dispute Resolution."

[15] Monahan, *Family Law in Australia.*

best interests and to encourage them to consider a range of shared parenting options.

Jieng family's customs expect that a woman is married to the man's family and if that marriage is ended, any children from the relationship will remain with the paternal family provided all the bride wealth was correctly paid. The research highlighted two very different sets of views of the use of Family Dispute Resolution depending on the participants' gender. The majority of males interviewed were dissatisfied with the family law system and normally blame the system for maximising disputes with their wives. In contrast, most women interviewed were thankful to the family law system for protecting their rights and their children. Atem further said:

> *Yeah I have tried in the past to seek help with Family Relationship Centre (FRC) but my wife did not respond and I was later told that they respect her right and they can only issue me a certificate to go to court. I have also tried with the family to try to resolve the matter within the family, we were brought together in a lengthy discussion but unfortunately it was unsuccessful because my wife was not willing to come to compromise. It always depends on individuals' understanding of the local culture, my wife took advantage of law and gave up the culture. I decided not to go to court and left my children with her, she is now isolated and not many people in the community like what she did to me including her family (Atem).*

This view is shared by many men in the Jieng community who have encountered separation and disputes over the care of children. The Jieng community expects that couples will have some problems in their relationship, but it is expected that they should resolve them, continue to live together for the sake of their children, and maintain the good name of their two families. Failure to adhere to these views normally leads to blame and eventually isolation of the party who chose to ignore the community expectations. According to Deng, the values of continued identity and influence through the lineage are both individual and communal; that is, they are equally competitive and cooperative.[16] This, in turn, dictates an emphasis on group solidarity and the resolution of conflicts through mediation and consensus building. As a result, the vast majority are generally reluctant to take issues relating to children to Family Dispute Resolution, as this process is seen to result in retributive outcomes which

[16] Deng, "The Cow and the Thing Called" What": Dinka Cultural Perspectives on Wealth and Poverty."

could harm or destroy social relations.[17] According to the survey conducted on Traditional Authority (TA) in South Sudan by the United Nations agency, it was revealed that the informants strongly emphasize "the need for dispute resolution with relatives and elders and that only when the process fails do they believe that the matter should be passed on to the headmen, sub-chiefs and chiefs."[18] The study found the dispute settlement procedure to be informal with local justice operating under a tree and substantial discussion amongst members and the public.[19] The study concluded that many people go to witness the hearing to judge whether it is fair and local people prefer to use local justice which tends to favour community interests over the rights of individuals.

In addition, there are issues that arise during separation and divorce of Jieng couples that cannot be addressed within the Family Dispute Resolution process. This is most clearly evident in relation to the issue of bride wealth. Bride wealth normally seals the marriage after a man and his family negotiate and pay a bride wealth to the woman's family in the form of cattle. It is considered a gift paid by the groom to the family of the bride,[20] and is usually done before the couple come together as husband and wife. In the event of a divorce, unless the marriage has resulted in having enough children (in which divorce may be more unlikely), bride wealth (cattle) and their offspring must be returned. Consequently, some of the cattle would have been passed on as the bride wealth of the other relatives, which means one divorce could threaten other marriages. Bride wealth is not illegal in Australia, but it is not practiced by mainstream communities; hence, there is no jurisdiction or ability to reclaim it in the event of divorce. Literature suggests that Jieng families in Australia practice bride wealth largely among themselves even with the other cross-marriages.[21] According to Jieng customary law, bride wealth is mainly paid with cattle but due to resettlement in the Western countries like Australia and the USA, there are now two options of payments. The girl's family can choose between the cattle and money. Most bride wealth is currently being paid by money in Australia. The majority of participants in the two focus groups in Adelaide and Melbourne clearly stated that the practice of bride wealth is currently

---

[17] Jok, Leitch, and Vandewint, "A Study of Customary Law in Contemporary Southern Sudan."

[18] Leonardi et al., *Local Justice in Southern Sudan.*

[19] Ibid.

[20] Deng, *The Dinka of the Sudan.*

[21] Springvale, "Comparative Analysis of South Sudanese Customary Law and Victorian Law."

working well but the difficulty comes when a marriage results in divorce. In most cases, the bride wealth is unlikely to be returned to the man's family due to the fear of the authority and the consequences that may ensue. During the interview, male participant Ajang stated the following:

> *I attempted mediation, but my ex-wife refused to attend, I was issued a certificate, but I don't believe a court will resolve my disputes as they will not be able to address my grievances. I married this woman and paid over 100 head of cattle to her family and this new man living with her did nothing to deserve staying with my wife and the children. I better leave this to God and maybe if he decided to go back to South Sudan, maybe I can talk to my family to get him arrested and pay my wealth back. My family and I worked hard to afford 100 head of cattle to marry her (Ajang).*

As stated by Ajang, the majority of men and their families work hard for many years to save resources for their son's marriages. It is expected that the woman getting married into a particular family will produce children which will carry forward the lineage of this particular individual. However, if such a marriage did not fulfil its obligations, it would be common to return the bride wealth to the man in question for him to remarry but in Australia, the expectations at FDR are for both parents to put the best interests of their children first.

In the context of family dispute resolution, acknowledgement of the parties' cultural and faith contexts may assume even more importance. Separation and divorce are always traumatic life events, but for parties from minority cultural and faith contexts, and especially for some women, there may be a great deal more at stake including social, spiritual and community consequences. Family dispute resolution processes may not be culturally appropriate for minority parents as stated below by Marial (not his real name) from the Adelaide focus group:

> *Family matters are not regulated by the government in our country and that is why it is surprise to many of us when you have a misunderstanding with your wife or husband which is obviously normal but those small argument would result in the attention of police. This is very shocking to me and I do not know if the mainstream society does experience those challenges too (Marial).*

As alluded to above by Marial, these parents may require assistance to access and understand FDR so that their participation is optimised, notwithstanding the limitations to the consensual FDR in court. Milos in her research argues that the resolution of disputes within the South Sudanese families follows the expectations of traditional gender roles, with men being the patriarchal head of the family.[22] However, the move to Australia often changes these traditional gender roles, as the roles of men and women or husbands and wives are quite different in the South Sudan and Australian cultures. South Sudanese women are expected to stay at home, have children, and take care of both, while men work and provide for the family.[23]

Family law disputing populations are already vulnerable in many ways, with higher levels of violence, substance abuse, mental health problems, and educational deficits; this implies limitations on capacity and suggesting power differentials between the parties. In addition, where parties are from minority cultural or faith backgrounds, there may be heightened party vulnerability, not only because of religious and community implications associated with separation, but also because of other needs including lack of English language proficiency, socio-economic disadvantage, and social exclusion.

According to Access to Justice Taskforce's Report, most people from CALD backgrounds will turn first to family and friends and non-legal professionals to resolve problems.[24] This trend may be particularly pronounced among people whose cultural norms are collectivistic. Collectivist cultural norms value family obligations over individual autonomy and are characterised by hierarchies based on age and gender and emphasise the role of the family and community in providing support. This may discourage approaching outsiders for assistance.[25] These norms will also influence help-seeking for legal problems. According to Armstrong, people who speak a language other than English at home are less likely to know about mainstream family mediation services as some believed mediation encouraged separation and family division.[26]

There is always a choice to make between one's own culture and the culture of wider community. Here is how a female participant Ayen (not her real name) put it:

> *I was caught between the two cultures, my parents want me to follow Jieng process, and on the other hand, my son's father only want the child and not*

---

[22] Milos, "South Sudanese Communities and Australian Family Law: A Clash of Systems."
[23] Ibid.
[24] Sackville, "Access to Justice: Towards an Integrated Approach."
[25] Ibid.
[26] Armstrong and Clearinghouse, *Enhancing Access to Family Dispute Resolution for Families from Culturally and Linguistically Diverse Backgrounds.*

> *me. My culture doesn't allow a woman to produce children without an official marriage or agreements from the two families, I have been trying to do the right thing by respecting my culture and the same time to ensure my ex-partner understand the cultural requirement, but he was not committed and opted to use the law into his advantage, now I lost my son into his full care. It is very sad (Ayen).*

It can be argued that not everyone from CALD communities would adhere to their culture. Some individuals would see cultural process as a barrier to their success and sometime would opt for mainstream ways to achieve what they want. The example above from Ayen demonstrated that, this father, would have not even seen his child if he listened to his family. According to Jieng customary law, if a man impregnated a girl and he did not want her as a wife, then the man and his family will pay a fine known in Jieng as "Aruok" to the girl's family. The aruok is normally six heads of cattle or the equivalent. The family will officially recognise the man as the father of the child and his right to have access and contact with the child. Whenever it is convenient for him, it will be granted. The father has the right to take the child into his care after the child turns seven years old or leave the child in the mother's care if he is happy with it.

Family law problems in the formal Australian legal system are decided on the principle of the best interests of the children. For the research participants, this principle was often misunderstood and did not necessarily sit well with Jieng values. As previously discussed in Chapter Three, in the Jieng normative approach, the two families and their extended families have a stake in the marriage and will bring pressure to bear on the couple to find a way to resolve their differences. The Jieng use the philosophy of "*cieng*" (which literally mean live together) that empathises unity and harmony which are experienced when a sense of balance and order is present and are highly valued. These concepts are expressed by the Jieng with the verb, which literally means "to live together" and "to look after." There is a caring element implied in cieng, which Deng describes in his book as a concept of ideal human relationships.[27] Cieng is nurtured or learned at home among family, yet it is idealised in the much broader sense of people living together in the village, community, or country. Cieng has the status of a moral code inherited from the ancestors.

Deng explains that "the social background of a man," his "physical appearance," "the way he walks, talks, eats, or dresses," and "the way he

[27] Deng, "The Cow and the Thing Called" What": Dinka Cultural Perspectives on Wealth and Poverty."

behaves towards his fellow men" are all factors in determining his considerations.[28] Cieng and dheeng (dheeng mean nobility) are closely related; a person would not be capable of acquiring the virtue of dheeng, if cieng did not define the moral standards required to achieve it.[29]

It is experienced as a state of dynamic equilibrium. The importance of this value to the Jieng is reflected in a common greeting within families.[30] Continuity of the lineage through procreation is of vital importance to the Jieng and is the most important function of marriage. Unity and harmony, which are experienced when a sense of balance and order is present, are highly valued in the Jieng cultures. On the other hand, dheeng also determines how one approaches social issues and his or her relationship with relatives and the community. It is dheeng and cieng that determine the outcome of the disputes between the couple, which means dheeng and cieng are maintained when the majority in the dispute resolution process decided on the outcome of the dispute, the Jieng man or woman will accept the outcome either against or in their favour for the respect of majority decision based on cieng and dheeng. The quote below, from one of the participants in the focus group in Melbourne referred to here as Garang (not his real name), explained the frustration from the families on how decisions regarding the care of the children are made.

> *Separation used to be difficult in South Sudan due to the nature of the care of the children which was dealt with through the customary law. Custody of the children was usually awarded to the man if the bride wealth was paid. But here in Australia, children normally are given to the woman as a primary carer and that made it easy for women to get out of marriage easily (Garang).*

The misfit between Jieng normative values and the principle of the best interests of the child is most clearly seen in the issue of co-parenting. Co-parenting is not commonly used among the Jieng as it does not apply after divorce. As previous discussed in Chapter Three, Jieng customary law takes a patriarchal approach when it comes to co-parenting or child custody in Jieng perspective. According to Jieng family customary law, it is the right of the husband to take full custody of the children if Aruok has not yet been

---

[28] Ibid.

[29] Deng, "Customary Law in the Cross-Fire of Sudan's War of Identities."

[30] Twining, "Human Rights: Southern Voices Francis Deng, Abdullahi an-Na'im, Yash Ghai and Upendra Baxi."

paid. If not, this requiring the maternal family to live with child/ren until all dues are paid.[31]

Furthermore, the man has the right to recover some of his bride wealth or property depending on the number of children from the marriage. Similarly, he is allowed to take full custody of the children after all the settlement is made, while in Australia the focus of most family dispute resolution is to help parents make decisions about their children's post separation care arrangements that will assist children to flourish. Children will rarely have any direct involvement in FDR, so mediators must frequently advocate for the child, and encourage parents to make decisions in their children's best interests. This includes the child's right to enjoy their culture, and thus to facilitate the child's capacity to shape their own cultural identity.

The majority of participants in both focus groups held in Adelaide and Melbourne expressed disappointment with the current number of separations and the fact that they have been helpless in trying to resolve those matters. During the interview, the female participant Abuk (not her real name) explains:

> *I am a widow and I had children with my late husband, though I am still young, I was not allowed to have sexual relationship with another man outside the family and when I did it few years ago, I was expected to keep the child as a child of my late husband but the biological father of this child took me to court and was ordered by family court to spend time with the child who the community sees socially as not his (Abuk).*

This example implied that there are different set of rights. There are legal rights that allow the biological father to spend time with the child regardless of the community views. On the other hand, there are social rights which according to Jieng customary law state that the widow is still bound by marriage after her husband's death and is not allowed to have children outside the deceased man's family. According to Jieng customary law, Abuk has committed adultery and the man who procreates with her should have been punished by paying six head of cattle or doing prison time if he was in South Sudan. In addition, he would not have the rights to the child.[32] Jieng customary law considered the father as "Thon Gauic" (out of wedlock) who would be seriously warned not to repeat the same mistake or

---

[31] Jok, Leitch, and Vandewint, "A Study of Customary Law in Contemporary Southern Sudan."

[32] Makec, *The Customary Law of the Dinka People of Sudan: In Comparison with Aspects of Western and Islamic Laws.*

else he may get hurt if he was found to continue having a relationship with the mother of the child. Nevertheless, since this case happened in Australia, the biological father of the child insisted and followed the legal process to have access to his child regardless of the series of warnings from both families of the widow and the in-laws. He initially went through mediation and when the mother refused to attend dispute resolution, the father was issued a S60I certificate which he lodged through the court. The father was ordered to spend time with his child. Abuk further stated that:

> *I was shocked when the judge ordered that he could spend time with my son, I screamed in the court and was carried away from the court room by the security guards. I could not imagine; it was going to be that way; I regret my decision. I thought the court will understand my cultural context. That decision made me insecure within my married family and the community at large. It is a taboo and serious matter for a man who is considered to have committed adultery to have access to a child (Abuk).*

Within the Australian legal context, Abuk is a widow who has a choice and legal rights to enter into a new relationship without seeking anyone's permission. However, because of cultural norms, her deceased husband's family gives her the choice to be inherited by the next of kin and if she refuses, she must look after the existing children and is not supposed to have any relationship outside the family. These notions are based on the lack of understanding of the system and the fact that the system here in Australia does not restrict anyone from leaving or entering a new relationship. The system here in Australia gives the biological parents equal responsibilities for the upbringing of the child. The parental responsibilities are based on the best interests of the child or the children, putting the needs of the children first. However, the Jieng families have different expectations which are contrary to what they think the best interests of the child mean to them.

The majority of participants would normally wish family disputes to be resolved within the family and, if necessary, by the community but not through the family court system or law enforcement agencies unless there is a genuine safety concern from one party. During the interview, Madut (not his real name) stated the following:

> *Though my wife left me, I am happy and thanks her for not taking my children with her. In Australia, I have no rights, the court would have given her the children, I have no problem with her now and if she wants to return any time, she is welcome, she is still my wife, and we have not yet divorced (Madut).*

Madut expressed his happiness toward his ex-wife for not taking the children with her. The notion of children is a major issue to Jieng families. The majority of men prefer family disputes to be resolved by relatives and that hope is fading due to a new environment and legal system. Here is a quote from Wal (not his real name), one of focus group participants from Melbourne:

> *Separation used to be difficult in South Sudan due to the nature of the care of the children which was dealt with according to customary law. Custody of the children was usually awarded to the men if the bride wealth was paid, but here in Australia, children are given to woman and that made it easy for women to get out of marriage easily (Wal).*

For many of the participants, especially males, the concept of rights did not fit well with their cultural understandings. For many of the male participants, the way in which women are able to exert rights within Australia is one of the major sources of family law disputes. The more independent the wife becomes, the more the structure of the family changes and weakens, as the traditional role of the wife and family is being undermined. In this way, access to education, employment, and even social security payments in the woman's name can all contribute to the breakdown of the traditional South Sudanese family in Australia. Men can feel that their role as the family provider and breadwinner is undermined, putting a strain on the marriage and family.[33]

In Australia, men and women of legal age have the right to marry, regardless of race, nationality, and religion.[34] They are entitled to equal rights both during the marriage and upon its dissolution. The Commonwealth has powers to legislate marriage, divorce, matrimonial causes, parental rights, the custody, and guardianship of infants.[35] Family law deals with divorce and the disputes over the care of children differently. It dissolves the bonds

[33] Milos, "South Sudanese Communities and Australian Family Law: A Clash of Systems."

[34] Parkinson and Parkinson, *Australian Family Law in Context : Commentary and Materials*.

[35] Patrick Parkinson, *Australian Family Law in Context : Commentary and Materials* (Pyrmont, N.S.W.: Pyrmont, N.S.W. : Thomson Reuters Professional Australia, 2012).

of marriage, but it does not deal with where children live, who supports them, or the division of the property.[36]

It is a legal requirement within Australian law that a couple must be separated for twelve months with no possibilities of a future reconciliation before they can apply to the court for divorce.[37] Within the Jieng communities in Australia, the decision to divorce is very difficult, due to the fact that it is collectively made by the couple and their two extended families. If one of the couples, either a man or a woman declares that they want to divorce, it is likely to meet a great deal of resistance within their family. For instance, the female participant Akon recounted that she was married here in Australia and had two children. Her ex-husband paid bride wealth to her family. The ex-husband was abusive and physically violent to her. Akon spoke with her mother who told her that every marriage has its own problems and that her husband's behaviour should be taken lightly. Her mother suggested that if the behaviour continued, that she talks to her in-laws to intervene. Akon claims that one time they had a small argument, and the ex-husband became aggressive and beat her up. She rang the police and when they arrived, she was bleeding. Police called an ambulance for her and she was rushed to hospital. She had a miscarriage but told the police that she fell in the bathroom. Despite her safety concerns, both families agreed to resolve the problem within the two families and initiate the reconciliation process and here she said:

> *I told my family that, I will not reunite with this man again if even it means you are going to disown me, so be it. When I refused the family reconciliation, he took me to court, and he lost the case due to evidence of violence and the safety of the children. He was only ordered to spend time with the children under supervision. I thank the court for teaching him a lesson (Akon).*

For instance, interview participant Atem described coming to Australia in the early 2000s as a single young man. He returned to South Sudan some years later to get married. He left his wife in Africa for five years and would visit each year. Atem and wife had three children before she came to Australia on a partner visa. Atem said his wife stayed only for three months when she started causing problems in the relationship by claiming that he was trying to kill her. She rang the police on him and when they arrived, she was bleeding from self-inflicted wounds. Atem explains that he was

---

[36] Eekelaar, "The Interests of the Child and the Child's Wishes: The Role of Dynamic Self-Determinism."

[37] Parkinson, *Australian Family Law in Context : Commentary and Materials*.

immediately arrested and later charged. Three months later, those charges were dropped as there was not enough evidence to pursue them.

Atem also explains how family disputes are usually resolved within Jieng communities contrary to his experiences with his wife:

> *Minor problems are normally resolved by the man's family starting with parents or older brother or uncles. You normally tell (call or tell) your mother or father or your uncle and let them know that there is misunderstanding between you and your wife, especially for the man you normally talk to your father and he will call two of you to discuss and resolve the matter. This is how Jieng people resolved family dispute (Atem).*

5.4.1. Lack of Resolution

All those complexities raise the question of whether Jieng normative expectations still apply here in Australia. With the older generation, there are still several obstacles with marriage, divorce and care arrangement for children after separation. During the interview, one of the female participants referred to here as Akuch stated that she arrived in Australia with her three children in the 2000s after spending many years in a refugee camp in Kenya. She said her husband was a soldier in South Sudan and due to his status as a high-ranking military man, he married three other wives. Consequently, their relationship was failing and she decided to apply for resettlement in Australia. She was fortunately granted a visa to come to Australia. She was still married because of the children and she did not wish to divorce as it could degrade her status and her family would be disappointed. As a result, she decided to raise her children alone but abstained herself from having another relationship. Below is the direct quote from her:

> *I got married back in South Sudan since 1980s. It was an arranged marriage as our parents were friends. Though my husband was twenty years older than me, our marriage was initially so great. Due to civil war in South Sudan, we lived away from our parents for many years and our parents were still in contact with us but my relationship with my husband was not very smooth after we had children. But because of my children, it was difficult to divorce him because my children would have been taken away and I would have been left empty handed to start a new difficult life in which I would have no respect. I can also lose my status within the family and the community at large. My husband has paid bride wealth and for that matter he has every right to take his children in accordance to Jieng customary law (Akuch).*

Akuch decided to remain a married woman for the sake of her children as she is no longer in an intimate relationship with her husband. Many women in her position do travel to South Sudan to spend a few months with their husbands and come back to Australia to look after the children, but for her, it is no longer relevant though she is not willing to divorce him. On the other hand, divorce according to Jieng customary law is the dissolution or ending of marriage,[38] which states that marriage should be legally ended or granted by the customary law court with the consent of all parties attached to the marriage agreements. The court process and divorce are made more difficult rather than easier as a means of retaining the families' ties.[39] When the South Sudanese arrived over two decades ago, particularly the Jieng speaking communities in Australia, they encountered enormous challenges in trying to integrate into a new culture which was significantly different to their own. Consequently, since Akuch marriage was arranged and would have been difficult for her to get the divorce granted from both families then, she decided to remain married for her children's sake.

During the focus groups' session in Adelaide, one of the participants refer to here as Wal reported:

> *Divorce was rarely an issue within the Jieng society in South Sudan and during those days in refugee camps but here in Australia, it happened every day to our families and when we the elders want to intervene, then the one in defensive position would threaten us to call the police on us. When the matter is left to them and the police to deal with it, apparently, they go nowhere and when they are faced with severe challenges, they come back again seeking help from the elders or the families but sometimes it would be too late to repair the damage. In most cases, there are successful stories where young families would testify that, they were misled by friends or service providers (Wal).*

Wal is concerned about the rate of divorce within the South Sudanese community and, particularly, the Jieng families. According to Wal, marriage to some extent is no longer an issue between the two families and their son and daughter. At the time of dispute, some individual couples may have had access to services where they could be given appropriate advice regarding their rights including their right to stand up for themselves and challenge the abusive behaviour from the partner. Consequently, such

---

[38] Fadlalla, Mohamed, 'Customary Laws in Southern Sudan: Customary Law of Jieng and Nuer' (2009) New York: iUniverse

[39] Fadlalla, "Customary Laws in Southern Sudan: Customary Law of Dinka and Nuer."

individuals can challenge the issue of collective responsibility of the marriage and may end it without the involvement of the two families. Second, the notion of bride wealth is not a great issue as no one is eventually obligated to pay back the bride wealth. It is no longer an issue for the women to stay in abusive relationship due to the constraints of bride wealth repayments. Third, the issue of co-parenting is no longer a win for the man and is handled differently in Australia.[40] It is expected that parents are in better position to make decisions about the care of their children, however, if they are not able to reach private arrangement, then they are required to seek mediation through family relationship centre in their respective state or territory before they go to court.[41]

As clearly stated by female participant Adeng from the focus group in Melbourne:

> *Jieng take into the account family status when getting married or taking leadership in the community and in most cases those values double the commitment to remain in a married relationship.*

As discussed in Chapter Three, the requirement to repay bride wealth always creates tensions. The re-collection of the bride wealth from the extended family comes with challenges and resentment as it is often shared amongst the woman's extended family and might have been redistributed to settle further marriages.[42] Consequently, families do have an incentive to ensure that marriages remain intact even if the woman is facing abuse and violence in her marriages, still she may be pressured by her family to reconcile with the husband despite the risks to her safety and wellbeing.[43]

As discussed in Chapter Three, despite the principles of cieng and dheeng, divorce still exists in Jieng customary law and it is only ended through the customary court to ensure that it is known to everyone that these families have ended their relationship, especially when adultery is involved.[44] In addition, the party to blame is publicised, making it difficult for him or her to remarry. It is particularly tougher for a woman to remarry than the man

---

[40] Milos, "South Sudanese Communities and Australian Family Law: A Clash of Systems."

[41] Fisher, *Mediating with Families.*

[42] Fadlalla, "Customary Laws in Southern Sudan: Customary Law of Dinka and Nuer."

[43] Twining, "Human Rights: Southern Voices Francis Deng, Abdullahi an-Na'im, Yash Ghai and Upendra Baxi."

[44] Deng, "Customary Law in the Cross-Fire of Sudan's War of Identities."

especially when misbehaviour or adultery was the cause of divorce. Jieng Customary law describes the legal effects of releasing the spouse of the obligation to continue their marital relationship, giving the woman the freedom to remarry again and vice versa.[45]

Regardless of divorce status, a man can easily remarry whether in a relationship or not, however, it is much difficult for a woman to remarry after separation. Very few women successfully remarry after divorce and the majority remain without a permanent husband or are married as a co-wife as it is cheaper to marry "aberdhec" (literally mean re-emerge). The majority of men are reluctant to marry aberdhec because a good family is valued by the nature and the circumstance of marriage. A woman who was previously married or had a sexual relationship with another man has low social status and those who married them as their first wife are not well regarded in Jieng society.

At the nullification of marriage, the man has the right to recover some of his bride wealth or property and at the same time, he can take full custody of the children after all the settlement is made. Consequently, if he did not pay all the cows required according to the number of children, then custody of children can be delayed until all payment of cattle is made. This is normally five head of cattle during the court decision or ten head of cattle (Aruok) per child, if the child is left to stay with the mother and her family for more than five years.[46] Kuol, one of the participants from focus group in Melbourne states:

> *Divorce exists in Jieng culture though it is very rare, Jieng do not have any word for practice of separation. We also do not have what is so called Intervention Orders because there is no person who can be dangerous to their own family, but we cannot deny the existing of conflict and misunderstanding in all the communities but with us the Jieng community, close relatives can provide sanction to the violent party especially is sometime a man. We used to have not much violence and rarely, there was no killing or harming (Kuol).*

---

[45] Fadlalla, *Customary Laws in Southern Sudan: Customary Laws of Dinka and Nuer*.

[46] Fadlalla, "Customary Laws in Southern Sudan: Customary Law of Dinka and Nuer."

Despite the existing structures of divorce court process, conflict usually arises in many cases during the recovery of the bride's price or property.[47] This is because the returned cattle usually include the offspring, or any cattle sold or diseased as a result of negligence or where death of cattle could not be proven. However, the proof of dead cattle includes the skin, or witnesses during the death, as a result, maintenance takes effect immediately after divorce.[48] On the other hand, many families and Jieng in particular have their own ways of handling domestic and family violence. Instead, they will always try to resolve the matter within the family or community and keep it from escalating. Danne claims the:

> South Sudanese dispute resolution has been described as placing a premium on improving the relations on the basis of equality, good conscience and fair play, rather than the strict legality associated with western statutory law.[49]

On the other hand, there are other issues where a cultural approach may not be considered such as in family and domestic violence and this is discussed in detail below:

> Under Jieng customary law, divorce is not widely accepted and only possible under extreme situations and only when the woman's family are willing to repay some portion of bride wealth to man's family. However, when the couple in question have children together, the repaying of bride wealth may be unlikely, but more emphasis is put on the future status of the children. In the Jieng perception, the children of divorce parents suffer discrimination and lack of respect from their peers and the wider community.[50]

Adeng, a female participant from Melbourne's focus group informed:

> *Divorce was difficult in South Sudan, because women do not want to leave their children behind and in addition, stepchildren do live a difficult life because Jieng measured the best family on the wealth, health, and characters of the parents toward each other and the public (Adeng).*

---

47 Ahmed El Mahd, "Some General Principles of Acquisition of Ownership of and Rights over Land by Customary Prescription in the Sudan."
48 Jok, Leitch, and Vandewint, "A Study of Customary Law in Contemporary Southern Sudan."
49 Danne, "Customary and Indigenous Law in Transitional Post-Conflict States: A South Sudanese Case Study."
50 Deng, *The Dinka of the Sudan.*

5.5. Conclusion

This chapter analysed why Jieng families do not use formal family dispute resolution and other services within the family law sector. It discussed how resolution processes were useful or not useful to the families using the emerging themes from the interviews and focus group. The chapter concluded that Jieng families were not utilising the current dispute resolution mechanism as many concluded they were not willing to take their family matters to the government agencies since they would not get the outcome that suited their family situations. The findings indicated that Jieng families faced several challenges in seeking help with family dispute issues, as they do not believe family conflict should be a legal matter but should be family business. It was concluded that families usually tried to resolve disputes within the family and community as the majority did not trust service providers and would rather give up access to children than going for unknown.

CHAPTER SIX

TRADITIONAL DISPUTE RESOLUTION MODEL

6.1 Introduction

This chapter presents further findings from the interviews and focus groups. Chapter Six examined the nature of family law problems experienced by participants and explored why formal resolution rarely works for Jieng communities. Chapter Seven presents participants' efforts to reach a resolution using traditional dispute resolution processes through families and communities. Efforts at resolution are largely contrary to the methods of resolution expected within the formal Australian legal system. In order to examine how Jieng communities resolve disputes outside the formal legal system, this chapter scrutinises each type of family dispute that arose from the interviews such as issues relating to bride wealth and co-parenting. Finally, this chapter critically assesses the use of traditional methods of resolution, highlighting problems with the use of these methods. Participants were asked what their family and marriage life were like before they came to Australia and what they think had changed since arrival. During the interviews and the focus groups, participants discussed specific issues relating to separation, divorce, and disputes over the care of children. Participants were asked additional questions in relation to the actions they took to resolve those problems, and their satisfaction with the outcome. These issues were then discussed in-depth, exploring the reasons behind the actions taken and any services that were helpful or unhelpful throughout the process.

The chapter raised the question of whether legal pluralism or restorative (community-based) dispute resolution normally led by elders may be an appropriate solution in resolving family disputes among South Sudanese families and other non-European groups particularly the Indigenous Australians.

6.2. Jieng Normative Approaches and their Pitfalls

When disputes arise between two individuals or a couple who are unable to resolve the dispute themselves, it takes a third neutral party or parties to facilitate its resolution. Every society or cultural group has its own ways of approaching dispute resolution. In traditional families like the Jieng, it is the responsibility of the nuclear or extended family (both paternal and maternal) and, to some extent, the community to step in and facilitate the resolution of the dispute if necessary. Among the Jieng of traditional South Sudan families, the resolution of disputes between the couples remains entirely the responsibility of the relatives, elders, and leaders.

Jieng communities of South Sudan address disputes of marriage, divorce, and matters regarding the care of children in accordance with their family traditions and customary law.[1] This tradition is based on customary oral laws passed down from one generation to another, implemented by the local chiefs and elders in a public, informal setting. Generally, disputes are not considered legal but rather familial and communal. Resolutions are not decided according to written legislation by judges, but according to the wellbeing of the individuals and of the community by its well-regarded chiefs and elders. As discussed in Chapter Three, the Jieng define marriage as a union between one man or his successor and one or more women for the purpose of sexual cohabitation.[2] It is further elaborated that marriage is a means of procreation and maintenance of the homestead. This is under the provision that such a union may take place between one barren or childless woman and another woman for whom male consorts are provided; it can also be described as a union between a deceased male person and one or more women through his successor.[3] Therefore, marriage in Jieng customary law is not only between a man and a woman or women, but it can be between a barren woman and another woman or women for the purpose of continuing family lineage. The definition also uses the term between a man and a woman or women implying a polygamous marriage which is allowed according to Jieng customary law.[4] There are no limits to

---

[1] Lola Akin Ojelabi et al., "A Cultural Assessment of Family Dispute Resolution: Findings About Access, Retention and Outcomes from the Evaluation of a Family Relationship Centre," *Journal of Family Studies* 17, no. 3 (2011).

[2] Fadlalla, "Customary Laws in Southern Sudan: Customary Law of Dinka and Nuer."

[3] Abu Rannat, "The Relationship between Islamic and Customary Law in the Sudan 1."

[4] Ibid.

the number of women a man can marry. In addition, the definition also uses the term "succession", which means one could enter marriage through "succession" in the event of death or infertility of the husband. Thus, this adds more complexity when trying to resolve any dispute regarding those kinds of marriages while in Australia where family law is formalised. These efforts at resolution sometime fall short of reaching an agreement due to several underlining issues. Resolution efforts initially start with restorative practices where relatives and elders try to reconcile the couple to forgive each other and move forward for the sake of the children and the two families.

This raises the question: what does this mean to families under those circumstances while in Australia? The following section discusses the conceptualisation of marriage and the connection with bride wealth among South Sudanese Jieng families:

6.2.1. Bride Wealth Resolutions

In the event of a divorce, unless the marriage has resulted in having enough children (in which divorce may be more unlikely), bride wealth (cattle) and the cattle's offspring must be returned. Consequently, some of these assets may have been passed on for the bride wealth of the other relatives, which means one divorce could threaten other marriages. Hence, divorce is viewed as a tragedy to be avoided except in the most compelling circumstances of extreme incompatibility. As stated in Chapters Five and Six, participants were given pseudonyms to ensure anonymity and any name referred to here with is not the interview participant's real name. Interviewee Ajang reported his disappointment that he paid over one hundred head of cattle to get married and moved to Australia in early 2000s with one child. While in Australia, they had another child. A few years later, his ex-wife left him for another man and took the two children. He tried to resolve this with his family and his ex-wife family but was unsuccessful. He stated he did not want to go to court because he believed the court would not resolve the matter as he knew the court would not give him the children and his bride wealth back. He stated the following:

> *My wife and children are with this man here in Australia and no one cares, I wish we were in South Sudan, this man would have not seen the Sun again in his whole life. I think he will never step foot in South Sudan otherwise, he will end up in jail (Ajang).*

The quote from Ajang illustrates how dispute resolution is complex with Jieng families. Formal family law in Australia is premised on the best interests of the children, and the issue of bride wealth will not be resolved here, as the cattle was paid to the woman's family in South Sudan. Consequently, there is no way the Australian courts can consider the hundred head of cattle as part of property settlement as the nature of these payments has no jurisdiction within the *Family Law Act 1975,* and it was paid to the woman's family outside Australia. Secondly, the parents of both Ajang and his ex-wife are not here in Australia. Ajang and his ex-wife only have their extended families and the issue of resolving bride wealth disputes can be discussed starting with their immediate families.

On the other hand, bride wealth makes divorce and separation more difficult for women as many women forfeit all their belongings if they separate or divorce. Under the Jieng customary law system, divorce is not widely accepted and is only possible when bride wealth is repaid to the husband's family. It is a requirement that can create tensions, especially because bride wealth is often shared amongst the bride's extended family.[5] Consequently, families have a financial incentive to ensure that a marriage remains intact even if the girl faces violence. Women who face violence in their marriage may face pressure to reconcile despite risks to their safety and wellbeing. In addition, a woman who leaves her husband without obtaining a divorce, and any man with whom she subsequently has a relationship, can be accused of adultery, an offence under south Sudan's penal code, punishable by customary compensation awards, court fines, or up to two years imprisonment.[6]

Jieng customary law looks at the rights granted by the custom patriarchy, giving males rights to full custody in the event of divorce.[7] The maternal family has the right to be paid remedies before children can live with their paternal family. During the two focus groups in Melbourne and Adelaide, the overall conclusion was that:

> *The majority of male participants stated that care of the children should be given to men as per the Jieng custom, we do pay the bride wealth and any*

[5] Armstrong, "Good Practices with Culturally Diverse Families in Family Dispute Resolution."
[6] Jok, Leitch, and Vandewint, "A Study of Customary Law in Contemporary Southern Sudan."
[7] Fadlalla, *Customary Laws in Southern Sudan: Customary Laws of Dinka and Nuer.*

child/children from the marriage are automatically affiliated with the paternal family (Marial).

Therefore, it would be argued that Jieng customary law does not consider children's position or the mother's, and this takes us to the next discussion on co-parenting within Jieng families.

6.2.2. Co-Parenting Resolutions (formerly Child Residence)

Jieng customary law takes a patriarchal approach when it comes to children's living arrangements. The Jieng use the term "*child custody*" which is no longer used in Australia. According to formal family law, residence of the child refers to where the child will reside. The term custody was dropped through the *Family Law Reform Act 2006*, in order to convey to families that children are not property.

For research participants, however, the concept of custody remains strong. The custody means one parent will permanently have the children after divorce. The issue of child custody also goes beyond this. According to Jieng family customary law, the man is at liberty to take full custody of the children, unless "Aruok" has not yet been paid, which would mean, the maternal family is allowed to live with the child(ren) until all dues are paid.[8] Further, the man has the right to recover some of his bride wealth or property depending on the number of children from the marriage and, at the same time, he can take full custody of the children after all the settlement is made. Below is a quote from one of the interview participants, Ajang:

After my wife was taken by another man, I could have been happy if she did not take my children with her. This man has no right to live with my children. I have paid bride wealth to her family and I deserved to take my children as per Jieng customary law, but the law here is not good with men (Ajang).

It is very clear here that many participants no longer have trust in their marriages and connection with their children. They fear that, someone in the wider community will exert undue influence over their wives, particularly in relation to "unfounded" freedom. and could happened any times that their only hope, which is the family is just gone without any genuine reason and never see their children again unless they go through mediation or family

[8] Jok, Leitch, and Vandewint, "A Study of Customary Law in Contemporary Southern Sudan."

court system which is unlikely to occur due to lack of trust in the system and fear of unknown outcome and potential hope of reconciliation.

Men do not want to relinquish their children for two reasons. First, children carry the family lineage and any Jieng man who does not have a family by middle-age is considered the living dead since he did not procreate to leave behind family lineage. Second, the payments of bride wealth are considered by the Jieng families as an incentive for the children's affiliation. Hence, children are automatically affiliated to their paternal family. For women, it is very clear from the Jieng perspective that their right to live with their children after divorce is always limited if they pursue dispute resolution through the Jieng customary law model. Consequently, some women chose to remain in a relationship for the children's sake. If they choose to follow the formalities of Australian family law to share parental responsibilities, then they may face some challenges with ongoing threats and demands to return to the relationship. If they chose to stop contact with the children to avoid potential family and domestic violence, then they can be isolated from their family and community. This issue of children affiliation and best interest of the children may play a challenging role in the children's relationships with both parents.

In contrast, Jieng customary law examines the rights granted by the customary patriarchy, giving males the rights to full custody of the children in the event of divorce.[9] Similarly, the woman's family has the similar right to be paid remedies before children can live with their paternal family. Therefore, it would be said that Jieng customary law does not consider children's position or the mother's and do not have the concept of shared parental responsibilities after divorce.

6.3. Jieng Dispute Resolution Model

During the interviews and two focus groups in Adelaide and Melbourne, the Jieng dispute resolution model was established as per Figure 6 below:

---

[9] Fadlalla, *Customary Laws in Southern Sudan: Customary Laws of Dinka and Nuer.*

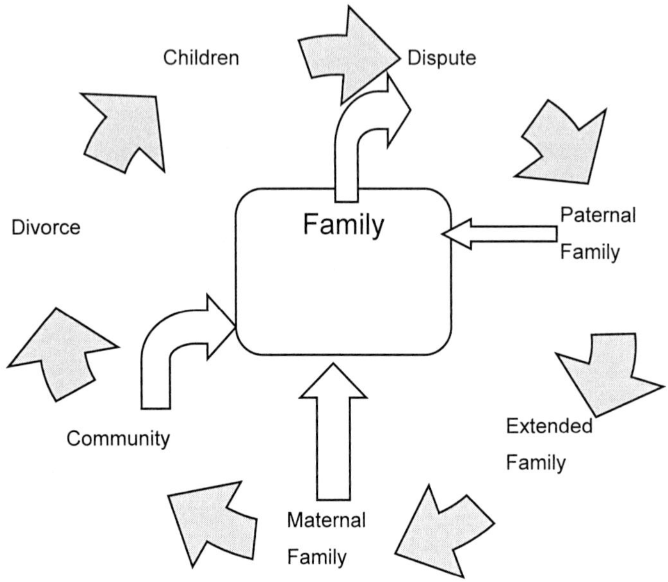

Figure 6: Family Dispute Resolution

In Australia and worldwide, it is common for a family or couple to encounter disputes and issues within their relationships, which can be either resolved by the couple themselves or with the help of professional through counselling or family dispute resolution services. However, in South Sudan particularly with Jieng (Dinka) families, dispute resolution remains the responsibility of couples themselves or the family, relatives, and the community at large. This process used to be followed smoothly when disputes arose between the couples back in the South Sudan. In the following section, the process of Jieng family dispute resolution and why it is often ineffective in Australia is briefly analysed.

6.4. Domestic Violence

With Jieng communities back in South Sudan and in Australia, domestic violence is not culturally acceptable. If it occurs, Jieng families always take a restorative approach to resolving the conflict by blaming and shaming the perpetrator and persuading the victim to forgive and reconcile. This is done for their children's sake, as well as to maintain the good names of the two parties' families. However, Jieng customary law uses the sanction as a form of deterrence for the perpetrator, although the deterrence is not based on the fear of imprisonment, but rather the fear of "Nhialic" (God), the fear of supernatural powers, the fear of public criticism, and the fear of revenge.[10] The fear of revenge is perhaps the most effective deterrent to violent crime, as revenge is collective and a whole clan can be held responsible for the wrongful actions of one member against another clan. Therefore, it is in the clan's best interest to prevent individuals from committing wrongs, and when a wrong is committed compensation to the wronged party is best paid "*within a reasonable time to prevent revenge*."[11]

Nevertheless, the Jieng do not have a specific consequence for domestic violence, only that a man could lose his social status in the community. This may mean that a man who is violent to women and children is considered as "*not man enough*" and, in most cases, may be excluded from important family and community matters.

6.4.1. Step One: Man's Family ("Koc Ke wa")

The Jieng traditional family takes a patrilineal lineage structure; when a man marries his wife, she is considered to have left her parents and their family lineage and to have become a member of her husband's family. In the event of any disputes, it is entirely the responsibility of the man's family to take appropriate measures to end the dispute. It is common among the Jieng family to seek help within the family when conflict arises. However, it is an obligation of the man's family to engage the couple in a dialogue setting which normally puts more emphasis on "cieng" (living together) as stated earlier. This process takes several days and many consultations with everyone who may be part of, or had any great influence in, the subject matter. Nevertheless, if the matter cannot be resolved by the man's family, it will be taken further to the in-law's (woman's) family for intervention. This normally happens by taking the woman back to her family with a specific message requesting her family members to discuss their daughters' concerns. This is done without giving the details or the nature of the conflict and feedback is to be delivered within a short period of time. This generally occurs if the woman is not happy with the outcome of the resolution concluded by her husband's family. This stage of the process is reached: if the woman wants to end the relationship; if she thinks she was not heard; or

[10] Makec, *The Customary Law of the Dinka People of Sudan: In Comparison with Aspects of Western and Islamic Laws.*
[11] Deng, "The Cow and the Thing Called" What": Dinka Cultural Perspectives on Wealth and Poverty."

if she believes the resolution was unfair on her and would like her family intervention. During the dispute resolution conducted by the man's family, emphasis is put on the nature of the issues as there are sensitive issues which do not require compromise. For instance, if the woman has insulted "kaat" (the lineage) with a taboo subject such as witchcraft, natural defects, or greediness, it is automatically taken to her family as the dispute is no longer between her family and her husband's but is a whole clan issue. During the interview, participant Mabior stated the following:

> *It is normal in Jieng culture, when issues arise within the families, you usually call your relatives to intervene, but, if the matter is difficult to resolve within the family by parents or closed relatives, then a woman can be returned to her family such that she could be investigated and returned with a specific message (Mabior).*

This leads us to the next stage of resolution which addresses how the woman's family would normally respond to the request from the in-laws.

6.4.2. Step Two: Woman's Family (Koc Ke nya - In-Laws)

In the Jieng marriage settlement, there are many stakeholders including: the couple, their two families; relatives, and the communities of origin. At the settlement of the marriage, everyone mentioned above has a say from the initial process until the settlement. In the same way when a marriage comes to an end or faces challenges, it is also expected that everyone involved will have an opportunity to make a comment regarding the future of the marriage. In Jieng traditions, there are two main protocols in dispute resolution: the first dictates that the family of the man is the initial contact in any dispute process; and the second, that if they are unable to resolve the matter, it is then taken to the woman's family. It is from this point that the meeting between two families would commence. During the interview, Atem stated the following:

> *My ex-wife was taken to her family after she refused to accept the resolution concluded by my family. Her family came back after three months with the message that they found, there was no major issue to end the marriage but regrettably she refused to reunite with me and they requested more time to consult with all the family members including her father and mother back in South Sudan (Atem).*

As stated above by Atem, his family resolved the dispute and wanted them to remain a married couple but his ex-wife refused to accept the resolution. This triggered Atem's family to seek the intervention of his ex-wife's family but this was unsuccessful as she made her position clear and she was no longer interested in the marriage. This example raises two questions: firstly, what would have happened if this case was resolved in South Sudan? To respond to this question, one has to look at the position presented by the ex-wife's family. There was no major issue to change their views that the marriage is in jeopardy and therefore, they only requested more time to resolve the matter which mean they will try to persuade her to change her mind. However, if she were in South Sudan, she would likely have been forced to accept the resolution. She would have had no choice but to accept the resolution because no one from the two families who was willing to stand with her. It may be different if her family stood with her and was ready to repay the bride wealth when necessary but unfortunately, her family disagreed and rejected her request to end the marriage. The second question would be, what would be the result be if she refused to accept the outcome of the resolution? Well, in Australia, there would be nothing else the family could do since she had the protection of the law and no one in her family could force her to do or accept anything that she was not happy with. Atem further explained that:

> *My ex-wife is now isolated as she has been disowned by her family after she refused to listen to them and my family are still hoping to welcome her back if she changes her mind, but for me it is over because she committed adultery and I don't think I can handle having a step child in my family. It is embarrassing (Atem).*

Atem states that his ex-wife is isolated from her family and his family because, it was their expectation that she should listen to them. At the same time, she also faced challenges in finding a new partner from the same community, as any man who having a sexual relationship with her would be considered as adulterer. He would also face isolation as her family would not accept to negotiate her remarrying anyone else since her divorce request had not yet been accepted by both families.

Generally, when a family encounters challenges in their relationship, it is common for them to separate for a short while they may reunite later if the matter is resolved, or they may choose to end the relationship permanently. In Jieng customary law, this process is not given the chance. The priority of every stakeholder is to make anything possible for the continuation of the marriage between the couple. When the woman is examined and found that she was at fault, the stakeholders may decide on the "awac" compensation for the wrong committed by the woman against her husband or his family. It is usually up to the man's family to accept the awac or reject it. But if the woman's family believe that she was not at fault then they will call for the meeting with her husband's family in the presence of the community to raise some of her concerns. The community here acts as a mediator between the two families.

In Jieng customary law, when a couple decides to end their marriage, they must go through a lengthy process.[12] Divorce, according to Jieng customary law, is the dissolution or ending of the marriage.[13] Marriage should be legally ended or granted by the court with the consent of all parties attached to the marriage agreements. The court process and divorce are made more difficult rather than easier as a means of retention of family ties.[14] During the Melbourne focus group, one of the participants, Matiop, informed that:

> *Divorce is not only difficult because of wealth pay back but it is also difficult because it's diminished the status of the man or both parents and their children consequently bear [the stigma] of being considered children from a dysfunctional family. Therefore, Jieng families are always careful to ensure that their families remain together for the betterment of their children's future and how they will be viewed by the society (Matiop).*

As stated earlier in this chapter, under Jieng customary law, divorce is not widely accepted and only possible under extreme situations and most likely when the woman's family are willing to repay some portion of bride wealth to the husband's family when couples have children together. The requirement of repaying bride wealth always creates tensions, especially since the bride wealth is shared amongst the bride's extended family.[15] Consequently, families have an incentive to ensure that marriages remain intact. Though domestic violence is not within the scope of this study, it is directly connected with marriage, divorce, and care of children disputes.

6.4. Conclusion

This chapter presented the findings from the interviews and the focus groups both in Adelaide and Melbourne. It showed the different dispute resolution mechanisms usually used by Jieng families back in South Sudan and explained why the same processes are not effective here in Australia. The

---

[12] Statistics, "Canberra."

[13] Fadlalla, Mohamed, 'Customary Laws in Southern Sudan: Customary Law of Jieng and Nuer' (2009) New York: iUniverse

[14] Fadlalla, "Customary Laws in Southern Sudan: Customary Law of Dinka and Nuer."

[15] Ibid.

findings have revealed that Jieng families have many challenges in trying to use their own dispute resolution process in resolving family disputes in Australia.

In this chapter, two main factors stood out: first, it is very clear that Jieng customary law gives custody of the children to their father as his customary legal rights are connected with the payments of bride wealth. Similarly, the family of the woman has a right to be fully compensated before children are allowed to stay with their paternal family. This demonstrated that the mother of the children and the children themselves have no rights throughout the process of determining living arrangements for the children. Therefore, there are some cultural processes that favour the rights of the father and do not incorporate the notion of the best interests of the child or children. Conversely, it could be concluded that the family law system does not consider cultural approaches when making decisions regarding the care of the children. This is also true of FDR which is only conducted by accredited family dispute resolution professionals, contrary to the cultural approaches of elders and aunties. Hence, both approaches have gaps in determining mutually agreed resolutions for South Sudanese Jieng families and other similar groups in Australia. The chapter concluded that there were many family law problems experienced among Jieng families in Australia and that the current approaches to their resolutions were not effective.

CHAPTER SEVEN

IS RESTORATIVE DISPUTE RESOLUTION A SOLUTION (COMMUNITY BASED MEDIATION)?

7.1. Introduction

This chapter examines whether the family law disputes of Australia's South Sudanese and other similar communities are best resolved through the formal family dispute resolution process, the incorporation of legal pluralism, or another more appropriate solution process. As discussed in Chapter Four, there is one nationwide system of law and no recognition of legal pluralism in the area of family law in Australia.[1] This is due to the unwillingness of policy makers to act on research and several legal reviews that recommend the recognition of customary law of Indigenous Australians and religious practice within family law through legal pluralism. It is unlikely that legal pluralism is a solution. Hence, this chapter offers another answer to the resolution of family disputes faced by South Sudanese Jieng families and other groups in Australia.

The chapter proposes a new dispute resolution model known as the restorative family dispute resolution model (RFDR). This is significant for migrants, refugees, and Indigenous communities as it offers a collective approach and provides healing and focus for future relationships with families. It also offers strategies to engage South Sudanese Jieng communities and other similar groups who resolve family law problems in the community through Community Based Mediation. Community Based Mediation is a form of restorative family dispute resolution mainly conducted by elders and leaders using a collective approach among families and relatives.

---

[1] Voyce and Possamai, "Legal Pluralism, Family Personal Laws, and the Rejection of Shari'a in Australia: A Case of Multiple or "Clashing" Modernities?."

7.2. Is Legal Pluralism an Alternative Answer to South Sudanese Family Dispute Resolution Problems?

There is only one legal system in Australia, which includes family law. This is in contrast to other Western legal systems where legal pluralism is allowed in the area of personal law.[2] This is due to unwillingness of policy makers to act on several research and legal reviews[3] that recommend the recognition of customary law of Indigenous Australians and religious practice within family law through legal pluralism. Thus, all attempts to recognise legal pluralism were unsuccessful. The Australian Law Reform Commission[4] delivered a report that suggested the Aboriginal and Torres Strait Islander's law be recognised in the family law jurisdiction but failed to conclude whether a separate legal approach is desirable for Indigenous people. Consequently, despite the Law Review Commission's recommendations, there was no action taken concerning their recommendations. Another report presented in the Western Australia against the recognition of Indigenous customary law,[5] stating that the practice of two personal legal system would encourage division among the Australia communities.[6]

The Australian Law Reform Commission compiled a similar report which promoted a process for the recognition of multiculturalism suggesting the elimination of bureaucratic obstacles and supporting of cross-cultural responsiveness.[7] This report did not support separate laws for different ethnic group within the Australian communities on the grounds the separate systems could be perceived as undermining equality and universality. On the other hand, researchers such as that of Humphrey, (Humphrey, 2007)[8] argue that the majority of Lebanese people feel that Australian law lacks

---

[2] Ibid.
[3] Parashar, "Australian Muslims and Family Law: Diversity and Gender Justice."
[4] Commission and Commission, *The Recognition of Aboriginal Customary Laws: Summary Report.*
[5] Horstman and Wightman, "Karparti Ecology: Recognition of Aboriginal Ecological Knowledge and Its Application to Management in North-Western Australia."
[6] Ibid.
[7] Voyce and Possamai, "Legal Pluralism, Family Personal Laws, and the Rejection of Shari'a in Australia: A Case of Multiple or "Clashing" Modernities?."
[8] Michael Humphrey, "Culturalising the Abject: Islam, Law and Moral Panic in the West," *Australian journal of social issues* 42, no. 1 (2007).

"*equality and universality*," and instead is prejudiced against multicultural communities and lacks transparency.[9]

Consequently, the Australian state and federal governments have repeatedly declined accepting the legal practices of Indigenous and multicultural groups. The *Family Law Act 1975* (Cth) Cth is the abbreviation for Commonwealth which mean it is a federal legislation not a state. is seen as the contemporary law protecting the rights of all Australian special regarding gender justice. For instance, the introduction of no-fault divorce within the family law promotes the equal division of family property after divorce or separation. The equal division of assets of marriage signifies the appreciation of the homemaking contribution of the two parties. The informal practices of some cultural groups within Australia may not fit with the formal legal system. .[10] Family customary law or personal religious law in some instances may not have a formal recognition by the state even though they may be in practice.

Recognising legal pluralism raises several issues. The South Sudanese customary law system is based on patriarchal values and is susceptible to human rights violations. In many cases women may be oppressed under this system, expected to follow traditional cultural practices that can be harmful, and may be blamed for family breakdowns. Atem stated in Chapter Seven:

> *My ex-wife is now isolated as she has been disowned by her family after she refused to listen to them and my family are still hopping to welcome her back if she change her mind, but for me it is over because she committed adultery and I don't think I can handle having step child in my family. It is embarrassing (Atem).*

Consequently, violence against women may be overlooked among the South Sudanese. This is due to the focus being on keeping the family together by arguing that problems are part of human life and can be resolved by families rather than strangers in a court of law who know nothing about the dynamics within that particular family. Recognising the customary law in its entirety under Australian family law would, in turn, provide less protection to vulnerable groups like women and children. As merry explains, culture often refers to traditions and customs that are justified by their roots in the past, and arguments about preserving culture become the basis for

---

[9] Ibid.

[10] Gordon R Woodman, "Alternative Law of Alternative Dispute Resolution, The," *C. de D.* 32 (1991).

defending control over women.[11] Therefore, the protection of women and the children is likely to be compromised with the notion of upholding cultural practices and keeping the families together, as this is the key element of the customary law approach.

Customary law and its dispute resolution approach, however, are considered by South Sudanese families as being more authentic,[12] and for many, would be seen to put the interests of family and particularly the children first above any other interest. Therefore, rather than accepting legal pluralism into the formal legal system, it seems that a middle ground that protects human rights, and especially protects against domestic violence, but still recognises the cultural norms and values of the South Sudanese community is necessary. This middle ground is best provided through the recognition of alternative dispute resolution alongside formal dispute resolution. This process may support and build trust among South Sudanese families and other similar groups in Australia.

The role of leaders is another significant issue with the customary legal system. Participants in this study highlighted the importance of community leaders and elders in resolving disputes, suggesting their powers be recognised and supported by the Australian family law sector. Milos, in her research, argued that community leaders are expected to make decisions and resolve conflict within the community based on customary practices and traditions. The involvement of leaders, however, must work alongside rather than against the formal legal system. Customary traditions and practices are based on patriarchal values, and community leaders can potentially exercise arbitrary power, oppressing the vulnerable groups within their communities, including women, young people, and small, unrepresented community groups.[13] It is further argued that recognising the role of community leaders would mean recognising the powers of unelected leaders to interpret customs based on patriarchal values and power hierarchy. Therefore, acknowledging and supporting the powers of community leaders without state control could lead to indiscriminate results and possible human rights violations.

---

[11] Merry, "Human Rights Law and the Demonization of Culture (and Anthropology Along the Way)."
[12] Jok, Leitch, and Vandewint, "A Study of Customary Law in Contemporary Southern Sudan."
[13] Milos, "South Sudanese Communities and Australian Family Law: A Clash of Systems."

Despite the problems arising out of recognition of plural legal orders, recognition of legal pluralism is not an impossible task, assuming the downfalls are addressed in an appropriate way. First and foremost, as the International Council on Human Rights Policy stresses, it is paramount to have a thorough understanding of the problems faced by the families, and of the context of community's laws if recognition of customary law is to be meaningful.[14] The importance, relevance and reliance on customary law need to be understood and appreciated before recognition of such law can begin. More importantly, the Australian family law system needs to recognise the shortcomings of the customary system and its elements and attempt to address these in that recognition.

7.3. Is Formal Family Dispute Resolution an Alternative Answer to South Sudanese Family Dispute Resolution Problems?

As discussed in Chapters Four, Six, and Seven, studies into family dispute resolution indicate that families from minority cultural backgrounds do not use FDR at a rate proportionate to their representation in the community.[15] Several reviews have concluded that the family law system does not meet the needs of people from culturally and linguistically diverse (CALD) backgrounds, and that a range of personal and systemic factors limit the ability of people from minority cultural backgrounds to access family law services.[16] The discussion from Chapter Seven revealed that, Jieng communities of South Sudan address disputes of marriage, divorce, and the care of children matters in accordance to their family traditions and customary law.[17] Resolution of family law problems is based on customary oral laws passed down from one generation to another, implemented by the local chiefs and elders in a public, informal setting. Generally, disputes are not considered legal but rather familial and communal, and resolutions are not decided according to written legislation by judges, but according to the wellbeing of the individuals and of the community by it well regarded chiefs and elders.

---

[14] Parashar, "Australian Muslims and Family Law: Diversity and Gender Justice."

[15] Armstrong, "Encouraging Conversations About Culture: Supporting Culturally Responsive Family Dispute Resolution1."

[16] Ibid.

[17] Ojelabi et al., "A Cultural Assessment of Family Dispute Resolution: Findings About Access, Retention and Outcomes from the Evaluation of a Family Relationship Centre."

Formal family dispute resolution has been an alternative solution to going to court among wider Australian mainstream communities since 2006. However, the literature suggests that families from CALD backgrounds are underrepresented within family dispute resolution services and do not understand how family disputes are resolved among those communities.[18] The available data indicates that families from minority cultural backgrounds do not use FDR at a rate proportionate to their representation in the community.[19] A number of reviews have concluded that the family law system does not meet the needs of people from culturally and linguistically diverse (CALD) backgrounds, and that a range of personal and systemic factors limits the ability of people from minority cultural backgrounds to access family law services.[20] In addition to the existing data, the findings from this book revealed that Jieng families do not trust government agencies or service providers with family dispute problems. As previously discussed, one of the interview participants states:

We have language and communication difficulties with government agencies and other service providers. I don't think taking family issues to strangers was useful. I decided to leave my children in the care of their mother because I don't want to have trouble with Police. If my wife understands the benefit of our children having their father around them, then, she will allow me to come back and live with my children again as family (Deng).

7.4. Restorative Family Dispute Resolution (RFDR)

The question arises whether restorative family dispute resolution may be a solution to Jieng families and others of similar cultural backgrounds including Indigenous Australians, religious groups, and other ethnic groups which practice customary law. This is the first time this new model has been proposed in Australia in relation to assisting South Sudanese families to resolve family disputes. There is no literature to suggest that the concept of restorative family dispute resolution has been proposed previously for

---

[18] Armstrong and Clearinghouse, *Enhancing Access to Family Dispute Resolution for Families from Culturally and Linguistically Diverse Backgrounds*.
[19] Armstrong, "Encouraging Conversations About Culture: Supporting Culturally Responsive Family Dispute Resolution1."
[20] Ibid.

resolving family law disputes. Instead, it is widely being used in the criminal justice systems of Australia and New Zealand[21]

Restorative justice is defined as a process whereby all parties with a stake in a dispute come together to resolve collectively how to deal with the aftermath of a disagreement and its implications for the future.[22] It is an approach that promotes fair or just restorative outcomes, separate from the formal legal system. It transforms conflict into co-operation, and the parties negotiate workable outcomes for themselves and their children; this results in fairer and more effective decision-making, the healing of individuals, and the resetting and restoring of relations.

The concept of restorative justice has existed for many years in one form or another among Indigenous and other cultures, it was initially used in its modern sense in the 1970s to refer victim-offender mediation programs in North America.[23] Restorative justice was adopted in the 1990s in New Zealand as an effective way of addressing juvenile offending through the introduction of Group Conferencing under the Children, Young person and their Families Act.[24] Consequently, all juvenile offences except murder and aggravated rape were dealt with by a family group conference, which was meant to bring together of the offender, victim and their families with the goal of repairing the harm caused.[25]

The development of restorative justice policies, procedures and programmes that are respectful of rights, needs and interests of victims, offenders, communities and all other parties was encouraged at the Tenth Session of the United Nations Congress on Crime prevention and Criminal Justice in 2000.[26] Restorative justice principles were then added on the United Nations agenda in 2002, where its basic principles on the use of

---

[21] Kelly Richards, "Police-Referred Restorative Justice for Juveniles in Australia," *Trends and Issues in Crime and Criminal Justice*, no. 398 (2010).

[22] Mark Umbreit and Howard Zehr, "Restorative Family Group Conferences: Differing Models and Guidelines for Practice," *Fed. Probation* 60 (1996).

[23] Heather Strang and John Braithwaite, *Restorative Justice and Family Violence* (Cambridge University Press, 2002).

[24] Murray Levine, "The Family Group Conference in the New Zealand Children, Young Persons, and Their Families Act of 1989 (Cyp&F): Review and Evaluation," *Behavioral sciences & the law* 18, no. 4 (2000).

[25] Ibid.

[26] Roger S Clark, *The United Nations Crime Prevention and Criminal Justice Program: Formulation of Standards and Efforts at Their Implementation* (University of Pennsylvania Press, 1994).

Restorative Justice Programmes in criminal matters were adopted by the Economic and Social Council.[27] The UN basic principles encourage member states to establish guidelines and standards that set out use of restorative justice programs appropriate to their legal system.[28]

Since 2001, restorative justice practice has become mainstream in the Australian juvenile criminal justice system and has been extended for use with adults' offenders.[29] Current literature suggests that restorative justice programs now expand conferencing for both young and adult offenders known as circle sentencing and victim-offender mediation.[30]

This book argues that since restorative justice programs are widely used and effective within the criminal justice system then, it would be of great benefit to extend the same concept to the family dispute resolution sector among the South Sudanese and other similar cultural groups who are currently under-represented in formal family dispute resolution.

7.4.1. Restorative justice family dispute resolution in South Sudanese communities

The potential value of restorative justice in resolving family law problems within the South Sudanese community is reflected in the comments of a participant from the Adelaide focus group:

Councils of elders should be formed and trained with Australia dispute resolution process such that they can be ready to arbitrate family dispute which are not criminal by nature - issues which may require counselling or family mediation (Malou).

Malou explained that in his own sub-community, there are three key elders whom they rely on when there is a problem between a couple or two people in their community. This approach works with people prioritising safety, doing no further harm, building trust, empowerment, and self-determination, and ensuring voluntariness. Restorative mediation is a style of mediation that seeks to allow the parties to reach their own resolution in partnership with a trained neutral practitioner and to find ways to restore the

---

[27] Paul McCold, "The Recent History of Restorative Justice: Mediation, Circles, and Conferencing," *Handbook of restorative justice: A global perspective* (2006).
[28] Ibid.
[29] Richards, "Police-Referred Restorative Justice for Juveniles in Australia."
[30] Gerry Johnstone, *Restorative Justice: Ideas, Values, Debates* (Routledge, 2013).

relationship between the parties to a more balanced level of civility. This concept is a core value of the South Sudanese customary law process of dispute resolution which, as discussed in Chapter Three, adopts a "conciliatory approach" to dispute resolution.[31] The objectives of South Sudanese customary law are not retributive but restitutive, and can be summarised as: "the maintenance of peace or equilibrium and the restoration of the status through the payment of damages."[32]

This differs from the goal of Western statutory law systems, which is to ascertain the truth, regardless of whether the truth brings satisfaction or resolution to the parties. A study conducted in Melbourne with Sudanese former refugee on how disputes are resolved in their community in Australia. The study results are consistent with the findings of this book, participants revealed that they struggles in getting appropriate approaches to resolve the different types of dispute faced in their community in Australia.[33] One of the participants pointed out that "it is painful to see a family break up and parents decide to go separate ways."[34] This view is common across the South Sudanese families as their priority is always to keep the family together by resolving the problem with aim to reconcile and reunite. Danne explains that, "African dispute resolution has been described as placing a premium on improving relations on the basis of equity, good conscience and fair play, rather than the strict legality often associated with Western justice."[35] Therefore, when a crime is committed, it is common for the court to order the defendant or accused to pay compensation to the victim's family to restore equilibrium. This is seen as more effective than applying penal sanctions, as it is said to induce obedience and enable society to maintain a strong sense of discipline.[36]

As evidenced in Chapters Six and Seven, Jieng families want to resolve family problems without recourse to the formal legal system. Participants

---

[31] Danne, "Customary and Indigenous Law in Transitional Post-Conflict States: A South Sudanese Case Study."

[32] Milos, "South Sudanese Communities and Australian Family Law: A Clash of Systems."

[33] Siew Fang Law, ""We Assumed That by Living in a Civilised Country Things Can Be Freer and Better": Counter Stories of Dispute Resolution in Australia," *Australasian Dispute Resolution Journal* 25, no. 1 (2014).

[34] Ibid.

[35] Danne, "Customary and Indigenous Law in Transitional Post-Conflict States: A South Sudanese Case Study."

[36] Makec, *The Customary Law of the Dinka People of Sudan: In Comparison with Aspects of Western and Islamic Laws.*

suggested a hierarchy of preferred dispute resolution avenues for family and relationship problems, with conciliation by extended family as a first step, and "arbitration" or mediation by a community or religious leaders or council of elders if this fails. South Sudanese Jieng participants, most of whom were community leaders, stressed that family cohesion is the main priority for Jieng families, and that the involvement of external services is seen as likely to lead to divorce rather than reconciliation. Going outside the community to family law services is regarded as a "last resort." One of the participants from the Adelaide focus group summed up this concern:

> *If you try to solve family problems outside the family, it usually gets bigger and becomes something else, everything becomes about the woman's safety and not the family's cohesion (Makuei).*

This concern reflects the perception that family relationship services are separation services, rather than relationship building services. In contrast, community-based dispute resolution or restorative resolution focus on preserving family relationships. Nevertheless, restorative dispute resolution offers an approach that brings together individuals, families, social networks, services, and government agencies, through informal and formal processes, to proactively build relationships to resolve, or prevent, conflict and wrongdoing.

Restorative dispute resolution is based on the philosophy of restorative justice. This philosophy provides a framework which is underpinned by values and beliefs that asks to approach wrongdoing differently. The focus is on community, relationships, and the healing process whereby all parties with a stake in a particular dispute come together to resolve collectively how to deal with the aftermath of the conflict and its implications for the future.[37]

The philosophy that underpins restorative justice philosophy holds that human beings are happier, more productive and cooperative, and more likely to make positive changes in their behaviour when those in positions of authority act with them rather than upon them or for them.[38] As revealed by the participants through interviews and focus groups, the majority of participants stated clearly that they did try to resolve their family problems including domestic and family violence themselves but were unsuccessful. This means Jieng families are using restorative family dispute resolution approaches in trying to resolve family law problems. Consequently, participants expressed a necessity and dedication to the Jieng customary law

---

[37] Richards, "Police-Referred Restorative Justice for Juveniles in Australia."

[38] Tony F Marshall, *Restorative Justice: An Overview* (Home Office London, 1999).

system, suggesting that it is still widely utilised throughout Australia among the Jieng communities. Other similar groups, including Indigenous Australians, are also practising a restorative dispute resolution approach.[39]

This is significant for other refugee communities within Australia, as well as other migrant and indigenous communities as it takes a collective approach and provides healing and focus for the future relationships with the families. Findings from a cultural assessment of family dispute resolution at one of family relationship centre revealed that participants in an Iraqi men group prefer the collective approach of dispute resolution over the individualist approach way of resolving the dispute in Australia.[40] The study pointed out that shame and face-saving were some of the factors preventing families from some CALD communities to seek help with formal family dispute resolution services.[41] With those factors in mind, it is very significant to look at the alternative ways of resolving disputes in the way that appropriate to their family's situation. A further report by the Family Law Council concluded that members of CALD communities have a preference for resolving family disputes privately with the assistance of extended family and community or religious leaders.[42] (Council, 2012)

Furthermore, this approach is widely used in South Sudan and other African countries among the local communities. Assefa pointed out that the Ethiopian legal system has adopted the use of the dispute resolution known as "Shimglina" (Shimglina is an Amharic word for elderliness), the process is preside over by the Shimagles (elders in Amharic) who are selected by the parties to the dispute or by their relatives on the merit basis that include age, kinship, integrity, religious authority and the knowledge of the custom of a given community.[43] The Shimglina process allows the parties to a dispute to present and explain their problem and respond to the question from the Shimagles. Kelemework argues that the objective of the Shimglina process is the reconciliation and forgiveness between the parties in a dispute and the wider community rather than the punishing the individual

---

[39] Larissa Behrendt, *Aboriginal Dispute Resolution: A Step Towards Self-Determination and Community Autonomy* (Federation Press, 1995).

[40] Ojelabi et al., "A Cultural Assessment of Family Dispute Resolution: Findings About Access, Retention and Outcomes from the Evaluation of a Family Relationship Centre."

[41] Ibid.

[42] Council, *Improving the Family Law System for Clients from Culturally and Linguistically Diverse Backgrounds: A Report to the Attorney-General.*

[43] Susanne Epple and Getachew Assefa, *Legal Pluralism in Ethiopia: Actors, Challenges and Solutions* (transcript Verlag, 2020).

responsible for the wrongs committed.[44] However, resolution concluded by the Shimagles does not aim for financial compensation or criminal punishment. The outcome may range from apology in low conflict cases and all other form of symbolic gesture of reconciliation which may involve customary ritual.[45] Similarly, in South Sudan custom, family disputes are generally resolved by the elders or leaders starting from family level to the larger community in few cases, according to Deng, conflict resolution in South Sudan is based on the mediation to restore social harmony and consensus within the respective community, rather than on strict legality or punishment. The ethos of customary law family dispute resolution mechanisms is thus conciliation.[46]

Restorative justice approaches to resolving disputes within communities where a community-oriented focus would be more culturally appropriate has been criticised. In particular, Indigenous Australians have been reluctant to be involved in family group conferences in the criminal law context, and the implementation of conferencing for Indigenous young offenders has not reduced the offending rate,[47] however, argues the success of restorative justice dispute resolution within the criminal justice system has been evaluated against criteria that is too narrow and bounded by colonialist assumptions. Instead, he suggests that restorative justice dispute resolution not only helps to restore relations between the direct participants, but also assists in opening a dialogue between oppressed social groups and the dominant culture.[48] Thus, restorative family dispute resolution may also assist in building more positive relations between the Jieng community, who have faced discrimination within Australia and a sense of alienation from the formal legal system, and the dominant culture.

7.4.2. Restorative Dispute Resolution and Family Violence

Family violence is common among the CALD communities, and family violence is often thought to be incompatible with restorative justice due to emphasis on face-to-face processes and reconciliation between the victim

---

[44] Kelemework Tafere Reda, "Social Organization and Cultural Institutions of the Afar of Northern Ethiopia," *International Journal of Sociology and Anthropology* 3, no. 11 (2011).
[45] Ibid.
[46] Deng, "Customary Law in the Cross-Fire of Sudan's War of Identities."
[47] Chris Cunneen, "Restorative Justice and the Politics of Decolonization," in *Restorative Justice: Theoretical Foundations* (Willan, 2012).
[48] Ibid.

and perpetrator which in most cases may not be suitable to the power in balance featured in family violence cases.[49] However, it has also been argued that restorative dispute resolution is often more appropriate for addressing family violence than traditional methods of dispute resolution. The main aims of restorative justice are broader than just face-to-face meetings regarding restorative justice. There is common understanding between the efforts to reduce family violence and restorative justice movement. It has been argued that both are greatly concerned with clear acknowledgement of the wrongness of the behaviour, with the message to the victims that they are not responsible or do not deserve what happened,[50] with a recognition that the community bears some responsibility for the broader social climate regarding the behaviour and with making both individual and the social changes which will end the behaviour.[51]

It is argued that community-based processes that emerged in the restorative justice movement offer the hope that in response to family violence a larger group of parties can be engaged to influence the offender, to create safety nets for victims and stimulate a larger community discussion about the origin of such behaviour.[52] Pranis further argues that individuals are responsible for their impact on others and on the larger whole of which they are a part. Which mean communities are responsible for the good of the whole, which includes the well-being of each member.[53] With the Jieng families back in South Sudan and in Australia, there is a shared value that the wellbeing of the whole community is the responsibility of every individual and the wellbeing of every individual is a responsibility of the whole community. Hence, there is a chance the restorative dispute resolution may effectively worked with Jieng families and other similar groups if leaders and elders' roles are recognised and given a specifics training and guidance to response to family violence situations.

---

[49] Kay Pranis, "Restorative Justice, Socialjustice, Andthe Empowerment of Marginalized Populations," *Restorative community justice: Repairing harm and transforming communities* (2001).
[50] Mary Achilles and Howard Zehr, "Restorative Justice for Crime Victims: The Promise, the Challenge," *Restorative and community justice cultivating common ground for victims, communities and offenders. Cincinnati, OH: Anderson* (2001).
[51] Kay Pranis, "Restorative Values," in *Handbook of Restorative Justice* (Willan, 2013).
[52] Ibid.
[53] Kay Pranis, "Restorative Values and Confronting Family Violence," *Restorative justice and family violence* (2002).

It has also been argued that restorative justice has, at its heart, values that assist in confronting family violence. Restorative justice has a focus on mutual responsibility, which hold individuals responsible for their impact on other family members, as well as being responsible for contributing to the good of the community as a whole.[54] It recognises moral authority, especially the authority of the community leaders, which is more likely to produce behavioural change than a dispute resolution process that is embedded in the recognition of legal authority.[55] It can increase the agency of vulnerable parties by providing the community support and ensuring that the community, and not just individuals, take responsibility for the safety of women and children.[56]

7.4.3. The Model (RFDR)

The empirical data from chapters Six and Seven suggested that community-based mediation with a similar approach referred to here as "Restorative Family Dispute Resolution" (RFDR) can be established as reflected in figure 8:

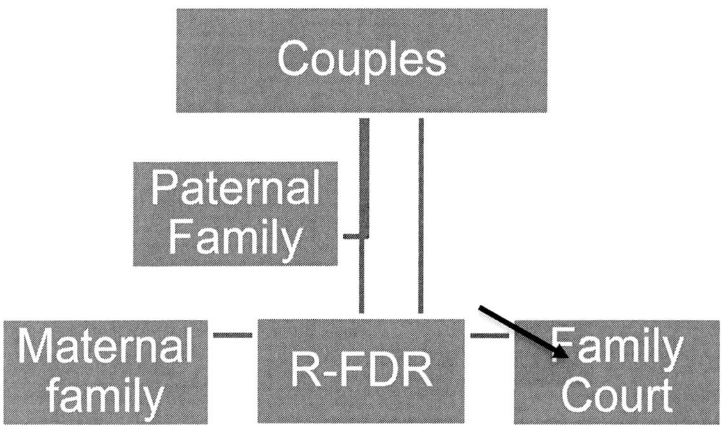

Figure 8: The RFDR Model

---

[54] Strang and Braithwaite, *Restorative Justice and Family Violence*.

[55] Ibid.

[56] Pranis, "Restorative Justice, Socialjustice, Andthe Empowerment of Marginalized Populations."

The desire to resolve family problems privately was a strong theme in both focus groups as well as for a majority of interview participants. Participants suggested a hierarchy of preferred dispute resolution avenues for family and relationship problems, with conciliation by extended family as a first step and "arbitration" or mediation by community or religious leaders or by a council of elders if this fails. South Sudanese Jieng participants, most of whom were community leaders, stressed that family cohesion is the main priority for the Jieng families, and that the involvement of external services is seen as likely to lead to divorce rather than reconciliation. Going outside the community to family law services is regarded as a "last resort." Therefore, the general perspective suggested that a community-based dispute resolutions model may be a solution to South Sudanese communities and other similar groups in Australia. This approach is not new among the Indigenous communities across the globe, literature suggested that the approach is popular among the native communities in Canada, New Zealand and more recently within the juvenile justice system in Australia.[57] For instance, the Navajo peace process which is a quintessential form of restorative justice as it involves the community in restoring people and groups to a state of wellbeing in a needs-meeting way. The needs of everyone in the healing process are the paramount. The findings from the interview participants and focus groups are consistence with the Navajo's perspective. Among the South Sudanese and Jieng families, conflict between parties normally affect the nuclear family, extended family and the larger community.

It is suggested that with the current sixty-five Family Relationship Centres (FRC) across Australia, there is a need to employ and train CALD-Family Dispute Resolution Practitioners in restorative dispute resolution approaches. They can then work in collaboration with elders and community leaders to ensure that appropriate assessment for family and domestic violence is conducted and that there is help in the facilitation of the restorative family dispute resolution process. Those mediations would be divided into stage one and stage two.

7.4.4. Stage One: Early Intervention

Stage one would be to use the restorative dispute resolution approach to resolve the conflict between the couples as they are about to separate or after they have already done so, but are still under the same roof and have not

[57] Dennis Sullivan and Larry Tifft, *Handbook of Restorative Justice: A Global Perspective* (Routledge, 2007).

made a final decision to end the relationship. This stage is equivalent to the current counselling undertaken by the mainstream Australians when they are faced with challenges in their relationship. This stage does not aim to resolve co-parenting. Rather, it aims for early intervention, which means resolving the conflict before proceeding to separation or divorce and if, indeed, the separation occurs then. The restorative dispute resolution practitioner then commences with stage two, whose goal is to amicably resolve issues related to the care of children in culturally appropriate ways that reflect the *Family Law Amendment (Shared Parental Responsibility) Act 2006* with the principal of shared care responsibility where this is in the best interests of the children.

For instance, let us use Ajang's example with his ex-wife. Ajang outlined his disappointment in Chapter Seven; that he paid over one hundred head of cattle to marry his ex-wife and moved to Australia in early 2000s with one child and while in Australia they had another child. A few years down the line, his ex-wife took off with another man and the two children. He tried to resolve this with his family and then the ex-wife family but was unsuccessful. He stated he does not want to go to court because he believes the court will not resolve the matter as he knows the court will not give him the children and his bride wealth back. He stated the following:

> *My wife and children are with this man here in Australia and no one cares, I wish we were in South Sudan, this man would have not seen the Sun again in his whole life. I think he will never step foot in South Sudan otherwise, he will end up in jail. (Ajang)*

Ajang's example had already involved the two families but there was no solution as his ex-wife had already decided to end her relationship with Ajang and re-partner. The new proposed restorative family dispute resolution approach would have done little to reunite Ajang and his ex-wife but instead could have made a referral to stage two for co-parenting. Extensive explanations would have been provided to both Ajang and his ex-wife such that they were informed of what was in the best interests of the child or children and the importance of shared responsibility in their children's up-bringing. Throughout the interviews and focus groups, almost all participants believed that the family law in Australia only gives a mother the rights to remain with the children at the family home while the father is taken away. However, there is no literature to prove this, just a mere perception among the CALD communities across Australia. If Ajang were given the opportunity to spend time with his children without going to court, he would not have been bitter about his bride wealth and the children since the main purpose of bride wealth is for the wife to procreate children who will carry forward the family lineage. Furthermore, further explanations would have proven significant for him to understand that both parents were important in the upbringing of the children. If these explanations had been communicated through elders emphasising co-parenting, he would have not felt like such a hopeless father. The majority of cases are unsuccessful because one grieving parent threatens the elders and community with the authority that what they were doing is illegal and is not known by the government. Consequently, this notion would change if the participation of elders and community leaders were to be recognised in the two stages of the dispute resolution process.

7.4.5. Stage Two: Co-Parenting

Stage two would be aimed at amicably resolving the care of children using culturally appropriate ways that adhere to the *Family Law Amendment (Shared Parental Responsibility) Act 2006* with the principal of shared care responsibility for the parents. Using Ajang's example above, the restorative family dispute resolution practitioner would do an intake and assess whether it was appropriate to proceed with RFDR through the use of the same screening tools employed by the mainstream services. The practitioner would explain in detail the best interest of the child and the expectations of the *Family Law Act (1975)* emphasising the importance of co-parenting to demystify this notion of one parent having more rights than the other one. The new model would allow both parties to bring along family members who are culturally important in the resolution process. This is meant to bring everyone on board as it was previously discussed in Chapters Six and Seven that any party who refused to accept a resolution facilitated by the elders or community is normally isolated and disowned by their own family and wider society.

The involvement of elders and the community are essential elements to this model. Participants recommended that in order to make family dispute resolution easier and more accessible to South Sudanese and similar groups, elders and community and religious leaders be given more formal dispute resolution responsibilities to play a leading role in non-complex dispute cases. These findings suggest that what is desirable for South Sudanese Jieng communities and other similar groups to make family law dispute accessible and appropriate is to deploy a different approach to what the Australian family law system is currently offering. Resolutions of family disputes among South Sudanese communities' means private issues to the families and communities, rather than a family law problem.

Elders and the community would also need to be involved at a deeper level than just mere attendance. Cunneen suggests that one of the reasons why restorative justice approaches within the criminal justice system have not been well-received within Indigenous communities is that too many assumptions had made about the format and process of conferences without genuine dialogue with Indigenous communities. For instance, it had been assumed that what would work within Maori communities in New Zealand could be simply transplanted to Australia without acknowledgement that Indigenous communities are culturally diverse. Therefore, the elders and the South Sudanese community should be involved as participants in restorative family dispute resolution conferences, they should also be full partners in setting up the conferences, with regards to determining the format, processes and norms upon which they need to be founded. This could also involve more support for South Sudanese people to become restorative family dispute resolution practitioners.

7.6. Conclusion

This chapter has provided a possible solution to the issue of family law dispute for South Sudanese Jieng families and other similar groups in Australia. That solution is referred to here as the restorative family dispute resolution approach which has been defined and explained. It was discussed how the restorative family dispute resolution approach was already in use by the Jieng and other similar groups in Australia. Although it is less effective due to the lack of recognition by the legal system in Australia, this chapter has suggested a recognition of the restorative family dispute resolution approach alongside current formal family dispute resolution may improve the level of dispute resolution services delivery among South Sudanese families and other similar groups across Australia.

CHAPTER EIGHT

CONCLUSION

This concluding chapter brings together the whole book, consisting of the previous seven central chapters which explored how disputes related to marriage, divorce, and co-parenting are resolved, or not resolved, among the South Sudanese Jieng communities in Australia. It offers some concluding remarks and strategies on the important perspectives on engaging with South Sudanese Jieng communities and other similar groups in Australia.

The aim of this book was to analyse the experiences and the ways in which Jieng families, now living in Australia, attempt to resolve disputes in relation to marriage, divorce, and disputes over the care of children. The book has examined the nature of Jieng customary law and how it differs to statutory law, focusing on the resolution of marriage, divorce and co-parents disputes in Jieng communities in South Sudan. It has provided a brief discussion on the evolution of Jieng customs and cultures as well as critiques. It explored the role of international human rights instruments under customary law in South Sudan and argued that the rights of women and children continue to be violated despite relevant legislation in South Sudan. There is enough evidence to suggest that ninety percent of court cases are handled by customary courts that have not yet modified their practices to be compliant with human rights standards.[1]

It was noted that Jieng customary law maintains these practices which are not being practiced in other cultures outside South Sudan. This causes legal consciousness with the Jieng families in their new countries of residence like Australia. Practices such as polygamy, arranged/forced, levirate, and ghost marriages are not commonly practised in many Western countries and may clash with the legal systems of countries like Australia where South Sudanese or Jieng communities have settled in the last few years. However, the definition of marriage and its validity encompassed three different categories in Jieng custom. In Jieng customary law, marriage is the

[1] Garcia, "The Future of South Sudanese Women: Restructuring Customary Law in South Sudan."

agreement between two families and their relatives. It can be concluded that South Sudanese Jieng communities are likely to continue to utilise their traditional marriage practices by resolving their marriage and other related disputes within their communities wherever they reside outside South Sudan including in Australia.[2] Scrutinising Jieng customary law in detail is important as it has provided a deep understanding of how communities prefer to resolve their problems. It also provides perspectives for the family law sector in Australia.

In contrast, it was noted that divorce was made difficult as it required the consensus of both families since marriage is an agreement between two families and not between individual couples. Furthermore, care of children was discussed from the Jieng community's perspective, and it was noted that children are traditionally affiliated to their paternal parents and could be taken by the father' family after divorce if all the "Hocke Thieek" or "Aruok" are paid.[3] This is highly significant for many Jieng families as children are their hope of continuing the family lineage and name for future generations.

The book has also briefly discussed the historical background of the South Sudanese especially during five decades of civil war between the periods 1955-1972 and 1983-2005. This resulted in a massive displacement from their homeland which, in turn, led to their eventual resettlement in Western countries including Australia, and resulted in their experiences in different refugee camps in neighbouring countries and beyond.

The book has discussed the historical background of family law in Australia and the subsequent progressive changes and amendments which took place over the years. Despite the diversity in Australian society, the family law does not in any way consider the recognition of customary law or legal pluralism. However, FDR may be an alternative avenue to address CALD and Indigenous family law disputes although the literature suggested under-representation of those groups in family dispute resolution services. This suggests that those groups may be using other means such as family and community to resolve family disputes including the care of children after separation.

It has also analysed the available literature which suggests that there are many family law issues faced by the South Sudanese community and other

[2] Hutchinson, "Researching and Writting in Law."

[3] Deng, "Customary Law in the Cross-Fire of Sudan's War of Identities."

similar groups here in Australia. It is unlikely these problems will have any policy impact in the Australian family law system.

The book has also identified several issues that hinder Jieng families' participation with mainstream family dispute resolution services. There was a general fear from the families that their concerns and problems may not be properly addressed by strangers as they believed family matters should be resolved by family members and not government agencies or professionals. For example, participants were unsure whether mainstream family dispute resolution services or family court would properly address the issues surrounding bride wealth and care of children in ways that would correspond with their cultural expectations and values. The majority of male participants believed that the laws only favour women, and they suggested it is not good to share family issues which are taboo topics with strangers.

This book is significant because it contributes to the growing body of research on non-Australian perspectives of South Sudanese settlement in Australia. While other researchers have highlighted some of the settlement problems faced by South Sudanese former refugees, none have focused on the important issues of how family law problems are resolved.

The book has analysed the possible use of culturally appropriate mediation and has identified strategies that may assist in the prevention and early intervention in Jieng families and other cultural groups before statutory Australian family law becomes necessary. Further, this research has also shed light on approaches to mediating conflicts between customary laws and Australian laws in the other cultural groups. Thus, this book has provided knowledge to service providers, practitioners, and communities about how to best support South Sudanese families and other groups with similar practices in Australia. It has examined disputes from their own perspectives, including their use of the family law system, and explored ways in which service providers with the family justice section, including family lawyers, mediators, and judges, can make family dispute resolution among the South Sudanese families more appropriate and relevant to their cultures and other minor groups in Australia. This book component is important because it contributes to the growing body of research on South Sudanese settlement in Australia, and also adds to research concerning the experiences of migrants and refugees when faced with navigating the Australian legal system. Previous research has identified that migrant and refugee communities do not use the formal legal system to resolve family law dispute but there has been little consideration as to why this is the case. This is the important gap as these groups are often vulnerable.

It is concluded that an alternative dispute resolution approach known as restorative family dispute resolution may be a solution to the family problems faced by South Sudanese Jieng families and other similar groups including the Indigenous Australians. This approach is currently being used in those communities, but due to its lack of recognition by the legal system, it has not been effective as its volunteer facilitators are sometime fearful of the consequences should their unrecognised roles catch the attention of the authorities. Therefore, the recognition of restorative family dispute resolution alongside current formal family dispute resolution would add credibility and may effectively maximise the participation of Jieng families and other similar groups in family dispute resolution process across Australia. Recognising the importance of the role of community and religious leaders, for instance, and providing community leaders with more formal dispute resolution powers could increase the participation of Jieng families and other similar groups in family dispute resolution services. Furthermore, formal recognition could ensure that the role of community and religious leaders is supervised more closely, ensuring that dispute resolution complies with Australian human rights protections.

BIBLIOGRAPHY

(ABS), Australia Bureau of Statistics. "Culturally Diversity in Australia." 2011 Census (2011).

Abu Rannat, Sayyid Muhammad. "The Relationship between Islamic and Customary Law in the Sudan 1." *Journal of African Law* 4, no. 1 (1960): 9-16.

Achilles, Mary, and Howard Zehr. "Restorative Justice for Crime Victims: The Promise, the Challenge." *Restorative and community justice cultivating common ground for victims, communities and offenders. Cincinnati, OH: Anderson* (2001): 87-100.

Ahmed El Mahd, Saeed Mohd. "Some General Principles of Acquisition of Ownership of and Rights over Land by Customary Prescription in the Sudan." *Journal of African Law* 20, no. 2 (1976): 79-99.

Akolawin, Natale Olwak. "Personal Law in the Sudan—Trends and Developments." *Journal of African Law* 17, no. 2: 149-95.

Akyeampong, emmanuel. "social history gender, ethnicity and social change on the upper slave coast: a history of the anlo-ewe. By sandra e. Greene. Portsmouth nh: heinemann; oxford: james currey, 1996.

Aldehaib, Amel. *Sudan's Comprehensive Peace Agreement Viewed through the Eyes of the Women of South Sudan.* Institute for Justice and Reconciliation, 2010.

Aldershot, England : Ashgate. *The Multi-Cultural Family.* Edited by Ann Laquer Estin. Aldershot, England: Aldershot, England: Ashgate, 2008.

Ali, Nada Mustafa. *Gender and Statebuilding in South Sudan.* US Institute of Peace, 2011.

Alier, Abel. *Southern Sudan: Too Many Agreements Dishonoured.* Vol. 13: Ithaca Press, 1992.

Alston, Philip, and Bridget Gilmour-Walsh. "The Best Interests of the Child: Towards a Synthesis of Children's Rights and Cultural Values." UNICEF Innocenti Research Centre, 1996.

An-na' Im, Abdullahi A., and Francis M. Deng. "Self-Determination and Unity: The Case of Sudan." *Law & Policy* 18 (1996): 199-223.

Anderson, G Norman. *Sudan in Crisis: The Failure of Democracy.* University Press of Florida, 1999.

Aplin, Sally. "Analysis of the Legal Needs of Horn of Africa People in Melbourne." (2002).

Armstrong, Susan. "Good Practices with Culturally Diverse Families in Family Dispute Resolution." *Family Matters*, no. 92 (2013): 48.

Armstrong, Susan, and Australian Family Relationships Clearinghouse. *Enhancing Access to Family Dispute Resolution for Families from Culturally and Linguistically Diverse Backgrounds.* Australian Institute of Family Studies, 2010.

Armstrong, Susan M. "Encouraging Conversations About Culture: Supporting Culturally Responsive Family Dispute Resolution1." *Journal of Family Studies* 17, no. 3 (2011): 233-48.

Ashkanasy, Neal M, Edwin Trevor-Roberts, and Louise Earnshaw. "The Anglo Cluster: Legacy of the British Empire." *Journal of World Business* 37, no. 1 (2002): 28-39.

Assembly, UN General. "Convention Relating to the Status of Refugees, 28 July 1951, United Nations, Treaty Series, Vol. 189." *Retrieved April* 20 (2015): 137.

Ayers, Alison J. "Sudan's Uncivil War: The Global–Historical Constitution of Political Violence." *Review of African Political Economy* 37, no. 124 (2010): 153-71.

Badal, Raphael Koba. "Religion and Conflict in the Sudan: A Perspective." *Bulletin of Peace Proposals* 21, no. 3 (1990): 263-72.

Bainham, Andrew. *Children, the Modern Law.* Edited by Stephen Michael Cretney. Bristol, England: Bristol, England: Family Law, 1993.

Banks, Cyndi. "Protecting the Rights of the Child: Regulating Restorative Justice and Indigenous Practices in Southern Sudan and East Timor." *The International Journal of Children's Rights* 19, no. 2 (2011): 167-93.

Bantekas, Ilias, and Hassan Abu-Sabeib. "Reconciliation of Islamic Law with Constitutionalism: The Protection of Human Rights in Sudan's New Constitution." *Afr. J. Int'l & Comp. L.* 12 (2000): 531.

Barbour, K Michael. "The Sudan since Independence." *The Journal of Modern African Studies* 18, no. 1 (1980): 73-97.

Barwick, Garfield. "The Commonwealth Marriage Act 1961." *Melb. UL Rev.* 3 (1961): 277.

Behrendt, Larissa. *Aboriginal Dispute Resolution: A Step Towards Self-Determination and Community Autonomy.* Federation Press, 1995.

Berry, John W, Uichol Kim, Thomas Minde, and Doris Mok. "Comparative Studies of Acculturative Stress." *International migration review* (1987): 491-511.

Beswick, S. F. "Islam and the Dinka of the Southern Sudan from the Pre-Colonial Period to Independence (1956)." *Journal of Asian and African Studies* 35, no. 4: 422.

Beswick, Stephanie. "We Are Bought Like Clothes": The War over Polygyny and Levirate Marriage in South Sudan." *Northeast African Studies* 8, no. 2 (2001): 35-61.

Bishop, Jessica Rebecca. *To Be a Family: Changes Experienced within South Sudanese Families in Australia.* University of Melbourne, Department of Social Work, 2011.

Boswell, A. "Sudan: Will the North Survive If the South Secedes." *Retrieved January* 24 (2011): 2011.

Brettell, Caroline B, and James F Hollifield. *Migration Theory: Talking across Disciplines.* Routledge, 2014.

Brown, Tim. "South Sudan Education Emergency." *Forced Migration Review* 24 (2006): 54.

Cadigan, R. Jean. "Woman-to-Woman Marriage: Practices and Benefits in Sub-Saharan Africa.(Special Issue: Comparative Perspectives on Black Family Life, Vol 1)." *Journal of Comparative Family Studies* 29, no. 1: 89.

Canavera, Mark, Kiryn Lanning, Katherine Polin, and Lindsay Stark. "'And Then They Left': Challenges to Child Protection Systems Strengthening in South Sudan." *Children & Society* 30, no. 5 (2016): 356-68.

Chisholm, Richard. "Making It Work: The Family Law Amendment (Shared Parental Responsibility) Act 2006." *Australian Journal of Family Law* 21, no. 2 (2007): 143-72.

Clark, Roger S. *The United Nations Crime Prevention and Criminal Justice Program: Formulation of Standards and Efforts at Their Implementation.* University of Pennsylvania Press, 1994.

Colic-Peisker, Val, and Iain Walker. "Human Capital, Acculturation and Social Identity: Bosnian Refugees in Australia." *Journal of Community & Applied Social Psychology* 13, no. 5 (2003): 337-60.

Collins, Robert O. *A History of Modern Sudan.* Cambridge University Press, 2008.

Commission, Australia. Law Reform, and Australian Law Reform Commission. *The Recognition of Aboriginal Customary Laws: Summary Report.* Australian Government Publishing Service, 1986.

Constantine, Stephen. "British Emigration to the Empire-Commonwealth since 1880: From Overseas Settlement to Diaspora?". *The Journal of Imperial and Commonwealth History* 31, no. 2 (2003): 16-35.

Correa-Velez, Ignacio, Sandra M Gifford, and Adrian G Barnett. "Longing to Belong: Social Inclusion and Wellbeing among Youth with Refugee Backgrounds in the First Three Years in Melbourne, Australia." *Social Science & Medicine* 71, no. 8 (2010): 1399-408.

Council, Family Law. *Improving the Family Law System for Clients from Culturally and Linguistically Diverse Backgrounds: A Report to the Attorney-General.* Attorney-General's Department, 2012.

Cowan, Jane K, Marie-Bénédicte Dembour, and Richard A Wilson. *Culture and Rights: Anthropological Perspectives.* Cambridge University Press, 2001.

Cunneen, Chris. "Restorative Justice and the Politics of Decolonization." In *Restorative Justice: Theoretical Foundations*, 54-71: Willan, 2012.

Daly, MW. "'Summing Up'islam and Politics in Sudan Islam, Secularism and Politics in Sudan since the Mahdiyya. By Gabriel Warburg. London: Hurst, 2003. Pp. 19.95, Paperback (Isbn 1-85065-590-1)." *The Journal of African History* 45, no. 02 (2004): 332-33.

Danne, Alexander P. "Customary and Indigenous Law in Transitional Post-Conflict States: A South Sudanese Case Study." *Monash University Law Review* 30, no. 2 (2004): 199-228.

De Waal, Alex. "When Kleptocracy Becomes Insolvent: Brute Causes of the Civil War in South Sudan." *African Affairs* 113, no. 452 (2014): 347-69.

Deal, Jeffery L. "Torture by 'Cieng': Ethical Theory Meets Social Practice among the Dinka Agaar of South Sudan." *American Anthropologist* 112, no. 4: 563-75.

Deng, FM. "The Cow and the Thing Calledwhat': Dinka Cultural Perspectives on Wealth and Poverty." *Journal of International Affairs* 52, no. 1 (1998): 101-29.

Deng, Francis. *Customary Law in the Modern World: The Crossfire of Sudan's War of Identities.* Routledge, 2009.

Deng, Francis M. "The Cow and the Thing Called 'What': Dinka Cultural Perspectives on Wealth and Poverty." *Journal of International Affairs* (1998): 101-29.

Deng, Francis Mading. *The Dinka of the Sudan.* New York: New York, Holt, Rinehart and Winston, 1972.

Deng, Santino Atem. "Fitting the Jigsaw: South Sudanese Family Dynamics and Parenting Practices in Australia." Victoria University, 2016.

Dennison, Gráinne. "Is Mediation Compatible with Children's Rights?". *Journal of Social Welfare & Family Law* 32, no. 2 (2010): 169-82.

Dersso, Solomon A. "International Law and the Self-Determination of South Sudan." *Institute for Security Studies Papers* 2012, no. 231 (2012): 12-12.

Detrick, Sharon. *A Commentary on the United Nations Convention on the Rights of the Child.* Martinus Nijhoff Publishers, 1999.

Diehl, Katharina, Ruben Madol Arol, and Simone Malz. "South Sudan: Linking the Chiefs' Judicial Authority and the Statutory Court System." In *Non-State Justice Institutions and the Law*, 55-79: Springer, 2015.

Donnelly, Jack. "Cultural Relativism and Universal Human Rights." *Hum. Rts. Q.* 6 (1984): 400.

Duany, Julia A, and Wal Duany. "War and Women in the Sudan: Role Change and Adjustment to New Responsibilities." *Northeast African Studies* 8, no. 2 (2001): 63-82.

Ebbeck, Marjory Anne, and Carmencita H Dela Cerna. "A Study of Child Rearing Practices Amongst Selected, Sudanese Families in South Australia: Implications for Child Care Service Selection." *Early Childhood Education Journal* 34, no. 5 (2007): 307-14.

Edward, Jane Kani. "South Sudanese Refugee Women: Questioning the Past, Imagining the Future." In *Women's Rights and Human Rights*, 272-89: Springer, 2001.

Eekelaar, John. "The Interests of the Child and the Child's Wishes: The Role of Dynamic Self-Determinism." *International Journal of Law, Policy and the Family* 8, no. 1 (1994): 42-61.

Epple, Susanne, and Getachew Assefa. *Legal Pluralism in Ethiopia: Actors, Challenges and Solutions.* transcript Verlag, 2020.

Fadlalla, Mohamed. "Customary Laws in Southern Sudan: Customary Law of Dinka and Nuer." *New York: iUniverse* (2009).

Fakhoury, Tamirace. "Multi-Level Governance and Migration Politics in the Arab World: The Case of Syria's Displacement." *Journal of Ethnic and Migration Studies* 45, no. 8 (2019): 1310-26.

Ferrell, Ruth M. "No-Fault Divorce." *Women Law. J.* 62 (1976): 27.

Finlay, H. L., Margaret Otlowski, and R. Bailey-Harris. *Family law in Australia*. University Of Tasmania, 1997.

Fisher, Linda. *Mediating with Families.* Edited by Mieke Brandon. Pyrmont, N.S.W.: Pyrmont, N.S.W. : Lawbook, 2009.

Flint, Julie, and Alex De Waal. *Darfur: A New History of a Long War.* Zed Books, 2008.

Fozdar, Farida, and Lisa Hartley. "Refugee Resettlement in Australia: What We Know and Need to Know." *Refugee Survey Quarterly* 32, no. 3 (2013): 23-51.

Fozdar, Farida, and Brian Spittles. "The Australian Citizenship Test: Process and Rhetoric." *Australian Journal of Politics & History* 55, no. 4 (2009): 496-512.

Furnes, H, MM El-Sayed, SO Khalil, and MA Hassanen. "Pan-African Magmatism in the Wadi El-Imra District, Central Eastern Desert, Egypt:

Geochemistry and Tectonic Environment." *Journal of the Geological Society* 153, no. 5 (1996): 705-18.
Garcia, Jaclyn Christine. "The Future of South Sudanese Women: Restructuring Customary Law in South Sudan." Brandeis University, 2011.
Genn, Hazel. "What Is Civil Justice for-Reform, Adr, and Access to Justice." *Yale JL & Human.* 24 (2012): 397.
Government, Australia. "Sudanese Community Profile." Canberra: Department of Immigration and Citizenship, 2007.
Government, Australia. *Family Law Handbook : Containing Family Law Act 1975 and Family Law Regulations Together with an Explanatory Summary and an Index to the Act and Regulations.* Edited by statutes etc Family Law Act Australia. Laws and Australia. Canb.
Canberra: Canb.: Aust. Govt. Pub. Serv., 1975 <https://trove.nla.gov.au/newspaper/title/1308#>.
Government of South Sudan. "Child Act 2008 and Penal Code 2008." Ministry Justice and legal Affiars, 2008.
Government, South Sudan. "Judiciary Act." (2008).
Government, Sudan. "5th Sudan Population and Housing Census 2008." 21-26. Khartoum Sudan: Central Bureau of Statistics, 2009.
Gray, Richard. "A History of the Southern Sudan, 1839-1889." (1961).
Griffiths, Anne. "Pursuing Legal Pluralism: The Power of Paradigms in a Global World." *The Journal of Legal Pluralism and Unofficial Law* 43, no. 64 (2011): 173-202.
Griffiths, Curt Taylor, and Ray Corrado. "Implementing Restorative Youth Justice: A Case Study in Community Justice and the Dynamics of Reform (Restorative Juvenile Justice: Repairing the Harm of Youth Crime, P 237-258, 1999, Gordon Bazemore and Lode Walgrave, Eds.--See Ncj-181924)." (1999).
Griffiths, John. "What Is Legal Pluralism?". *The journal of legal pluralism and unofficial law* 18, no. 24 (1986): 1-55.
Guarak, Mawut Achiecque Mach. *Integration and Fragmentation of the Sudan: An African Renaissance.* AuthorHouse, 2011.
Guttmann, Egon. "The Reception of the Common Law in the Sudan." *International & Comparative Law Quarterly* 6, no. 03 (1957): 401-17.
Harris-Short, Sonia. "International Human Rights Law: Imperialist, Inept and Ineffective? Cultural Relativism and the Un Convention on the Rights of the Child." *Human rights quarterly* 25, no. 1 (2003): 130-81.
Harte, Elizabeth Wendy. "Settlement Geography of African Refugee Communities in Southeast Queensland: An Analysis of Residential Distribution and Secondary Migration." (2010).

Hassan, Abdelsalam. "History of Law Reform in Sudan." *REDRESS*, no. Khartoum. Sudan (2008).

Hathaway, James C. *The Rights of Refugees under International Law.* Cambridge University Press, 2005.

Hebbani, Aparna, Levi Obijiofor, and Helen Bristed. "Intercultural Communication Challenges Confronting Female Sudanese Former Refugees in Australia." *The Australasian Review of African Studies* 31, no. 1 (2010): 37-61.

Heger Boyle, Elizabeth, and Ahmed Ali. "Culture, Structure, and the Refugee Experience in Somali Immigrant Family Transformation." *International Migration* 48, no. 1 (2010): 47-79.

Herieka, E, and J Dhar. "Female Genital Mutilation in the Sudan: Survey of the Attitude of Khartoum University Students Towards This Practice." *Sexually Transmitted Infections* 79, no. 3 (2003): 220-23.

Hessbruegge, Jan Arno. "Customary Law and Authority in a State under Construction: The Case of South Sudan." *African Journal of Legal Studies* 5, no. 3 (2012): 295-311.

Higgins, Tracy E. *Future of African Customary Law.* Edited by Paolo Galizzi and Jeanmarie Fenrich. Cambridge University Press, 2011.

Hill, Richard Leslie. "On the Frontiers of Islam: Two Manuscripts Concerning the Sudan under Turco-Egyptian Rule 1822-1845." (1970).

Hinz, Manfred. "The Ascertainment of Customary Law: What Is Ascertainment of Customary Law and What Is It For? The Experience of the Customary Law Ascertainment Project in Namibia." *The Experience of the Customary Law Ascertainment Project in Namibia (July 19, 2012). Oñati Socio-Legal Series* 2, no. 7 (2012).

Holborn, Louise Wilhelmine, Philip Chartrand, and Rita Chartrand. *Refugees, a Problem of Our Time: The Work of the United Nations High Commissioner for Refugees, 1951-1972.* Vol. 2: Scarecrow Press, 1975.

Holt, Peter Malcolm. *A Modern History of the Sudan: From the Funj Sultanate to the Present Day.* London: Weidenfeld & Nicolson, 1961.

Holt, Peter Malcolm, and Martin W Daly. *A History of the Sudan: From the Coming of Islam to the Present Day.* Routledge, 2014.

Horstman, Mark, and Glenn Wightman. "Karparti Ecology: Recognition of Aboriginal Ecological Knowledge and Its Application to Management in North-Western Australia." *Ecological Management & Restoration* 2, no. 2 (2001): 99-109.

Howell, Paul Philip. *A Manual of Nuer Law: Being an Account of Customary Law, Its Evolution and Development in the Courts Established by the Sudan Government.* Routledge, 2018.

Humphrey, Michael. "Culturalising the Abject: Islam, Law and Moral Panic in the West." *Australian journal of social issues* 42, no. 1 (2007): 9-25.

Hutchinson, Terry. *Researching and Writing in Law*. Thomson Reuters Lawbooks, 2001.

Idris, Amir H. *Sudan's Civil War: Slavery, Race, and Formational Identities*. Lewiston: Edwin Mellen Press, 2001.

Jackson, Ivor C. "The 1951 Convention Relating to the Status of Refugees: A Universal Basis for Protection." *Int'l J. Refugee l.* 3 (1991): 403.

Jacobs, Keith. *Experience and Representation: Contemporary Perspectives on Migration in Australia*. Routledge, 2016.

Jansen, Bram J. "Between Vulnerability and Assertiveness: Negotiating Resettlement in Kakuma Refugee Camp, Kenya." *African Affairs* 107, no. 429 (2008): 569-87.

Jenson, Jane. "Paradigms and Political Discourse: Protective Legislation in France and the United States before 1914." *Canadian journal of political science* 22, no. 02 (1989): 235-58.

Johnson, Douglas H. "Judicial Regulation and Administrative Control: Customary Law and the Nuer, 1898–1954." *J. Afr. Hist.* 27, no. 1 (2003): 59-78.

Johnson, Douglas Hamilton. *The Root Causes of Sudan's Civil Wars: Peace or Truce*. Boydell & Brewer Ltd, 2011.

Johnson, Hilde F. *South Sudan: The Untold Story from Independence to the Civil War*. IB Tauris, 2016.

Johnstone, Gerry. *Restorative Justice: Ideas, Values, Debates*. Routledge, 2013.

Jok, Akechak, R Leitch, and Carrie Vandewint. "A Study of Customary Law in Contemporary Southern Sudan." *Juba: World Vision International and the South Sudan Secretariat of Legal and Constitutional Affairs* (2004).

Jok, Jok Madut. *Diversity, Unity, and Nation Building in South Sudan*. US Institute of Peace, 2011.

Jok, Jok Madut, and Sharon Elaine Hutchinson. "Sudan's Prolonged Second Civil War and the Militarization of Nuer and Dinka Ethnic Identities." *African Studies Review* 42, no. 02 (1999): 125-45.

Jolaade, Adeogun Tolulope, and Isola Abidemi Abiola. "Patriarchy and Customary Law as Major Cogs in the Wheel of Women's Peace Building in South Sudan." *Journal of Gender, Information and Development in Africa (JGIDA)* 5, no. 1 (2016): 53-75.

Juuk, Buol. "South Sudanese Dinka Customary Law in Comparison with Australian Family Law: Legal Implications for Dinka Families." *Australasian Review of African Studies, The* 34, no. 2 (2013): 99.

Juuk, Buol Garang Anyieth. *From Tyranny to Triumph : Once a Sudanese Refugee, Now a Proud Citizen of Australia and South Sudan / Buol Garang Anyieth Juuk ; Edited by Don Sinnott.* Edited by D. H. Sinnott. West Lakes, S.Aust: Seaview Press, 2011.

Khalil, Mohammed Ibrahim. "Sudan Legal System and Problem of Law Reform." Paper presented at the Sudan Law Reform, Odmurman, 2008.

Khawaja, Nigar G., and Karla Milner. "Acculturation Stress in South Sudanese Refugees: Impact on Marital Relationships." *International Journal of Intercultural Relations* 36, no. 5 (2012): 624-36.

Kok, Peter Nyot. "The Customary Law of the Dinka People of Sudan: In Comparison with Aspects of Western and Islamic Laws." (1990): 1008.

Krieger, Heike. "A Conflict of Norms: The Relationship between Humanitarian Law and Human Rights Law in the Icrc Customary Law Study." *Journal of Conflict and Security Law* 11, no. 2 (2006): 265-91.

Lacey, Elizabeth. "It Takes Two Hands to Clap Conflict, Peacebuilding, and Gender Justice in Jonglei, South Sudan." (2013).

Law, Siew Fang. "“We Assumed That by Living in a Civilised Country Things Can Be Freer and Better”: Counter Stories of Dispute Resolution in Australia." *Australasian Dispute Resolution Journal* 25, no. 1 (2014): 45-54.

Layish, Aharon, and Gabriel R Warburg. *The Reinstatement of Islamic Law in Sudan under Numayrī: An Evaluation of a Legal Experiment in the Light of Its Historical Context, Methodology, and Repercussions.* Brill, 2002.

Lejukole, James Wani-Kana Lino. "'We Will Do It Our Own Ways': A Perspective of Southern Sudanese Refugees Resettlement Experiences in Australian Society." 2009.

Leonardi, Cherry, Leben Nelson Moro, Martina Santschi, and Deborah H Isser. *Local Justice in Southern Sudan.* United States Institute of Peace, 2010.

Levine, Murray. "The Family Group Conference in the New Zealand Children, Young Persons, and Their Families Act of 1989 (Cyp&F): Review and Evaluation." *Behavioral sciences & the law* 18, no. 4 (2000): 517-56.

Logo, Kuyang. "Exploring Linkages of Traditional and Formal Mechanism of Justice and Reconciliation in South Sudan." *Available at SSRN 3102242* (2018).

Lokosang, LB. *South Sudan: The Case for Independence and Learning from Mistakes.* London: Xlibris Corporation, 2010.

Losoncz, Ibolya. "Blocked Opportunity and Threatened Identity: Understanding Experiences of Disrespect in South Sudanese

Australians." *Australasian Review of African Studies, The* 32, no. 2 (2011): 118.
Lubin, Peter, and Dwight Duncan. "Follow the Footnote or the Advocate as Historian of Same-Sex Marriage." *Cath. UL Rev.* 47 (1997): 1271.
Machar, Riek. "South Sudan: A History of Political Domination-a Case of Self-Determination." *Nairobi: November* (1995): 26-37.
MacLachlan, Malcolm, Mutamad Amin, Hasheem Mannan, Shahla El Tayeb, Nafisa Bedri, Leslie Swartz, Alister Munthali, *et al.* "Inclusion and Human Rights in Health Policies: Comparative and Benchmarking Analysis of 51 Policies from Malawi, Sudan, South Africa and Namibia." *PLoS ONE* 7, no. 5.
Madut, Kon K. "Determinants of Early Marriage and Construction of Gender Roles in South Sudan." *SAGE Open* 10, no. 2 (2020): 2158244020922974.
Majavu, Mandisi. "The 'African Gangs' Narrative: Associating Blackness with Criminality and Other Anti-Black Racist Tropes in Australia." *African and Black Diaspora: An International Journal* 13, no. 1 (2020): 27-39.
Makec, John Wuol. *The Customary Law of the Dinka (Jieng): A Comparative Analysis of an African Legal System.* Khartoum: J. W. Makec, 1986.
Marlowe, Jay. *Belonging and Transnational Refugee Settlement: Unsettling the Everyday and the Extraordinary.* Routledge, 2017.
Marlowe, Jay M. "Beyond the Discourse of Trauma: Shifting the Focus on Sudanese Refugees." *Journal of refugee studies* 23, no. 2 (2010): 183-98.
Marshall, Tony F. *Restorative Justice: An Overview.* Home Office London, 1999.
Mason, Gail, and Mariastella Pulvirenti. "Former Refugees and Community Resilience 'Papering Over'domestic Violence." *British Journal of Criminology* 53, no. 3 (2013): 401-18.
Massoud, Mark Fathi. *Law's Fragile State: Colonial, Authoritarian, and Humanitarian Legacies in Sudan.* Cambridge University Press, 2013.
Matthews, Julie. "Schooling and Settlement: Refugee Education in Australia." *International studies in sociology of education* 18, no. 1 (2008): 31-45.
Mbano, Noah T. *The Perceptions of African Refugee Background Students: Their Schooling in Wa and Their Adjustment to the Australian Cultural Context.* Curtin University., 2012.

McCold, Paul. "The Recent History of Restorative Justice: Mediation, Circles, and Conferencing." *Handbook of restorative justice: A global perspective* (2006): 23-51.

McLachlan, Campbell. "The Recognition of Aboriginal Customary Law: Pluralism Beyond the Colonial Paradigm: A Review Article." *International and Comparative Law Quarterly* (1988): 368-86.

Mennen, Tiernan. "Legal Pluralism in Southern Sudan: Can the Rest of Africa Show the Way?". *Africa Policy Journal* 3, no. 1 (2007): 49-73.

Merry, Sally Engle. "Human Rights Law and the Demonization of Culture (and Anthropology Along the Way)." *PoLAR* 26 (2003): 55.

Metz, Helen Chapin. *Republic of the Sudan: Country Studies.* Edited by Congress Library Of. Washington, DC: Federal Research Division, Library of Congress, 2001.

Migration and Refugee Law : Principles and Practice in Australia. Edited by John Vrachnas. Port Melbourne, Vic.: Port Melbourne, Vic. : Cambridge University Press, 2008.

Mills, Eithne, and Marlene. *Family Law.* Chatswood, N.S.W.: Chatswood, N.S.W.: LexisNexis Butterworths, 2012.

Milos, Danijela. "South Sudanese Communities and Australian Family Law: A Clash of Systems." *Australasian Review of African Studies, The* 32, no. 2 (2011): 143-59.

Mkandawire, Paul, Katie MacPherson, Kon Madut, Odwa D Atari, Andrea Rishworth, and Isaac Luginaah. "Men's Perceptions of Women's Reproductive Health in South Sudan." *Health & place* 58 (2019): 102157.

Mohammed, Arifeen. "Child Marriage and Problems." *Pakistan & Gulf Economist* 33, no. 20 (2014).

Monahan, Lisa Young & Geoff. *Family Law in Australia.* Sydney: Ligar Pity Ltd, 2009.

Moore-Harell, Alice. "The Turco-Egyptian Army in Sudan on the Eve of the Mahdiyya, 1877-80." *International Journal of Middle East Studies* 31, no. 1 (1999): 19-37.

Moran, Anthony. "Post-Multicultural Australia? Cosmopolitanism Critique and the Future of Australian Multiculturalism." In *The Public Life of Australian Multiculturalism*, 241-68: Springer, 2017.

The Multi-Cultural Family. Edited by Ann Laquer Estin. Aldershot, England: Aldershot, England: Ashgate, 2008.

Murphy-Berman, Virginia, Helen L Levesque, and John J Berman. "Un Convention on the Rights of the Child: A Cross-Cultural View." *American Psychologist* 51, no. 12 (1996): 1257.

Murphy, Claire. "Asylum Seeker Policy in Australia: Sending Refugees Back to Persecution." Murdoch University, 2014.

Murray, Kate E. "Sudanese Perspectives on Resettlement in Australia." *Journal of Pacific Rim Psychology* 4, no. 01 (2010): 30-43.

Mwambene, Lea. "Custody Disputes under African Customary Family Law in Malawi: Adaptability to Change?". *International Journal of Law, Policy and the Family* 26, no. 2 (2012): 127-42.

Nasong'o, Shadrack Wanjala, and Godwin Rapando. "Lack of Consensus on Constitutive Fundamentals: Roots of the Sudanese Civil War and Prospects for Settlement." *African and Asian Studies* 4, no. 1 (2005): 51-82.

The Nature of Customary Law. Nature of Customary Law : Legal, Historical and Philosophical Perspectives. Edited by Amanda Perreau-Saussine and James Bernard Murphy. Cambridge: Cambridge : Cambridge University Press, 2007.

Neumann, Klaus, Sandra M Gifford, Annika Lems, and Stefanie Scherr. "Refugee Settlement in Australia: Policy, Scholarship and the Production of Knowledge, 1952– 2013." *Journal of Intercultural Studies* 35, no. 1 (2014): 1-17.

Newman, Edward, and Joanne Van Selm. "Refugees and Forced Displacement." *International Security, Human Vulnerability, and the State, UNU Press, Tokyo Japan* (2003).

Nicholson, Alastair, and Margaret Harrison. "Family Law and the Family Court of Australia: Experiences of the First 25 Years." *Melb. UL Rev.* 24 (2000): 756-61.

Nielson, Laura Beth, and Robert L Nelson. "Rights Realized-an Empirical Analysis of Employment Discrimination Litigation as a Claiming System." *Wis. L. Rev.* (2005): 663.

Njambi, Wairimu Ngaruiya, and William E O'Brien. "Revisiting 'Woman-Woman Marriage': Notes on Gikuyu Women." *NWSA Journal* 12, no. 1 (2000): 1-23.

Nolan, David, Karen Farquharson, Violeta Politoff, and Timothy Marjoribanks. "Mediated Multiculturalism: Newspaper Representations of Sudanese Migrants in Australia." *Journal of Intercultural studies* 32, no. 6 (2011): 655-71.

Ojelabi, Lola Akin, Thomas Fisher, Helen Cleak, Alikki Vernon, and Nikola Balvin. "A Cultural Assessment of Family Dispute Resolution: Findings About Access, Retention and Outcomes from the Evaluation of a Family Relationship Centre." *Journal of Family Studies* 17, no. 3 (2011): 220-32.

Olowu, 'Dejo. "Protecting Children's Rights in Africa: A Critique of the African Charter on the Rights and Welfare of the Child." *Int'l J. Child. Rts.* 10 (2002): 127.

Parashar, Archana. "Australian Muslims and Family Law: Diversity and Gender Justice." *Journal of Intercultural Studies* 33, no. 5 (2012): 565-83.

Parkinson, Patrick. *Australian Family Law in Context : Commentary and Materials.* Pyrmont, N.S.W.: Pyrmont, N.S.W.: Thomson Reuters Professional Australia, 2012.

Parkinson, Patrick, and Patrick Parkinson. *Australian Family Law in Context : Commentary and Materials.* Pyrmont, N.S.W.: Pyrmont, N.S.W. : Thomson Reuters Professional Australia, 2012.

Pavlish, Carol, and Anita Ho. "Human Rights Barriers for Displaced Persons in Southern Sudan.(World Health)." *Journal of Nursing Scholarship* 41, no. 3 (2009): 284.

Pimentel, David. "Rule of Law Reform without Cultural Imperialism? Reinforcing Customary Justice through Collateral Review in Southern Sudan." *Hague Journal on the Rule of Law* 2, no. 01 (2010): 1-28.

Pinaud, Clemence. "South Sudan: Civil War, Predation and the Making of a Military Aristocracy." *African Affairs* 113, no. 451 (2014): 192-211.

Poggo, Scopas S. "General Ibrahim Abboud's Military Administration in the Sudan, 1958-1964: Implementation of the Programs of Islamization and Arabization in the Southern Sudan." *Northeast African Studies* 9, no. 1 (2002): 67-101.

Pranis, Kay. "Restorative Justice, Socialjustice, Andthe Empowerment of Marginalized Populations." *Restorative community justice: Repairing harm and transforming communities* (2001): 287.

Reda, Kelemework Tafere. "Social Organization and Cultural Institutions of the Afar of Northern Ethiopia." *International Journal of Sociology and Anthropology* 3, no. 11 (2011): 423-29.

Renzaho, André, Julie Green, David Mellor, and Boyd Swinburn. "Parenting, Family Functioning and Lifestyle in a New Culture: The Case of African Migrants in Melbourne, Victoria, Australia." *Child & family social work* 16, no. 2 (2011): 228-40.

Rhoades, Helen L. "Improving the Family Law System for Clients from Culturally and Linguistically Diverse Backgrounds. (Australia). Australian Journal of Family Law,." *Australian Journal of Family Law*, no. 3 (2012): 240-53.

Richards, Kelly. "Police-Referred Restorative Justice for Juveniles in Australia." *Trends and Issues in Crime and Criminal Justice*, no. 398 (2010): 1.

Roberts, Simon. "Introduction: Some Notes on "African Customary Law"." *Journal of African Law* 28, no. 1-2 (1984): 1-5.
Robins, Melinda B. "'Lost Boys' and the Promised Land Us Newspaper Coverage of Sudanese Refugees." *Journalism* 4, no. 1 (2003): 29-49.
Robinson, Julie. "Sudanese Heritage and Living in Australia: Implications of Demography for Individual and Community Resilience." *Australasian Review of African Studies, The* 32, no. 2 (2011): 25.
Rolandsen, Øystein H, and Martin W Daly. *A History of South Sudan: From Slavery to Independence.* Cambridge University Press, 2016.
Sackville, Ronald. "Access to Justice: Towards an Integrated Approach." Paper presented at the Judicial Review: Selected Conference Papers: Journal of the Judicial Commission of New South Wales, The, 2011.
Santschi, Martina. "Traditional Authorities, Local Justice and Local Conflict Resolution Mechanisms in South Sudan." In *Is Local Beautiful?*, 43-63: Springer, 2014.
Schweitzer, Robert, Fritha Melville, Zachary Steel, and Philippe Lacherez. "Trauma, Post-Migration Living Difficulties, and Social Support as Predictors of Psychological Adjustment in Resettled Sudanese Refugees." *Australian and New Zealand Journal of Psychiatry* 40, no. 2 (2006): 179-87.
Shakespeare-Finch, Jane, and Kylie Wickham. "Adaptation of Sudanese Refugees in an Australian Context: Investigating Helps and Hindrances." *International migration* 48, no. 1 (2010): 23-46.
Shteir, Sarah. "The Institution & Practice of 'Bride Wealth' in Southern Sudan." *Refuge: Canada's Journal on Refugees* 26, no. 2 (2007).
Silbey, Susan S. "After Legal Consciousness." *Annu. Rev. Law Soc. Sci.* 1 (2005): 323-68.
Spaaij, Ramón. "Cultural Diversity in Community Sport: An Ethnographic Inquiry of Somali Australians' Experiences." *Sport Management Review* 16, no. 1 (2013): 29-40.
Springvale, Monash Legal Service Inc. "Comparative Analysis of South Sudanese Customary Law and Victorian Law." 47. Melbourne Australia: Springvale Monash Legal Service Inc., 2008.
Statistics, Australian Bureau. "Canberra." *Australian Bureau of Statistics* (2011).
Strang, Heather, and John Braithwaite. *Restorative Justice and Family Violence.* Cambridge University Press, 2002.
Studies, La Trobe University. National Centre for Socio-Legal, and Lawrence Moloney. *Managing Differences: Federally-Funded Family Mediation in Sydney: Outcomes, Costs and Client Satisfaction.* Attorney-General's Department, 1996.

SUDAN, BUILDING A NEW. "The Sudan People's Liberation Movement/Army." *Rebel Rulers: Insurgent Governance and Civilian Life during War* (2011): 129.

Sudan, Government of South. "Child Act 2008 and Penal Code 2008." Ministry Justice and legal Affiars 2008.

Sudan, Government of Southern. "Civil Procedure Act 2003." South Sudan, 2003.

Sudan Tribune. "High Court Judge to Lose Seat over Pregrancy Sentencing." <https://sudantribune.com/article38194/>

Sullivan, Dennis, and Larry Tifft. *Handbook of Restorative Justice: A Global Perspective.* Routledge, 2007.

Tamanaha, Brian Z. "Understanding Legal Pluralism: Past to Present, Local to Global." *Sydney L. Rev.* 30 (2008): 375.

Tønnessen, Liv, and Liv Tønnessen. "Gendered Citizenship in Sudan: Competing Debates on Family Laws among Northern and Southern Elites in Khartoum." *The Journal of North African Studies* 13, no. 4: 455-69.

Toubia, Nahid. "Female Genital Mutilation." *Women's Rights, Human Rights: International Feminist Perspectives* (1995): 224-37.

Twining, William. "Human Rights: Southern Voices Francis Deng, Abdullahi an-Na'im, Yash Ghai and Upendra Baxi." *Law, Social Justice and Global Development Journal.*

Twining, William, and William Twining. "Human Rights: Southern Voices Francis Deng, Abdullahi an-Na'im, Yash Ghai and Upendra Baxi." *Law, Social Justice and Global Development Journal.*

Umbreit, Mark, and Howard Zehr. "Restorative Family Group Conferences: Differing Models and Guidelines for Practice." *Fed. Probation* 60 (1996): 24.

Vanner, Catherine, Spogmai Akseer, and Thursica Kovinthan. "Learning Peace (and Conflict): The Role of Primary Learning Materials in Peacebuilding in Post-War Afghanistan, South Sudan and Sri Lanka." *Journal of Peace Education* 14, no. 1 (2017): 32-53.

Vidmar, Jure. "South Sudan and the International Legal Framework Governing the Emergence and Delimitation of New States." *Tex. Int'l LJ* 47 (2011): 541.

von Benda-Beckmann, Franz, Keebet von Benda-Beckmann, and Anne Griffiths. "Mobile People, Mobile Law: An Introduction." In *Mobile People, Mobile Law*, 13-38: Routledge, 2017.

Voyce, Malcolm, and Adam Possamai. "Legal Pluralism, Family Personal Laws, and the Rejection of Shari'a in Australia: A Case of Multiple or

"Clashing" Modernities?". *Democracy and Security* 7, no. 4 (2011): 338-53.

Warburg, Gabriel R. "Historical Discord in the Nile Valley." London: Hurst, 1992.

Webb, Lindsey. "Legal Consciousness as Race Consciousness: Expansion of the Fourth Amendment Seizure Analysis through Objective Knowledge of Police Impunity." *Seton Hall L. Rev.* 48 (2017): 403.

Weller, M., B. Metzger, N. Johnson, and U.C.C.I.C. Studies. *Settling Self-Determination Disputes: Complex Power-Sharing in Theory and Practice.* Martinus Nijhoff Publishers, 2008.

Westoby, Peter. "Developing a Community-Development Approach through Engaging Resettling Southern Sudanese Refugees within Australia." *Community development journal* 43, no. 4 (2008): 483-95.

White, Roger, and Bedassa Tadesse. "Immigration Policy, Cultural Pluralism and Trade: Evidence from the White Australia Policy." *Pacific Economic Review* 12, no. 4 (2007): 489-509.

Wilmsen, Brooke. "Family Separation: The Policies, Procedures, and Consequences for Refugee Background Families." *Refugee Survey Quarterly* 30, no. 1 (2011): 44-64.

Windle, Joel. "The Racialisation of African Youth in Australia." *Social identities* 14, no. 5 (2008): 553-66.

Wohler, Yvonne, and Jaya AR Dantas. "Barriers Accessing Mental Health Services among Culturally and Linguistically Diverse (Cald) Immigrant Women in Australia: Policy Implications." *Journal of Immigrant and Minority Health* 19, no. 3 (2017): 697-701.

Wooditch, Alese. "Human Trafficking Law and Social Structures." *International Journal of Offender Therapy and Comparative Criminology* 56, no. 5 (2012): 673-90.

Woodman, Gordon R. "Alternative Law of Alternative Dispute Resolution, The." *C. de D.* 32 (1991): 3.

Young, Lisa, Geoff Monahan, Adiva Sifris, and Robyn Carroll. *Family Law in Australia.* LexisNexis Butterworths, 2012.

Zambakari, Christopher. "In Search of Durable Peace: The Comprehensive Peace Agreement and Power Sharing in Sudan." *The Journal of North African Studies* (2012): 1-16.

Zimmermann, Andreas, Jonas Dörschner, and Felix Machts. *The 1951 Convention Relating to the Status of Refugees and Its 1967 Protocol: A Commentary.* Oxford University Press, 2011.